Learn Japanese: College Text, Volume II

「満 林 花」康 成

written by Mr. Yasunari Kawabata, who is
the author of many well-known novels, including *Yukiguni*. Mr. Kawabata received in 1961
the "Bunka Kunshō," an imperial award to
distinguished men of letters, and is now
president of the Japan Pen Club.

LEARN JAPANESE

COLLEGE TEXT   **VOLUME II**

By John Young and Kimiko Nakajima

Published for
University College, University of Maryland

The University Press of Hawaii Ⴟ
Honolulu

This volume is another in a series of Japanese language textbooks prepared by the Far East Division of the University College, University of Maryland, and published by The University Press of Hawaii. It was first published and copyrighted in Japan under the Universal Copyright Convention. This edition is an authorized U.S. reprint.

First published by the East-West Center Press 1968
Second printing 1968
Third printing 1969
Fourth printing 1970
Fifth printing by The University Press of Hawaii 1972
Sixth printing 1973
Seventh printing 1975
Eighth printing 1977
Ninth printing 1978
Tenth printing 1979
Eleventh printing 1980
Twelfth printing 1982

Library of Congress Catalog Card Number 67-64871

ISBN 0-8248-0069-9

Manufactured in the United States of America

Table of Contents

ACKNOWLEDGMENTS

The authors are deeply indebted to the Japanese language faculty and administrative staff members of the University of Maryland's Far East Division and of the University of Hawaii who assisted in the preparation of this book.

We especially wish to mention the following people whose assistance was the most valuable:

Miss Yoshiko Ando, who assisted us in preparing the text and enriched it with her practical and valuable suggestions.

Dr. Edgar A. Austin, who proofread the material and gave us his valuable suggestions.

Dr. Ivan Benson, who edited the English portion of the text and offered his valuable suggestions.

Mr. Keiichiro Okutsu, who reviewed our notes and gave us his valuable suggestions.

Mr. Setsuo Sugimura, who provided his fine illustrations.

Mr. Shozo Kurokawa and Mr. Keiichiro Okutsu, who gave us permission to use freely and adapt the content of LEARN JAPANESE — *Pattern Approach.*

Shirayuri ya

Nikei utsurite

Ike kaoru

— Seien —

The elegant reflection
Of two white lilies;
Now the pond is fragrant.

INTRODUCTION

This is the second volume of LEARN JAPANESE — *College Text*. It begins where Volume I ends. The use of Rōmaji — Romanized Japanese — is limited to a minimum, with Kana and Kanji used instead.

In this volume, a total of 91 Kanji characters with 110 different readings are introduced. Any Kanji that has appeared in a previous lesson with a different reading, or any compound Kanji whose reading is especially derived as a result of a combination, is introduced with the number with which it was originally introduced. Most of the Kanji first appear in presentations and dialogs, but there are some that first occur in notes or drills. They are identified with an asterisk.

In addition to the Kanji for "active" learning, we are introducing Kanji for "passive" learning, and to these Kanji, *furigana* — readings of the Kanji in small Hiragana characters — are attached. The student is required to identify and possibly reproduce the "active" Kanji, but the "passive" Kanji need not be memorized until they are introduced as the Kanji for active learning.

It should be remembered that the introduction of Kanji is not meant to interfere with the student's efforts in building up his oral-aural capability, which is the focal target of this volume. Therefore, reproduction of Kanji should not be overemphasized at this stage.

Lessons 1 through 3, 5 through 7, 9 through 11, and 13 and 14 constitute the main texts, while Lessons 4, 8, 12, and 15 are review lessons.

The lesson arrangement of Volume I has been followed, with these exceptions:
(1) A Presentation section has been introduced for each regular lesson, replacing the Useful Expression section of Volume I. This will enable the student to acquaint himself with the narrative style, leading eventually to the written style.
(2) The Hiragana Practice section has been replaced by a Kanji section.
(3) The Pronunciation Drill has been omitted. However, pronunciation practice should be pursued continually and any error must be corrected immediately.
(4) Capital letters have been used for a segment of pattern sentences in order to indicate structural points to be taught in a lesson.
(5) At the end of each main lesson, a section called Situational Conversation has been added to make sure that the student does not stay at the mim-mem stage but goes beyond it. Unless the student develops the so-called "selection" ability in generating utterances, he has not yet learned the language. This section should help the student to develop this ability after overlearning the lesson through dialog and drills. The situation described in the section should be read by the student before he comes to his class and he should be able to enact it in Japanese before his teacher.

LESSON 1

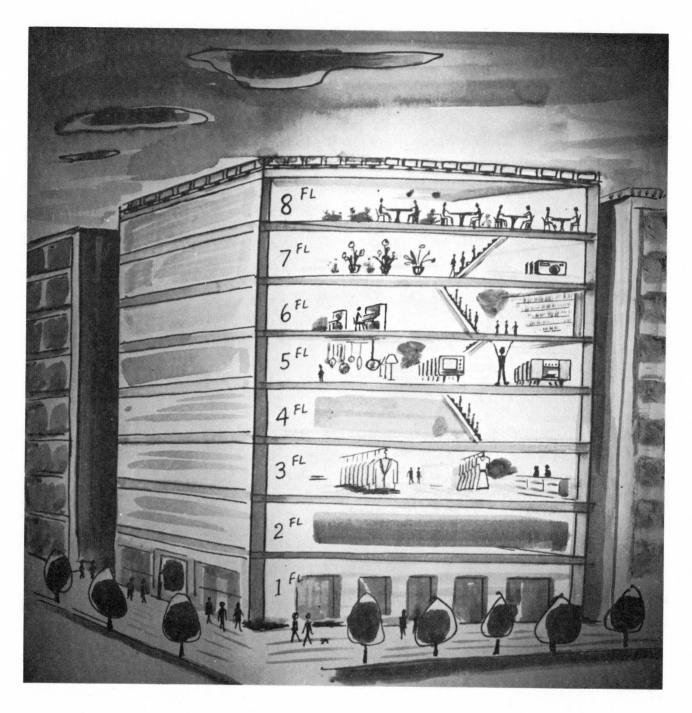

1.1 PRESENTATION

ーかいものー

日本の　デパートなどの　店員の　ことばは、　たいへん　ていねいです。　つぎは、
店員と　客の　かいわです。

1.2 DIALOG

店員　「いらっしゃいませ。　なにを　さしあげましょう*1か*2。」

女の客*3　「レインコートが　ほしい*4んですが*5……。」

店員　「お客*6さま*7のですね?」

女の客　「ええ、　わたくしの*7です。　それを　みせて*8ください*9。」

店員　「はい、　どうぞ。」

女の客　「この　レインコートは　いくら*10ですか。」

店員　「三千六百円*11です。」

女の客　「ちょっと　きてみましょう*12。　すこし　ちいさいですね。」

店員　「では、　これは　いかがですか。　四千三百円です。　サイズは　ちょうど
　　　いいですね。」

女の客　「ええ。　じゃあ、　これを　いただきます*13。　それから、　百円ぐらいの*14
　　　ハンカチを　二まい　ください*9。」

店員　「ありがとうございます。　レインコートは　はこに　いれましょう*2か。」

女の客　「ええ、　そう　してください。　それから、　ネクタイを　みせてください。」

店員　「ネクタイは　二かいで*15　うっています*16。」

女の客　「じゃあ、　あとで　いってみましょう。　ぜんぶで*17　いくらですか。」

店員　「四千五百円です。　どうも　ありがとうございました*18。」

1.3 PATTERN SENTENCES

1.3.1

N	R
sore	o

→

V	E
miseTE	KUDASAI

"Please show me that one."

1.3.2

N	R	N	R
anata	no	( )	o

→

V	E
kiTE	MIMASU

"I will try on yours."

1.4 NOTES

1.4.1 *Sashiagemasu* is a polite equivalent of *agemasu* "give." See Lesson 12 of Vol. I in which *agemasu* and *sashiagemasu* are explained.

$$\text{Nominative} + \textbf{\textit{ni}} + \text{Nominative} + \textbf{\textit{o}} + \begin{cases} \textit{agemasu} \\ \textit{sashiagemasu} \end{cases}$$

Nani o sashiagemashoo ka ?   "What shall I give to [you]?"

Ano kata ni kippu o sashiagemashita.   "[I] gave a ticket to that person."

1.4.2 *Sashiagemashoo ka*? means in this instance "Shall I give it?" In some situation such as this, *-mashoo ka*? may refer to the speaker's doing something without involving the hearer and means "Shall I . . .?" instead of "Shall we . . .?" The affirmative answer to this question is often an expression of "please do such and such," which is introduced in Note 1.4.9.

Nani o sashiagemashoo ka ?   "What shall I give to [you]?"

Hako ni iremashoo ka ?   "Shall I put it into a box?"

Watakushi ga ikimashoo ka?   "Shall I go?"

Moo ichido iimashoo ka ?   "Shall I say it once more?"

Ee, moo ichido itte kudasai.   "Yes, please say it once more."

1.4.3 *On'na no kyaku* means "lady customer." *On'na* "female" and *otoko* "male" form many phrases as follows:

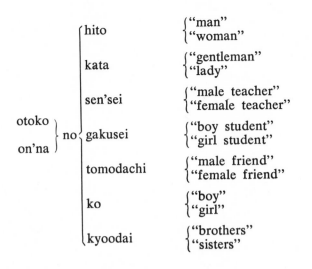

otoko, on'na	no	hito	"man" / "woman"
		kata	"gentleman" / "lady"
		sen'sei	"male teacher" / "female teacher"
		gakusei	"boy student" / "girl student"
		tomodachi	"male friend" / "female friend"
		ko	"boy" / "girl"
		kyoodai	"brothers" / "sisters"

1.4.4 *Hoshii* is an Adjective meaning "something is wanted," "desire to have something," or "want." Therefore, like ~ *ga suki desu,* an item that is wanted is followed by the Relational *ga.* (See Note 5.4.13, Vol. I.)

Nominative + *wa* + Nominative + *ga* + *hoshii desu*
(person)

(watakushi wa) {rein'kooto / okane} *ga* {hoshii (n) desu / hoshiku arimasen / hoshikatta (n) desu / hoshiku arimasen deshita} "a raincoat" / "money" {is / is not / was / was not} wanted (by me)"

Eiga no kippu ga nimai hoshii n desu ga, arimasen ka ? — "I want two movie tickets; don't you have any?"

Ima ocha wa hoshiku arimasen. — "I don't want tea now."

Kono kodomo wa okashi ga hoshii n desu. — "This child wants some candy."

1.4.5 The clause Relational *ga* usually connects two clauses and means "but" or "and." Sometimes, *ga* appears without any clause following it. In such a case, *ga* is used to soften the directness of the expression, to show the speaker's hesitation, or to suggest an implication of the statement.

Rein'kooto ga hoshii n desu ga.... — "I want a raincoat, but will you let me see some?"

1.4.6 The *-sama* is a polite equivalent of the dependent Nominative *-san.* The *-sama* is used in very polite speech or regularly used in superscribing a letter. (See Lesson 14, Presentation.)

okyakusan ...... okyakusama
okusan ...... okusama
otoosan ...... otoosama
Ishii san ...... Ishii sama

4

1.4.7 *Okyakusama no desu ne?* means "Is it the customer's*?" or "Is it (one) for the customer?" A Nominative *rein'kooto* after *no* has been omitted because it is understood. When the implication is clear, a Nominative following *no* may be omitted.

watakushi no	"mine"
anata no	"yours"
ano hito no	"that person's," "his," "hers"
dare no	"whose?"
hyakuen no	"the one hundred yen one"
kono mise no	"this store's"

Kore wa anata no kutsu desu ka ?   "Are these your shoes?"

Ee, watakushi no desu.   "Yes, they are mine."

Nisen'en no seetaa ga arimasu ka ?   "Do you have sweaters for 2,000 yen?"

Iie, nisen'en no wa arimasen.   "No, we don't have any for 2,000 yen."

* As already explained in Note 5.4.9, Vol. I, *okyakusama* may be said directly to the second person who is a customer or a guest.

1.4.8 *Misete* is the TE form of the Verb *misemasu ←— miseru*. This form is used in various patterns, some of which are introduced in this lesson and in some of the following lessons, and it is important for you to familiarize yourself with this form. A grammatical note is given in Note 1.4.19 to explain how the TE forms are formed.

Here is a list of the TE forms of the Verbs you have studied in Vol. I and in this lesson.

agemasu	"give"	⟶	agete
ben'kyoo shimasu	"study"	⟶	ben'kyoo shite
dekakemasu	"go out"	⟶	dekakete
den'wa shimasu	"make a phone call"	⟶	den'wa shite
hairimasu	"enter"	⟶	haitte
hanashimasu	"talk"	⟶	hanashite
hikimasu	"play (a piano)"	⟶	hiite
iimasu	"say"	⟶	itte
ikimasu	"go"	⟶	itte
imasu	"be"	⟶	ite
iremasu	"put in"	⟶	irete
itadakimasu	"receive"	⟶	itadaite
kaerimasu	"go back"	⟶	kaette
kaimasu	"buy"	⟶	katte
kaimono shimasu	"do shopping"	⟶	kaimono shite
kakimasu	"write"	⟶	kaite
karimasu	"borrow"	⟶	karite
kekkon shimasu	"marry"	⟶	kekkon shite
ken'butsu shimasu	"see the sights of"	⟶	ken'butsu shite

kikimasu	"listen"	$\longrightarrow$	kiite
kimasu	"come"	$\longrightarrow$	kite
kimasu	"wear"	$\longrightarrow$	kite
machimasu	"wait"	$\longrightarrow$	matte
mimasu	"see"	$\longrightarrow$	mite
misemasu	"show"	$\longrightarrow$	misete
moraimasu	"receive"	$\longrightarrow$	moratte
naraimasu	"learn"	$\longrightarrow$	naratte
nomimasu	"drink"	$\longrightarrow$	non'de
ryokoo shimasu	"travel"	$\longrightarrow$	ryokoo shite
sagashimasu	"look for"	$\longrightarrow$	sagashite
sashiagemasu	"give"	$\longrightarrow$	sashiagete
shimasu	"do"	$\longrightarrow$	shite
tabemasu	"eat"	$\longrightarrow$	tabete
urimasu	"sell"	$\longrightarrow$	utte
wasuremasu	"forget"	$\longrightarrow$	wasurete
yarimasu	"give"	$\longrightarrow$	yatte
yomimasu	"read"	$\longrightarrow$	yon'de
(arimasu*	"be"	$\longrightarrow$	atte*)
(chigaimasu*	"differ"	$\longrightarrow$	chigatte*)
(furimasu*	"fall"	$\longrightarrow$	futte*)
(kuremasu*	"give"	$\longrightarrow$	kurete*)

* TE forms of these Verbs are listed here, but the use of them is rather limited. They seldom occur in the patterns introduced in this lesson.

1.4.9 *Misete kudasai* means "Please show it to me or us." The TE form of a Verb plus the Predicate Extender *kudasai,* Verb(-*te*)+*kudasai,* formulates the polite imperative "please do such and such."

Verb(-*te*) + *kudasai*

Sore o misete kudasai.   "Please show it to me."

Kore o tabete kudasai.   "Please eat this."

Chotto matte kudasai.   "Please wait for a minute."

When *kudasai* is used as a Predicate by itself, without being preceded by the TE form, it is the imperative form of the Verb *kudasaimasu,* the polite equivalent of *kuremasu* "give to me," which has been introduced in Note 12.4.3, Vol. I. *Kudasai* without being preceded by the TE form means "please give me or us." The direct object of the Predicate *kudasai* will be followed by the Relational *o* and the indirect object will be followed by *ni*.

Watakushi ni sore o kudasai.   "Please give that to me."

Mittsu kudasai.   "Please give me three."

1.4.10 *Ikura* is the interrogative Nominative meaning "how much?" The way *ikura* is used is the same as that of *ikutsu* "how many?"

Kono rein'kooto wa ikura desu ka?	"How much is this raincoat?"
Kore wa ikura deshita ka?	"How much was this?"
Okane ga ikura arimasu ka?	"How much money is there?" "How much money do you have?"
Ikura kaimashita ka?	"How much did you buy?"

1.4.11   *-En* is the counter for "yen," the unit for Japanese currency. Counters for American currency units are *-doru* "dollar" and *-sen'to* "cent."

Sore wa ikura desu ka?	"How much is that?"
Gosen'en desu.	"It is five thousand yen."
Chichi kara hyakudoru moraimashita.	"I was given a hundred dollars by my father."
Gosen'to kudasai.	"Give me five cents."

Like *-satsu* and *-sai*, some of the combinations of a numeral and *-sen'to* make sound change as follows:

1	issen'to	6	rokusen'to
2	nisen'to	7	nanasen'to
3	san'sen'to	8	hassen'to; hachisen'to
4	yon'sen'to	9	kyuusen'to
5	gosen'to	10	jissen'to; jussen'to

1.4.12   *Kite* mimashoo* here means "I think I'll try it on." The TE form plus the Predicate Extender *mimasu* ←— *miru* "try" forms the connotation "someone will do something and find out." The Extender *mimasu* conjugates like a Verb.

$$\text{Verb}(-te) + \begin{cases} \textit{mimasu} \\ \textit{mimasen} \\ \textit{mimashita} \\ \textit{mimasen deshita} \\ \textit{mimashoo} \\ \textit{mite kudasai} \end{cases}$$

Chotto kite mimashoo.	"I think I'll try it on for a short time."
Kore o tabete mimashoo.	"Let's eat this one and find out how it is."
Kono supootsu shatsu o kite mimasen ka?	"Won't you wear this sport shirt and see how it fits you?"

* The Verb *kimasu* "come" has the same TE form, *kite*, as the Verb *kimasu* "wear." The accent patterns and the Predicate Modifiers preceding *kite mimasu* will make it clear which meaning is called for.

| Kore o kite mimasen ka / | "Won't you try this on?" |
| Uchi e kite mimasen ka / | "Won't you come to my house and find out?" |

1.4.13 *Itadakimasu* means "I'll receive it." *Itadakimasu* is a polite equivalent of *moraimasu* "receive; get." This word may be used to a superior or even to an equal to show politeness.

Nominative + *kara* + Nominative + *o* + $\begin{cases} itadakimasu \\ moraimasu \end{cases}$
(person)

Kore o itadakimasu. "I will get [take] this one."

Donata kara itadakimashita ka? "From whom did you get it?"

1.4.14 The *-gurai* used immediately after a number is a dependent Nominative that indicates an approximate number or amount. *-Gurai* will correspond to "about," or "approximately." *-Gurai* may sometimes be pronounced *-kurai* by some Japanese.

Hyakuen gurai desu. "It is about a hundred yen."

Kono kyooshitsu ni gakusei ga nan'nin imasu ka? "How many students are there in this classroom?"

Juunin gurai imasu. "There are about ten."

Sono zasshi wa ikura desu ka? "How much is that magazine?"

Nihyakuen gurai deshoo. "I presume it will cost about two hundred yen."

Note that *-gurai* is never used to indicate approximate point of time. (See Note 2.4.18.)

1.4.15 *Nikai* is the combination of *ni* "two" and *-kai*, counter for "floor" or "story" as in "2nd floor" or "two storied house." *-Kai* may mean either a specific floor or number of floors.

1	ikkai*	6	rokkai*
2	nikai	7	nanakai; shichikai
3	san'gai	8	hakkai*; hachikai
4	yon'kai	9	kyuukai
5	gokai	10	jikkai*; jukkai

*The combination for these numbers is always *-kkai*.

The basement is called *chika*: Basement 2 is *chika nikai*.

Nikai de utte imasu. "They sell it on the second floor."

San'gai e ikimashoo. "Let's go to the third floor."

Ano tatemono wa nanakai desu. "That building has seven floors."

Pan ya koohii wa chika ni arimasu. "Bread and coffee are in the basement."

1.4.16 *Utte imasu* means "(they) sell." The pattern, the TE form plus *imasu*, will be explained in Note 2.4.2.

1.4.17 *Zen'bu de* means "for everything" or "for all." The function of the Relational *de* after a quantity Nominative is often to totalize.

8

Zen'bu de ikura desu ka ?   "How much for everything?"

Ichidaasu de sen gohyakuen desu.   "They are 1,500 yen for a dozen."

Kore wa mittsu de hyakuen desu.   "These cost a hundred yen for three."

1.4.18 *Doomo arigatoo gozaimashita* means "Thank you very much for what you have done." This expression is the perfect tense form of *Doomo arigatoo gozaimasu* and is used to express someone's having done something (here, for the customer's having bought some articles).

1.4.19 Verb Classification

All Verbs are classified into the following four categories:

1. Vowel Verb: the ending of the Base*1 form is a vowel.

2. Consonant Verb: the ending of the Base form is a consonant. (When Verbs are *naraimasu, kaimasu, chigaimasu,* etc., only the Pre-Nai*2 form of these Verbs contains a consonant as the ending of the Base. These Verbs should still be classified as Consonant Verbs.)

3. *shimasu* ←—— *suru* (Irregular Verb)

4. *kimasu* ←—— *kuru* (Irregular Verb)

The following is a list of some forms of Vowel Verbs and Consonant Verbs:

classification	Dictionary*3 form	Base form	Stem*4 form	Pre-Nai form
Vowel Verb	taberu	tabe	tabe(masu)	tabe(nai)
	miru	mi	mi(masu)	mi(nai)
Consonant Verb	ka(w)u	ka(w)	ka(w)i(masu)	kawa(nai)
	kaku	kak	kaki(masu)	kaka(nai)
	oyogu	oyog	oyogi(masu)	oyoga(nai)
	matsu /matu/	mat /mat/	machi(masu) /mati/	mata(nai)
	kaeru	kaer	kaeri(masu)	kaera(nai)
	hanasu	hanas	hanashi(masu) /hanasi/	hanasa(nai)
	asobu	asob	asobi(masu)	asoba(nai)
	nomu	nom	nomi(masu)	noma(nai)
	shinu	shin	shini(masu)	shina(nai)

*1 The Base of each Verb is the part that stays constant, after deleting the inflected part.
*2 The Pre-Nai form is the form that appears before *-nai*.
*3 The Dictionary form is the form that appears in dictionaries.
*4 The Stem or Pre-Masu form of a Verb is the form that occurs with *-masu*.

The student may have difficulty making a distinction between a Consonant Verb and a Vowel Verb. Some hints for the classification are given as follows:

(1) If the Dictionary form of a Verb does not end in *-eru*, or *-iru*, it is a Consonant Verb (except *suru* and *kuru*).

(2) If a Verb ends in *-eru* or *-iru*, you can not immediately know whether it is a Consonant Verb or a Vowel Verb until you check the TE form or the plain perfect tense form (TA form) of the Verb.

(3) The Derivatives *-masu* and *-nai* can be used as criteria for determining whether a Verb is a Vowel Verb or a Consonant Verb. If the two forms before *-masu* and *-nai* are identical, it is a Vowel Verb. If the two forms are not identical, the Verb is classified as a Consonant Verb.

The TE form of each Verb is formed in one of the following manners:

(a) Vowel Verb ...... Stem form + *te*
   e.g. *i(masu)* ⟶ *ite*
      mi(masu) ⟶ *mite*
      tabe(masu) ⟶ *tabete*

(b) Consonant Verb depends on the final syllable of the Stem form of the Verb.
   When the final syllable of the Stem form is:

   (1) *-i(masu)* ...... *tte* replaces *-i*
      e.g. *kai(masu)* ⟶ *katte*
         narai(masu) ⟶ *naratte*

   (2) *-ki(masu)* ...... *ite* replaces *-ki*
      e.g. *kaki(masu)* ⟶ *kaite*
      Ikimasu is the only exception to this rule and becomes *itte*.

   (3) *-gi(masu)* ...... *ide* replaces *-gi*
      e.g. *oyogi(masu)* ⟶ *oyoide*
         isogi(masu) ⟶ *isoide*

   (4) *-chi(masu)*, or *-ri(masu)* ...... *tte* replaces *-chi* or *-ri*
      e.g. *machi(masu)* ⟶ *matte*
         kaeri(masu) ⟶ *kaette*

   (5) *-shi(masu)* ...... add *te* to *-shi*
      e.g. *hanashi(masu)* ⟶ *hanashite*

   (6) *-bi(masu)*, *-mi(masu)*, or *-ni(masu)* ...... *n'de* replaces *-bi*, *-mi*, or *-ni*
      e.g. *asobi(masu)* ⟶ *ason'de*
         nomi(masu) ⟶ *non'de*
         shini(masu) ⟶ *shin'de*

(c) Irregular Verb
   (1) *shimasu* ⟶ *shite*
   (2) *kimasu* ⟶ *kite*

1.5 VOCABULARY

Presentation

など	-nado	...... Nd	etc.; and the like
店員 (てんいん)	ten'in	...... N	(shop) clerk
ことば	kotoba	...... N	speech; word; language
たいへん	taihen	...... Adv.	very (formal equivalent of *totemo*)
ていねい	teinei	...... Na	polite
つぎ	tsugi	...... N	next; following
客 (きゃく)	kyaku	...... N	customer; guest; visitor
かいわ	kaiwa	...... N	dialog; conversation

Dialog

さしあげましょう	sashiagemashoo	 V	I shall give (see 1.4.1 and 1.4.2) (OO form of *sashiagemasu* ← *sashiageru*)
女 (おんな)	on'na	...... N	female (see 1.4.3)
レインコート	rein'kooto	...... N	raincoat
ほしい	hoshii	...... A	want; is desirous (see 1.4.4)
さま	-sama	...... Nd	polite equivalent of *-san* (see 1.4.6)
みせて	misete	 V	TE form of *misemasu* ← *miseru* – show (see 1.4.8)
ください	kudasai	...... E	please (do) (see 1.4.9)
いくら	ikura	...... Ni	how much? (see 1.4.10)
三千六百円 (えん)	san'zen roppyakuen	.... N	three thousand six hundred yen
きて	kite	 V	TE form of *kimasu* ← *kiru* – wear
みましょう	mimashoo	...... E	I think I'll try (OO form of *mimasu* ← *miru*) (see 1.4.12)
では	dewa	...... SI	then; well (formal equivalent of *jaa*)
四千三百円 (えん)	yon'sen san'byakuen	.... N	four thousand three hundred yen
サイズ	saizu	...... N	size
ちょうど	choodo	...... Adv.	just; exactly
いただきます	itadakimasu	 V	get; receive (normal form of *itadaku*) (see 1.4.13)
百円 (えん)	hyakuen	...... N	hundred yen
ぐらい	-gurai	...... Nd	about; approximately (see 1.4.14)
ハンカチ	han'kachi	...... N	handkerchief
ください	kudasai	 V	please give (me) (see 1.4.9)
はこ	hako	...... N	box; case
いれましょう	iremashoo	 V	I shall put it in (OO form of *iremasu* ← *ireru*)
して	shite	 V	TE form of *shimasu* ← *suru* – do

ネクタイ	nekutai	. . . . . .	N	necktie
二かい	nikai	. . . . . .	N	second floor (see 1.4.15)
うって	utte	. . . . . .	V	TE form of *urimasu* ← *uru* – sell
います	imasu	. . . . . .	E	(see 1.4.16)
あとで	ato de	. . . . . .	PM	later
いって	itte	. . . . . .	V	TE form of *ikimasu* ← *iku* – go
ぜんぶ	zen'bu	. . . . . .	N	all; everything
で	de	. . . . . .	R	totalizing (see 1.4.17)

Notes

ど	-do	. . . . . .	Nd	time(s)
おとこ	otoko	. . . . . .	N	male (see 1.4.3)
こ	ko	. . . . . .	N	child (usually preceded by a modifier, e.g. *otoko no ko* "boy")
ほしく	hoshiku	. . . . . .	A	KU form of *hoshii* – is desirous; want
ほしかった	hoshikatta	. . . . . .	A	TA form of *hoshii* – was desirous; wanted
くつ	kutsu	. . . . . .	N	shoes
セーター	seetaa	. . . . . .	N	sweater
くださいます	kudasaimasu	. . . . . .	V	give me (or us) (polite equivalent of *kuremasu*) (normal form of *kudasaru*) (see 1.4.9)
円	-en	. . . . . .	Nd	unit for Japanese currency (see 1.4.11)
ドル	-doru	. . . . . .	Nd	dollar(s) (see 1.4.11)
セント	-sen'to	. . . . . .	Nd	cent(s) (see 1.4.11)
みます	mimasu	. . . . . .	E	I'll try (after TE form) (normal form of *miru*)
スポーツシャツ	supootsu shatsu	. . . . . .	N	sport shirt
くらい	-kurai	. . . . . .	Nd	about; approximately (see 1.4.14)
かい	-kai	. . . .	Nd	floor; stories (see 1.4.15)
ちか	chika	. . . . . .	N	basement (lit. underground)
たてもの	tatemono	. . . . . .	N	building
ダース	-daasu	. . . . . .	Nd	dozen

Drills

かたかな	katakana	. . . . . .	N	the square Japanese syllabary
すし	sushi	. . . . . .	N	vinegar-treated rice flavored primarily with sea food, usually raw

1.6 KANJI

Each of the *kanji* in this section is introduced for:

(1) reading: *on*-pronunciation in capitals, *kun*-pronunciation in italics. Sound-change is shown in brackets and *hiragana* following *kanji* in parentheses.

(2) meaning

(3) classifier and/or phonetic element (Some books call these forms "radicals.")

(4) stroke order

(5) examples of usage

1.6.1 一   (1) ICHI, *hito(tsu)*   (2) one   (3) forms the classifier 一   (4) 一

      (5) 一ドル、一まい、一つ、一ぱい *ippai*、一ぽん *ippon*、一かい *ikkai*

1.6.2 二   (1) NI, *futa(tsu)*   (2) two   (3) forms the classifier 二   (4) 一 二

      (5) 二じ、二円、二つ

1.6.3 三   (1) SAN, *mit(tsu)*   (2) three   (3) classifier 一   (4) 一 二 三

      (5) 三にん、三さい、三つ

1.6.4 四   (1) SHI, *yon, yo-, yot(tsu)*   (2) four   (3) classifier 口

      (4) 丨 冂 冃 四 四   (5) 四セント、四にん、四つ

1.6.5 五   (1) GO, *itsu(tsu)*   (2) five   (3) classifier 二   (4) 一 丁 开 五

      (5) 五はい、五じ、五つ

1.6.6 六   (1) ROKU, *mut(tsu)*   (2) six   (3) classifier 八   (4) 丶 亠 亠 六

      (5) 六さい、六にん、六つ、六ぱい *roppai*、六ぽん *roppon*、六かい *rokkai*

1.6.7 七   (1) SHICHI, *nana(tsu)*   (2) seven   (3) classifier 一   (4) 一 七

      (5) 七まい、七はい、七つ

1.6.8 八   (1) HACHI, *yat(tsu)*   (2) eight   (3) forms the classifier 八   (4) 丿 八

      (5) 八円、八にん、八つ、八ぱい *happai*、八ぽん *happon*、八かい *hakkai*

1.6.9 九   (1) KU, KYUU, *kokono(tsu)*   (2) nine   (3) classifier 乙   (4) 丿 九

      (5) 九にん、九じ、九つ

1.6.10 十   (1) JUU, *too*   (2) ten   (3) forms the classifier 十   (4) 一 十

      (5) 十円、十ドル、十ぱい *jippai; juppai*、十ぽん *jippon; juppon*、十かい *jikkai; jukkai*

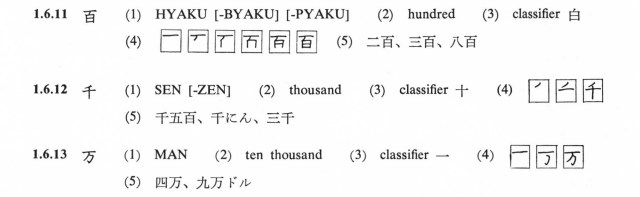

1.6.11　百　(1) HYAKU [-BYAKU] [-PYAKU]　(2) hundred　(3) classifier 白

　　　　　　(4) 一 ノ 了 万 百 百　(5) 二百、三百、八百

1.6.12　千　(1) SEN [-ZEN]　(2) thousand　(3) classifier 十　(4) ′ 二 千

　　　　　　(5) 千五百、千にん、三千

1.6.13　万　(1) MAN　(2) ten thousand　(3) classifier 一　(4) 一 丁 万

　　　　　　(5) 四万、九万ドル

1.7　DRILLS

1.7.1　Pattern Drill

1. Sore o misete kudasai.

2. Chotto kite mimashoo.

3. Sore kara, hyakuen gurai no han'kachi o nimai kudasai.

4. Soo shite kudasai.

5. Sore kara, nekutai o misete kudasai.

6. Jaa, ato de itte mimashoo.

1.7.2　Transformation Drill

1. はこに　いれます。　　　　　　　　⟶　はこに　いれてください。
2. ピアノを　ひきます。　　　　　　　⟶　ピアノを　ひいてください。
3. この　セーターを　うります。　　　⟶　この　セーターを　うってください。
4. デパートで　かいます。　　　　　　⟶　デパートで　かってください。
5. 日本語で　はなします。　　　　　　⟶　日本語で　はなしてください。
6. あなたのを　みせます。　　　　　　⟶　あなたのを　みせてください。
7. あした　うちに　います。　　　　　⟶　あした　うちに　いてください。
8. ここへ　きます。　　　　　　　　　⟶　ここへ　きてください。
9. レインコートを　きてみます。　　　⟶　レインコートを　きてみてください。
10. これを　たべてみます。　　　　　　⟶　これを　たべてみてください。

1.7.3　Transformation Drill

1. ちょっと　これを　きましょう。　　⟶　ちょっと　これを　きてみましょう。
2. てんぷらを　たべました。　　　　　⟶　てんぷらを　たべてみました。

14

3. ブラウンさんと いきました。　　　　　⟶　ブラウンさんと いってみました。

4. これを のみましょう。　　　　　　　　⟶　これを のんでみましょう。

5. スージーさんに はなしました。　　　　⟶　スージーさんに はなしてみました。

6. かたかなで かきませんか。　　　　　　⟶　かたかなで かいてみませんか。

7. ピアノを ひきましょう。　　　　　　　⟶　ピアノを ひいてみましょう。

8. うちで さがしましょう。　　　　　　　⟶　うちで さがしてみましょう。

9. あした でんわしてください。　　　　　⟶　あした でんわしてみてください。

10. その 本を よんでください。　　　　　⟶　その 本を よんでみてください。

1.7.4　Transformation Drill

1. お客さまの レインコートですね？　　　⟶　お客さまのですね？

2. あなたの コーヒーです。　　　　　　　⟶　あなたのです。

3. だれの カメラでしたか。　　　　　　　⟶　だれのでしたか。

4. 百円の ハンカチを ください。　　　　⟶　百円のを ください。

5. 三千円ぐらいの セーターが ほしいんです。　⟶　三千円ぐらいのが ほしいんです。

6. 店の はこに いれました。　　　　　　⟶　店のに いれました。

7. こどもの ハンカチを みせてください。　⟶　こどものを みせてください。

8. えい語の しんぶんを ください。　　　⟶　えい語のを ください。

9. つぎの かいわを きいてください。　　⟶　つぎのを きいてください。

10. いくらの くつが ほしいですか。　　　⟶　いくらのが ほしいですか。

1.7.5　Transformation Drill

1. なにを あげますか。　　　　　　　　　⟶　なにを さしあげますか。

2. せんせいに これを あげます。　　　　⟶　せんせいに これを さしあげます。

3. あなたの おとうさんから もらいました。　⟶　あなたの おとうさんから いただきました。

4. ごしゅじんに おちゃを あげました。　⟶　ごしゅじんに おちゃを さしあげました。

5. わたしに なにを くれますか。　　　　⟶　わたしに なにを くださいますか。

6. この かたが くれました。　　　　　　⟶　この かたが くださいました。

7. あとで お客さまに あげてください。　⟶　あとで お客さまに さしあげてください。

8. あの 女の かたから もらいます。　　⟶　あの 女の かたから いただきます。

9. やまもとさんが ぜんぶ くれました。　⟶　やまもとさんが ぜんぶ くださいました。

10. おくさんから すこし もらいました。　⟶　おくさんから すこし いただきました。

1.7.6 E-J Mixed Drill

1. ほしい(ん)です。

   tea   .... おちゃが　ほしい(ん)です。

   I   .... わたくしは　おちゃが　ほしい(ん)です。

   wanted   .... わたくしは　おちゃが　ほしかった(ん)です。

2. ほしかった(ん)です。

   what   .... なにが　ほしかった(ん)ですか。

   yesterday   .... きのう　なにが　ほしかった(ん)ですか。

   Kazuko   .... かずこさんは　きのう　なにが　ほしかった(ん)ですか。

3. ほしい(ん)です。

   don't want   .... ほしくありません。

   not at all   .... ちっとも　ほしくありません。

   money   .... おかねが　ちっとも　ほしくありません。

   I   .... わたくしは　おかねが　ちっとも　ほしくありません。

4. ほしくありません。

   didn't want   .... ほしくありませんでした。

   raincoat   .... レインコートが　ほしくありませんでした。

   that person   .... あの　ひとは　レインコートが　ほしくありませんでした。

1.7.7 Substitution Drill

A. さけを　一ぱい　のみました。

1. 三ばい　　……　さけを　三ばい　のみました。
2. おちゃ　　……　おちゃを　三ばい　のみました。
3. 六ぱい　　……　おちゃを　六ぱい　のみました。
4. 二はい　　……　おちゃを　二はい　のみました。
5. みず　　　……　みずを　二はい　のみました。
6. 九はい　　……　みずを　九はい　のみました。
7. コーヒー　……　コーヒーを　九はい　のみました。
8. 四はい　　……　コーヒーを　四はい　のみました。
9. 十ぱい　　……　コーヒーを　十ぱい　のみました。
10. なんばい　……　コーヒーを　なんばい　のみましたか。

B. コカコーラが　三ぼん　ほしいんです。

1. 一ぽん　　……　コカコーラが　一ぽん　ほしいんです。
2. えんぴつ　……　えんぴつが　一ぽん　ほしいんです。

3. 四ほん 　　……　えんぴつが 四ほん ほしいんです。

4. 六ぽん 　　……　えんぴつが 六ぽん ほしいんです。

5. 十ぽん 　　……　えんぴつが 十ぽん ほしいんです。

6. 五ほん 　　……　えんぴつが 五ほん ほしいんです。

7. ネクタイ 　　……　ネクタイが 五ほん ほしいんです。

8. 八ぽん 　　……　ネクタイが 八ぽん ほしいんです。

9. 一ダース 　　……　ネクタイが 一ダース ほしいんです。

10. なんぼん 　　……　ネクタイが なんぼん ほしいんですか。

C. レインコートは 二かいで うっていますか。

1. 五かい 　　……　レインコートは 五かいで うっていますか。

2. 七かい 　　……　レインコートは 七かいで うっていますか。

3. 一かい 　　……　レインコートは 一かいで うっていますか。

4. ちか 二かい……　レインコートは ちか 二かいで うっていますか。

5. レコード 　　……　レコードは ちか 二かいで うっていますか。

6. 四かい 　　……　レコードは 四かいで うっていますか。

7. 三がい 　　……　レコードは 三がいで うっていますか。

8. 六かい 　　……　レコードは 六かいで うっていますか。

9. 八かい 　　……　レコードは 八かいで うっていますか。

10. なんがい 　　……　レコードは なんがいで うっていますか。

1.7.8　Response Drill

1. この 本を かいましょうか。 　　……　ええ、(この 本を) かってください。

2. 日本語を べんきょうしましょうか。 …… ええ、(日本語を) べんきょうしてください。

3. あした きましょうか。 　　……　ええ、(あした) きてください。

4. しんぶんを よみましょうか。 　　……　ええ、(しんぶんを) よんでください。

5. わたなべさんを まちましょうか。 　　……　ええ、(わたなべさんを) まってください。

6. すずきさんに あげましょうか。 　　……　ええ、(すずきさんに) あげてください。

7. ひらがなで かきましょうか。 　　……　ええ、(ひらがなで) かいてください。

8. お客さまに さしあげましょうか。 　　……　ええ、(お客さまに) さしあげてください。

9. デパートへ いってみましょうか。 　　……　ええ、(デパートへ) いってみてください。

10. ピアノを ひきましょうか。 　　……　ええ、(ピアノを) ひいてください。

1.7.9　E-J Substitution Drill

ハンカチを 三まい ください。

1. one 　　.... ハンカチを 一まい ください。

2.	four	.... ハンカチを 四まい ください。
3.	water	.... みずを 四はい ください。
4.	one	.... みずを 一ぱい ください。
5.	three	.... みずを 三ばい ください。
6.	dictionary	.... じしょを 三さつ ください。
7.	four	.... じしょを 四さつ ください。
8.	one	.... じしょを 一さつ ください。
9.	candy	.... おかしを 一つ ください。
10.	four	.... おかしを 四つ ください。
11.	three	.... おかしを 三つ ください。
12.	necktie	.... ネクタイを 三ぼん ください。
13.	one	.... ネクタイを 一ぽん ください。
14.	four	.... ネクタイを 四ほん ください。

1.7.10 E-J Response Drill

1. これは　だれの　本ですか。
   mine ....　わたくしのです。

2. ハンカチは　はこに　いれましょうか。
   please do so ....　そう　してください。

3. これは　女の　こですか。
   no, boy's ....　いいえ、おとこの　こです。

4. いくらですか。
   10,000 yen for everything ....　ぜんぶで　一万円です。

5. どなたに　あげましょうか。
   please give it to me ....　わたくしに　ください。

6. いくらの　ネクタイが　ほしいんですか。
   3,000 yen ....　三千円のが　ほしいんです。

7. なにを　さしあげましょうか。
   please give me three pencils ....　えんぴつを　三ぼん　ください。

8. なにを　たべてみましたか。
   tempura ....　てんぷらを　たべてみました。

9. どなたが　くださいましたか。
   that person ....　あの　かたが　くださいました。

10. どなたから　いただきますか。
    Mr. Watanabe's wife ....　わたなべさんの　おくさんから　いただきます。

18

1.7.11 E-J Transformation Drill

A. 1. はこに　いれます。
   please put it into a box　　　　　.... はこに　いれてください。

2. ピアノを　ひきます。
   please play the piano　　　　　.... ピアノを　ひいてください。

3. あした　うちへ　きます。
   please come to my house tomorrow　.... あした　うちへ　きてください。

4. 日本語で　はなします。
   please speak in Japanese　　　.... 日本語で　はなしてください。

5. レインコートを　みせます。
   please show me a raincoat　　.... レインコートを　みせてください。

B. 1. これを　きます。
   I'll try this on　　　　　　　.... これを　きてみます。

2. この　ネクタイを　かいます。
   I'll buy this tie and see　　.... この　ネクタイを　かってみます。

3. おすしを　たべましょう。
   let's try sushi　　　　　　　.... おすしを　たべてみましょう。

4. きょうとへ　いきます。
   I'll try to go to Kyōto　　　.... きょうとへ　いってみます。

5. 日本語を　べんきょうしました。
   I tried to study Japanese　　.... 日本語を　べんきょうしてみました。

1.8 EXERCISES

1.8.1 Transform the following into the polite imperative ……てください：

1. まいにち　日本語を　べんきょうします。
2. その　レインコートを　みせます。
3. あした　うちへ　きます。
4. ひらがなで　かきます。
5. セーターを　はこに　いれます。
6. あとで　さがします。

1.8.2 Express the following in Japanese:

1. Let's go to the third floor of that building and see.

2. I don't want coffee.

3. I will try this coat on.

4. I will have [receive] black tea later.

5. I want a man's sport shirt and a lady's sweater.

6. Mr. Watanabe wanted three tickets.

7. The size is just right.

8. Shall I put these records in a box?

9. Please read [the book on] page 10.

1.8.3 What would you say when you ask the hearer:

1. to give you a dollar and fifty cents?

2. to write it two more times?

3. to show you a sweater for 2,500 yen?

4. to telephone you tomorrow morning?

5. to try to speak Japanese?

1.8.4 Answer the following questions in Japanese:

1. これは いくらですか。
   670 yen

2. いくらの セーターが ほしいんですか。
   for about 3,500 yen

3. ぜんぶで いくらですか。
   $425.25

4. そこに おかねが いくら ありますか。
   $83.10

1.8.5 Write the following in *kanji:*

1. せん きゅうひゃく ろくじゅう しち

2. はっぴゃく よんじゅう いち

3. ひゃく さんじゅう く

4. ごせん さんびゃく じゅう に

5. よんまん ななせん ろくじゅう はち

1.8.6 Write in *katakana:*

1. saizu

2. rein'kooto

3. doru

4. nekutai

5. daasu

6. han'kachi

7. supootsu shatsu

8. sen'to

9. seetaa

1.9 SITUATIONAL CONVERSATION

Using the patterns and expressions of this lesson, carry on the following conversation.

1.9.1   In a shop

A sales clerk greets a customer.

The customer wants to buy a raincoat for himself.

The customer tries on one and finds it is a little small.

The clerk recommends a larger one.

The customer decides to buy it.

The clerk tells its price.

1.9.2   In the same shop

A customer asks for two handkerchiefs and a tie.

A sales clerk shows them to the customer and the customer decides to buy them.

The customer asks the total price. Then the customer asks where he can find shoes.

1.9.3   Same as 1.9.1. The customer wants to buy a pair of shoes.

1.9.4   Free conversation under the topic of shopping.

LESSON 2

2.1 PRESENTATION

― 大 学 生 ―

一郎は　大学の　四年生です。　きょういく学を　べんきょうしています。[*2]

日本の　大学生は、　なつやすみに、[*3]　よく　アルバイトを[*4]　します。　大学の
なつやすみは　七月と[*5]　八月です。　一郎は、　七月に　アルバイトを　しました。

2.2 DIALOG

林　　「一郎くん、　しばらく。」[*6]

一 郎　「あ、　林さん、　しばらくですねえ。」

林　　「きみは　まだ　学生でしょう？」

一 郎　「ええ、　四年です。　林さんは、　いま、　なんの　しごとを[*7]
　　　　　していますか。」[*2]

林　　「デパートに　つとめています。」[*8]

一 郎　「そうですか。　ぼくも　なつやすみに[*3]　デパートで　はたらきましたよ。」[*9]

林　　「一郎くん、　あしたの　ばん、　うちへ　来ませんか。　ゆっくり[*10]
　　　　　はなしましょう。」

一 郎　「ええ、　ぜひ　うかがいます。」[*11]

林　　「わたしの　ところは　しっていましたね？[*12][*13]　いまも　まえの　ところに
　　　　　すんでいます。」[*14]

一 郎　「ええと……。　しぶやでしたね？」[*13]

林　　「そう、　すぐ　わかりますよ。[*15]　じどうしゃで　来ますか。」

一郎 「いいえ、 じどうしゃは もっていません。 なん時に うかがい *16 *3

ましょうか。」

林 「五時はんは どうですか。」 *17

一郎 「ええ、 いいです。」

林 「では、 五時はんごろ まっていますよ。」 *18

一郎 「ええ。 じゃあ、 また あした。」 *19

林 「さようなら。」

2.3 PATTERN SENTENCES

2.3.1

N	R	N	R
mae	no	tokoro	ni

→

V	E
sun'DE	IMASU

"I am living in the same place where I used to live."

2.3.2

N	R
nan'ji	NI

→

V	SP
ukagaimashoo	ka

"What time shall I visit you?"

2.4 NOTES

2.4.1 *Yonen'sei* means "fourth-year student," or "senior of a college." *Yonen'sei* can be shortened to *yonen.* *-Nen* is a counter for "year." *Nan'nen* may mean either "how many years?" or "what year?"

1	ichinen	6	rokunen
2	ninen	7	shichinen; nananen
3	san'nen	8	hachinen
4	yonen	9	kyuunen; kunen
5	gonen	10	juunen

Boku wa Tookyoo Daigaku no yonen'sei desu.

"I am a senior at Tōkyō University."

Ima nan'nen'sei desu ka ?

"What year are you in?"

Sen kyuuhyaku rokujuu rokunen ni   "He came to Japan in 1966."
   Nihon e kimashita.

Nan'nen Nihon ni imasu* ka ?   "How many years have you been in Japan?"

* As explained in Note 3.4.4, Vol. I, the imperfect tense form indicates that an action or a status has not been completed. Since the person is still in Japan, *imasu* is used. When he is not in Japan any more, *imashita* will be used.

2.4.2   *Ben'kyoo shite imasu* means "is studying," and is the combination of the TE form of the Verb *ben'kyoo shimasu* ⟵ *ben'kyoo suru* and the imperfect tense form of the Predicate Extender *imasu* ⟵ *iru*. The Extender *imasu* conjugates as the Verb *imasu* does.

$$
\textbf{(Predicate Modifier)} + \textbf{Verb}(\textit{-te}) + \begin{cases} \textit{imasu} \\ \textit{imasen} \\ \textit{imashita} \\ \textit{imasen deshita} \\ \textit{imashoo} \\ \textit{ite kudasai} \end{cases}
$$

This combination conveys either one of the following two meanings. The first meaning of the two should be studied thoroughly in this lesson. Only some of the second will be introduced in this lesson. Verbs such as *arimasu* and *imasu* do not have this combination however.

(1) an action is continuing or going on: "someone is doing such and such."

Here is a list of *-te imasu* combinations that carry this connotation:

agemasu	⟶ agete imasu	"is giving"
arubaito shimasu	⟶ arubaito shite imasu	"is doing a side-job"
ben'kyoo shimasu	⟶ ben'kyoo shite imasu	"is studying"
den'wa shimasu	⟶ den'wa shite imasu	"is making a phone call"
furimasu	⟶ futte imasu	"is raining" ["snowing," etc.]
hanashimasu	⟶ hanashite imasu	"is talking"
hatarakimasu	⟶ hataraite imasu	"is working"
hikimasu	⟶ hiite imasu	"is playing (the piano)"
iimasu	⟶ itte imasu	"is saying"
iremasu	⟶ irete imasu	"is putting in"
kaimasu	⟶ katte imasu	"is buying"
kaimono shimasu	⟶ kaimono shite imasu	"is shopping"
kakimasu	⟶ kaite imasu	"is writing"
ken'butsu shimasu	⟶ ken'butsu shite imasu	"is sightseeing"
kikimasu	⟶ kiite imasu	"is listening"
kimasu	⟶ kite imasu	"is wearing"
machimasu	⟶ matte imasu	"is waiting"
mimasu	⟶ mite imasu	"is watching"
misemasu	⟶ misete imasu	"is showing"
naraimasu	⟶ naratte imasu	"is learning"

nomimasu	⟶	non'de imasu	"is drinking"
ryokoo shimasu	⟶	ryokoo shite imasu	"is traveling"
sagashimasu	⟶	sagashite imasu	"is looking for"
shimasu	⟶	shite imasu	"is doing"
sumimasu	⟶	sun'de imasu	"is living"
tabemasu	⟶	tabete imasu	"is eating"
tsutomemasu	⟶	tsutomete imasu	"is employed"
urimasu	⟶	utte imasu	"is selling" "sell"
yomimasu	⟶	yon'de imasu	"is reading"

(2) the result of an action exists or the state resulting from an action exists: "something has been done, and the result of that action exists," or "something is done." This usage is common among Verbs which are not continuative.

chigaimashita	......	chigatte imasu	"is different"
hairimashita	......	haitte imasu	"is in"
karimashita	......	karite imasu	"have borrowed"
kekkon shimashita	......	kekkon shite imasu	"is married"
kikimashita*	......	kiite imasu	"have heard"
kimashita*	......	kite imasu	"wear"
mochimashita	......	motte imasu	"have"
shirimashita	......	shitte imasu	"know"
wakarimashita	......	wakatte imasu	"is understood"
wasuremashita	......	wasurete imasu	"have forgotten"

* Most of the Verbs listed under the first usage may also indicate "the result of an action" under certain limited circumstances. Verbs such as *kikimasu* and *kimasu*, however, are used in either one of the two meanings rather regularly. The context usually makes it clear which meaning is called for.

Chichi wa ima gin'koo ni tsutomete imasu.	"My father is working for the bank now."
Boku wa ima arubaito o shite imasen.	"I'm not working (I don't have a part-time job) now."
Yamamoto san wa mae Kyooto ni sun'de imashita.	"Mr. Yamamoto was living (used to live) in Kyōto before."
Eki de matte ite kudasai.	"Please be waiting at the station."
Kinoo no kuji goro nani o shite imashita ka ?	"What were you doing around nine o'clock yesterday?"
Terebi o mite imashita.	"I was watching television."

2.4.3 The Relational *ni* as in *natsuyasumi ni* or *nan'ji ni* is used to indicate a specific point of time. *Ni* corresponds to "at" as in "at three o'clock," "in" as in "in 1966," or "on" as in "on Monday." The Relational *wa* or *mo* may follow *ni,* forming multiple Relationals. (See 9.4.11, Vol. I.)

yasumi		"on vacation" "on a holiday"
haruyasumi		"during the spring vacation"
natsuyasumi		"during the summer vacation"
akiyasumi		"during the fall vacation"
fuyuyasumi		"during the winter vacation"
kugatsu	ni	"in September"
nan'gatsu		"in what month?"
yoji		"at four o'clock"
nan'ji		"at what time?"
sen kyuuhyaku rokujuu rokunen		"in 1966"
nan'nen		"in what year?"

Natsuyasumi ni nani o shimasu ka? "What are you going to do during the summer vacation?"

Kuji ni mo kite kudasai. "Please come at nine o'clock also."

Note the difference between time Nominatives that require the time Relational *ni* and those which are used alone, such as *kinoo, rainen,* etc.

2.4.4 *Arubaito (o) shimasu* means "(a student's) work (for money)," or "do a side-job." *Arubaito* comes from "arbeit," a German word for "work."

2.4.5 *Shichigatsu* means "July," and *hachigatsu* "August." The name of months is the combination of a numeral and the dependent Nominative *-gatsu*.

ichigatsu	"January"	shichigatsu	"July"
nigatsu	"February"	hachigatsu	"August"
san'gatsu	"March"	kugatsu	"September"
shigatsu	"April"	juugatsu	"October"
gogatsu	"May"	juuichigatsu	"November"
rokugatsu	"June"	juunigatsu	"December"

Nan'gatsu is the word for "what month?"

Nan'gatsu ni ryokoo shimashoo ka? "In what month shall we take a trip?"

Kon'getsu wa nan'gatsu desu ka? "What month is this month?"

Kon'getsu wa kugatsu desu yo. "This month is September."

Sen kyuuhyaku rokujuu rokunen (no) shigatsu ni Yooroppa e ikimashita. "I went to Europe in April, 1966."

2.4.6 *Shibaraku (desu nee)* is used in the meaning of "It's been a long time since I last saw you," or "I haven't seen you for a long time."

2.4.7 Unlike in English, the name of a person such as *Hayashi san* can be used instead of *anata* or *kimi* "you" in Japanese. Here *Hayashi san* is used in a sentence directly addressed to Mr. Hayashi instead of *anata*. It is not hard to know whether the speaker is referring to the third person or the second person.

| Ichiroo kun wa doko ni sun'de imasu ka ? | (1) "Ichirō, where are you living?" (2) "Where is Ichirō living?" |

2.4.8 The Verb *tsutomemasu* means "is employed," "serve in," or "work for (an organization)." The organization such as *depaato* "department store," *gin'koo* "bank" is always followed by *ni*.

| Anata wa doko ni tsutomete imasu ka ? | "What (organization, company, bank) are you working for?" |
| Tookyoo Gin'koo ni tsutomete imasu. | "I am working for the Bank of Tōkyō." |

2.4.9 *Hatarakimasu* is a word for "work," or "labor." While *tsutomete imasu* means "is employed (by an organization) and work (for it)," *hataraite imasu* merely means "is working" and often "is working physically." *Hatarakimasu* cannot be used in the meaning of "study."

| Depaato de hatarakimashita. | "I worked at a department store." |
| Haha wa ima niwa de hataraite imasu. | "My mother is now working in the garden." |

2.4.10 *Yukkuri* is an Adverb meaning "leisurely," "slowly," or "take (one's) time." *Yukkuri hanashimashoo* here means "Let's talk it over leisurely."

| Yukkuri hanashite kudasai. | "Please speak slowly." |

2.4.11 *Ukagaimasu* here is a polite equivalent of "visit (someone else's house)," or "go (to someone else's house)." *Ukagaimasu* is a motion Verb and is used like *ikimasu*.

| Zehi (anata no uchi e) ukagaimasu. | "I will visit (your house) by all means." |
| Kinoo sen'sei no tokoro e ukagaimashita. | "I went to the teacher's (place) yesterday." |

2.4.12 *Shitte imasu* means "[I] know it." The Verb *shirimasu* ← *shiru* is somewhat different in usage from other Verbs. *Shirimasu* means "get to know," or "come to know." Therefore, the state "someone does not know it" is expressed by the negative imperfect *shirimasen* "you haven't come to know," but never *shitte imasen*. Note that the negative expressions of "know" are formed differently from the affirmative expressions.

shitte imasu	"know"
shirimasen	"do not know"
shitte imashita	"knew"
shirimasen deshita	"did not know"

| Nihon'go o shitte imasu ka ? | "Do you know the Japanese language?" |

Hai, sukoshi shitte imasu.   "Yes, I know a little."

Iie, shirimasen.   "No, I don't know it."

2.4.13 *Watashi no tokoro wa shitte imashita ne*? may mean not only "you KNEW my address, didn't you?," but it also can mean "you KNOW my address, don't you?" The reason why this Japanese sentence has the Predicate in the perfect tense is that it carries the connotation of "that WAS my understanding or memory."

Anata wa daigakusei deshita ne ?   (1) "You were a college student, weren't you?"
(2) "According to my understanding, you are a college student. Am I right?"

The situation usually makes it clear which meaning is called for.

2.4.14 The expression "is living in (a place)" is expressed as ~ *ni sun'de imasu*. The Verb *sumimasu* "live" does not need any specific action except to be in that place and it represents something inactive like *imasu* and *arimasu*. Consequently, a place where one lives is never followed by *de* but by *ni*. (See 4.4.2, Vol. I.)

Mae no tokoro ni sun'de imasu.   "I am living in the same place where I used to live."

Doko ni sun'de imasu ka ?   "Where are you living?"

Ima Oosaka ni sun'de imasu.   "I am now living in Ōsaka."

2.4.15 The Verb *wakarimasu* means "can find," "understand," or "is clear," and is an intransitive Verb. Therefore, WHAT is understood or WHAT can be found has to be followed by the subject Relational *ga* or *wa*.

Watashi no uchi wa sugu wakarimasu yo.   "You will discover my house easily."

When it is necessary to mention WHO understands, the Relational *wa* follows the person.

Anata wa nihon'go ga wakarimasu ka ?   "Do you understand Japanese?"

2.4.16 *Motte imasen* means "do not have," and is a transitive Verb. Note that the Verb *mochimasu* ← *motsu* means an action, "hold," "own," etc. Therefore, the state of "have" would be expressed by *motte imasu*, the result of *motsu*, to hold.

Jidoosha wa motte imasen.   "I don't have a car."

Anata wa okane o motte imasu ka ?   "Do you have some money?"

Iie, motte imasen.   "No, I don't."

2.4.17 *-Han* is a dependent Nominative meaning "half," and is often attached to numbers such as *goji* "five o'clock," *ichinen* "one year," etc., to express the meaning "five-thirty," "one year and a half," etc.

Ima nan'ji desu ka?			"What time is it now?"
Yojihan desu.			"It's four-thirty."
Nihon ni ichinen'han sun'de imashita.			"I was living in Japan a year and a half."

2.4.18 *-Goro* is a dependent Nominative that occurs immediately after a time expression, and means an approximate point of time or "about." The time Relational *ni* that has been introduced in Note 2.4.3 may be replaced by *-goro*, or both *-goro* and *ni* may occur. In the latter case, *-goro* always precedes *ni*.

Nan'ji ni kimashita ka?	"What time did you come?"
Niji goro (ni) kimashita.	"I came here about two o'clock."

Do not confuse the *-goro* "approximate point of time" with *-gurai* and *-kurai* "approximate amount or number."

Ohiru goro uchi e kaerimasu.	"I am going home about noon."
Gohyakunin gurai imashita.	"There were about five hundred persons."

2.4.19 *Jaa, mata ashita* is used casually to mean "Well, see you tomorrow." *Jaa, mata* may be used as equivalent to "See you (again)," or "So long."

2.5 VOCABULARY

Presentation

大学生	daigakusei	......	N	college student
一郎	Ichiroo	......	N	boy's first name
四年生	yonen'sei	......	N	a senior student; fourth year student (see 2.4.1)
きょういく学	kyooiku-gaku	......	N	study of education; pedagogy
べんきょうして	ben'kyoo shite	......	V	TE form of *ben'kyoo shimasu* ← *ben'kyoo suru* – study (see 2.4.2)
います	imasu	......	E	normal form of *iru* (see 2.4.2)
やすみ	yasumi	......	N	vacation; leave; holiday; (day) off
に	ni	......	R	at; in; on (time Relational) (see 2.4.3)
よく	yoku	......	Adv.	often
アルバイト	arubaito	......	N	(student's) work (for money) (see 2.4.4)
アルバイトします	arubaito shimasu	......	V	do a side-job
七月	shichigatsu	......	N	July (see 2.4.5)
八月	hachigatsu	......	N	August

Dialog

林 はやし	Hayashi	......	N	family name
四年	yonen	......	N	fourth year (see 2.4.1)
しごと	shigoto	......	N	work; job
つとめて	tsutomete	......	V	TE form of *tsutomemasu* ← *tsutomeru* – is employed (see 2.4.8)
はたらきました	hatarakimashita	......	V	worked; labored (TA form of *hatarakimasu* ← *hataraku*) (see 2.4.9)
ゆっくり	yukkuri	......	Adv.	leisurely; slowly; take one's time (see 2.4.10)
ぜひ	zehi	......	Adv.	by all means; without fail
うかがいます	ukagaimasu	......	V	visit; go (to someone's house) (normal form of *ukagau*) (see 2.4.11)
ところ	tokoro	......	N	place; address
しって	shitte	......	V	TE form of *shirimasu* ← *shiru* – know (see 2.4.12)
いました	imashita	......	E	TA form of *imasu* ← *iru*
すんで	sun'de	......	V	TE form of *sumimasu* ← *sumu* – live (see 2.4.14)
ええと	eeto	......	SI	let me see; well
しぶや	Shibuya	......	N	a district of Tōkyō
わかります	wakarimasu	......	V	find; understand; is clear (see 2.4.15)
もって	motte	......	V	TE form of *mochimasu* ← *motsu* – have; hold; possess (see 2.4.16)
いません	imasen	......	E	negative form of *imasu* ← *iru*
五時はん じ	gojihan	......	N	five-thirty (see 2.4.17)
ごろ	-goro	......	Nd	about (time); approximately (see 2.4.18)

Notes

いましょう	imashoo	......	E	OO form of *imasu* ← *iru* (see 2.4.2)
いて	ite	......	E	TE form of *imasu* ← *iru* (see 2.4.2)
九月	kugatsu	......	N	September
一月	ichigatsu	......	N	January
二月	nigatsu	......	N	February
三月	san'gatsu	......	N	March
四月	shigatsu	......	N	April
五月	gogatsu	......	N	May
六月	rokugatsu	......	N	June
十月	juugatsu	......	N	October
十一月	juuichigatsu	......	N	November
十二月	juunigatsu	......	N	December

つとめます	tsutomemasu	 V	is employed; work for (an organization) (see 2.4.8)
はたらいて	hataraite	 V	TE form of *hatarakimasu* ← *hataraku* (see 2.4.9)
しります	shirimasu	 V	get to know; come to know (see 2.4.12)
しりません	shirimasen	 V	do not know (see 2.4.12)
すみます	sumimasu	 V	live (see 2.4.14)
大阪（おおさか）	Oosaka	...... N	the biggest city in western Japan
もちます	mochimasu	 V	hold; own; possess (see 2.4.16)
はん	-han	...... Nd	half (see 2.4.17)

2.6 KANJI

2.6.1 大 (1) DAI (2) big; large; great (3) forms the classifier 大 (4) 一 ナ 大
(5) 大すき、大きらい

2.6.2 学 (1) GAKU (2) learning; study (3) classifier 子
(4) ⎧ ⎧ ⎧ ⎧ ⎧ 学 学 (5) 大学、メリーランド大学、ハワイ大学

2.6.3 生 (1) SEI (2) beings; life; birth; person (3) forms the classifier 生
(4) ノ ヒ 牛 牛 生 (5) 先生（せん）、学生

2.6.4 年 (1) NEN (2) year (3) classifier 干 (4) ノ ヒ 午 午 年 年
(5) 一年、四年生、なん年、まい年

2.6.5 日 (1) NICHI [NI for NIHON] (2) sun; day; daytime (3) forms the classifier 日
(4) l 冂 日 日 (5) まい日、日本

2.6.6 本 (1) HON (2) origin; book (3) classifier 木 (4) 一 十 才 木 本
(5) 日本、本や、日本語の本

2.6.7 月 (1) -GATSU (2) counter for name of month; moon - *tsuki* (3) forms the classifier
月 (4)) 几 月 月 (5) 七月、九月、十二月、なん月

2.7 DRILLS

2.7.1 Pattern Drill

1. Ichiroo wa kyooiku-gaku o ben'kyoo shite imasu.

2. Nihon no daigakusei wa, natsuyasumi ni, yoku arubaito o shimasu.

3. Ichiroo wa, shichigatsu ni arubaito o shimashita.

4. Hayashi san wa, ima, nan no shigoto o shite imasu ka?

5. Depaato ni tsutomete imasu.

6. Boku mo natsuyasumi ni depaato de hatarakimashita yo.

7. Watashi no tokoro wa shitte imashita ne?

8. Ima mo mae no tokoro ni sun'de imasu.

9. Jidoosha wa motte imasen.

10. Nan'ji ni ukagaimashoo ka?

11. Dewa, gojihan goro matte imasu yo.

2.7.2 Transformation Drill

1. きょういく学を　べんきょうします。　　──→　きょういく学を　べんきょうしています。

2. ぎんこうに　つとめます。　　　　　　　──→　ぎんこうに　つとめています。

3. 一郎くんが　日本語で　はなします。　　──→　一郎くんが　日本語で　はなしています。

4. おんがくを　ききます。　　　　　　　　──→　おんがくを　きいています。

5. 大阪を　けんぶつします。　　　　　　　──→　大阪を　けんぶつしています。

6. えきで　まちます。　　　　　　　　　　──→　えきで　まっています。

7. 日本語の　本を　さがします。　　　　　──→　日本語の　本を　さがしています。

8. ゆっくり　しんぶんを　よみます。　　　──→　ゆっくり　しんぶんを　よんでいます。

9. ドイツ語を　ならいます。　　　　　　　──→　ドイツ語を　ならっています。

10. にわで　はたらきます。　　　　　　　　──→　にわで　はたらいています。

11. ピアノを　ひきます。　　　　　　　　　──→　ピアノを　ひいています。

12. アメリカに　すみます。　　　　　　　　──→　アメリカに　すんでいます。

2.7.3 Response Drill

1. いま　日本語を　ならっていますか。

　　はい　　　　　　　　　　　……　はい、　いま　日本語を　ならっています。

　　いいえ　　　　　　　　　　……　いいえ、　いま　日本語を　ならっていません。

2. きょ年　ハワイに　すんでいましたか。

　　はい　　　　　　　　　　　……　はい、　きょ年　ハワイに　すんでいました。

　　いいえ　　　　　　　　　　……　いいえ、　きょ年　ハワイに　すんでいませんでした。

3. いま　デパートで　はたらいていますか。

　　はい　　　　　　　　　　　……　はい、　いま　デパートで　はたらいています。

　　いいえ　　　　　　　　　　……　いいえ、　いま　デパートで　はたらいていません。

4. ごしゅじんは　ぎんこうに　つとめていますか。

　　はい　　　　　　　　　…… はい、　しゅじんは　ぎんこうに　つとめています。

　　いいえ　　　　　　　　…… いいえ、　しゅじんは　ぎんこうに　つとめていません。

5. きのうの　よる　あめが　ふっていましたか。

　　はい　　　　　　　　　…… はい、　きのうの　よる　あめが　ふっていました。

　　いいえ　　　　　　　　…… いいえ、　きのうの　よる　あめが　ふっていませんでした。

6. けいこさんは　スージーさんを　まっていますか。

　　はい　　　　　　　　　…… はい、　けいこさんは　スージーさんを　まっています。

　　いいえ　　　　　　　　…… いいえ、　けいこさんは　スージーさんを　まっていません。

2.7.4　Relational Checking Drill

デパートで　はたらいています。

1. 日本　　　　　　　　　…… 日本で　はたらいています。
2. べんきょうしています　…… 日本で　べんきょうしています。
3. 大学　　　　　　　　　…… 大学で　べんきょうしています。
4. ならっています　　　　…… 大学で　ならっています。
5. まっています　　　　　…… 大学で　まっています。
6. ぎんこう　　　　　　　…… ぎんこうで　まっています。
7. アルバイトしています　…… ぎんこうで　アルバイトしています。
8. つとめています　　　　…… ぎんこうに　つとめています。
9. どこ　　　　　　　　　…… どこに　つとめていますか。
10. すんでいましたか　　　…… どこに　すんでいましたか。

2.7.5　Relational Checking Drill

なつやすみに　いきましたか。

1. いつ　　　　　…… いつ　いきましたか。
2. なん月　　　　…… なん月に　いきましたか。
3. 九月　　　　　…… 九月に　いきましたか。
4. きのう　　　　…… きのう　いきましたか。
5. なん年　　　　…… なん年に　いきましたか。
6. なん時　　　　…… なん時に　いきましたか。
7. 千九百六十年　…… 千九百六十年に　いきましたか。
8. きょ年　　　　…… きょ年　いきましたか。
9. ふゆやすみ　　…… ふゆやすみに　いきましたか。

10. けさ   …… けさ　いきましたか。

11. まい日   …… まい日　いきましたか。

12. 七時はん   …… 七時はんに　いきましたか。

13. 四月   …… 四月に　いきましたか。

14. まいしゅう   …… まいしゅう　いきましたか。

15. まい年   …… まい年　いきましたか。

2.7.6　E-J Transformation Drill

1. じむしょで　はたらきます。

  I'm working   …… じむしょで　はたらいています。

  I'm not working   …… じむしょで　はたらいていません。

  I was working   …… じむしょで　はたらいていました。

  please be working   …… じむしょで　はたらいていてください。

2. しります。

  do you know   …… しっていますか。

  I don't know   …… しりません。

  I knew   …… しっていました。

  I didn't know   …… しりませんでした。

3. 大阪に　すみます。

  I'm not living   …… 大阪に　すんでいません

  I was living   …… 大阪に　すんでいました。

  are you living   …… 大阪に　すんでいますか。

  I was not living   …… 大阪に　すんでいませんでした。

4. じどうしゃを　もちます。

  I have   …… じどうしゃを　もっています。

  I don't have   …… じどうしゃを　もっていません。

  did you have   …… じどうしゃを　もっていましたか。

  I didn't have   …… じどうしゃを　もっていませんでした。

5. てがみを　かきます。

  I am writing   …… てがみを　かいています。

  I was not writing   …… てがみを　かいていませんでした。

  I was writing   …… てがみを　かいていました。

6. デパートで　うります。

  (they) were selling   …… デパートで　うっていました。

34

(they) are not selling ...... デパートで　うっていません。

(they) are selling ...... デパートで　うっています。

(they) were not selling ...... デパートで　うっていませんでした。

2.7.7　E-J Response Drill

1. なん年に　日本へ　来ましたか。
   in 1966   ...... 千九百六十六年に　来ました。

2. いつ　アルバイトを　しましたか。
   during the spring vacation   ...... はるやすみに　しました。

3. いつ　きょうとへ　いきますか。
   next month   ...... らいげつ　いきます。

4. なん時に　うちへ　来ますか。
   about six o'clock   ...... 六時ごろ(に)　来ます。

5. いつ　ぎんこうで　はたらいていましたか。
   last year   ...... きょ年　はたらいていました。

6. なん月に　りょこうしますか。
   in October   ...... 十月に　りょこうします。

7. いつ　先生の　ところへ　うかがいましょうか。
   tomorrow   ...... あした　うかがいましょう。

8. なつやすみは　いつですか。
   July and August   ...... 七月と　八月です。

2.7.8　E-J Response Drill

1. いま、　なんの　しごとを　していますか。
   working for a bank   ...... ぎんこうに　つとめています。

2. あなたは　まえ、　どこに　すんでいましたか。
   Shinjuku   ...... しんじゅくに　すんでいました。

3. きのうの　よる　七時ごろ　なにを　していましたか。
   watching T.V.   ...... テレビを　みていました。

4. きょ年の　ふゆ　なにを　べんきょうしていましたか。
   studying Japanese at the University   ...... 大阪大学で　日本語を　べんきょうしていました。
   of Ōsaka

5. あなたは　まだ　学生ですか。
   yes, a junior at the University ...... はい、　ハワイ大学の　三年(生)です。
   of Hawaii

6. やまださんの　ところを　しっていますか。
no　　　　　　　　　　　　　…… いいえ、　しりません。

7. じどうしゃを　もっていますか。
no　　　　　　　　　　　　　…… いいえ、　もっていません。

8. いま　なにを　していますか。
reading a newspaper　　　　…… しんぶんを　よんでいます。

9. 林さんは　けっこんしていますか。
no　　　　　　　　　　　　　…… いいえ、　けっこんしていません。

10. レインコートは　どこで　うっていますか。
basement　　　　　　　　　…… ちかで　うっています。

2.7.9　Transformation Drill (Review)

1. ここで　はたらいています。　　　　⟶ ここで　はたらいていてください。
2. えきで　まっています。　　　　　　⟶ えきで　まっていてください。
3. コーヒーを　のんでいます。　　　　⟶ コーヒーを　のんでいてください。
4. ジャズを　きいています。　　　　　⟶ ジャズを　きいていてください。
5. この　本を　よんでいます。　　　　⟶ この　本を　よんでいてください。
6. うちで　べんきょうしています。　　⟶ うちで　べんきょうしていてください。
7. テレビを　みています。　　　　　　⟶ テレビを　みていてください。
8. あの　レストランで　たべています。⟶ あの　レストランで　たべていてください。

2.8　EXERCISES

2.8.1　Insert an appropriate form in each blank, according to the English equivalent:

1. けさ　なにを　（　　　　　　　　　　　）。
What were you doing this morning?

2. にわで　（　　　　　　　　　）。
He is not working in the garden.

3. だれを　（　　　　　　　　）。
Whom are you waiting for?

4. ジャズを　（　　　　　　　　　）。
I was not listening to jazz.

5. 二かいで　（　　　　　　　）。
They are selling it on the second floor.

36

6. やまださんは　こうちゃを　（　　　　　　　　　　　　　）。
   Mr. Yamada is not drinking black tea.

7. なに語を　（　　　　　　　　　　　　　　　）。
   What language do you know?

2.8.2　Answer the following questions in Japanese:

1. あなたは　大学生ですね？
2. どこの　学生ですか。
3. いま　なん年生ですか。
4. 日本語を　しっていますか。
5. いま　フランス語を　ならっていますか。
6. なつやすみは　なん月ですか。
7. きょ年の　なつやすみに　アルバイトを　しましたか。
8. いま　どこに　すんでいますか。
9. かぞくと　いっしょに　すんでいますか。
10. じどうしゃを　もっていますか。

2.8.3　Insert an appropriate Relational in blank, if necessary:

1. 千九百六十五年（　　）日本（　　）来ました。
2. やすみ（　　）どこ（　　）はたらきましたか。
3. みちこさんが　四時（　　）えき（　　）まっていますよ。
4. きょ年（　　）どこ（　　）すんでいましたか。
5. けさ（　　）七時はん（　　）大阪（　　）でかけました。
6. なん月（　　）ハワイ（　　）かえりますか。
7. 五月（　　）六月（　　）学校（　　）アルバイト（　　）しました。
8. まい日（　　）コーヒー（　　）ほしいですねえ。
9. いま（　　）どこ（　　）つとめていますか。
10. 林さん（　　）えい語（　　）わかりません。

2.8.4　Write the underlined *hiragana* in *kanji*:

1. わたしは　くがつに　だいがくへ　いきます。
2. 一郎は　だいがくせいです。　いま、　よねんせいです。
3. いつ　にほんへ　来ましたか。　きょねんの　じゅうにがつに　来ました。

2.9 SITUATIONAL CONVERSATION

2.9.1   Two friends meet in the street

They haven't seen each other for a long time.

They ask each other what they are doing and where they are living, etc.

One is a sophomore at college and one is a bank employee.

The student had a part-time job at a restaurant during the winter vacation.

The bank employee invites the student for dinner at his home.

They set time and day for dinner.

2.9.2   Same as 2.9.1. Change the two friends' profession or job, living place, etc.

2.9.3   Free conversation under the topic of college life.

LESSON 3

3.1 PRESENTATION

— か ぶ き —

「かぶき」は 千六百年ごろに はじまりました。 その ころ、「かぶき」は
しょみんの ごらくでした。

いまは、 日本の だいひょう的な^{*1} 芸術の 一つです。^{*2}

3.2 DIALOG

井上 「もしもし、 森さんの おたくですか。」

よし子 「はい、 そうです。」

井上 「よし子さんは いらっしゃいますか。^{*3}」

よし子 「わたくしですが……。^{*4}」

井上 「あ、 よし子さん。 ぼく、^{*5} 井上です。」

よし子 「あら、 こんにちは。」

井上 「金曜日に^{*6} あなたに^{*7} あいたかったんですが、^{*8} 学校に^{*9} 来ませんでしたね?
　　　びょうきでしたか。」

よし子 「ええ。 じゅぎょうを やすみたくありませんでしたが、^{*10} かぜで きぶんが^{*11}
　　　わるかったんです。」

井上 「まだ わるいんですか。」

よし子 「いいえ。 きのうは 一日中^{*12} ねていましたが、^{*13} きょうは もう
　　　だいじょうぶです。」

井上 「それは よかったですね。 じつは、 らいしゅうの^{*14} 土曜日の かぶきの
　　　きっぷを もっています。 よし子さんは かぶきを 見たくありませんか。」

よし子 「ええ、 ぜひ 見たいです。」

井上 「じゃあ、ごご *15 四時十五分 *16 ごろ、 かぶきざで あいましょう。 ぼくは、
ともだちを ひとり つれていきます。」 *17

よし子 「らいしゅうの 土曜日、 四時十五分ですね? わかりました。 どうも
ありがとう。」

井上 「いいえ。 じゃあ、 また。」

よし子 「さようなら。」

3.3 PATTERN SENTENCES

3.3.1

Adv.
zehi

V	Da	(PC)	C
mi	TAI	n	desu

"I should very much like to see it."

3.3.2

N	R
kin'yoobi	ni

N	R
anata	ni

V	Da	(PC)	C
ai	TAKATTA	n	desu

"I wanted to see you on Friday."

3.3.3

N	R
kabuki	o

V	Da	E
mi	TAKU	ARIMASEN

"I don't want to see *kabuki*."

3.3.4

N	R
jugyoo	o

V	Da	E	C
yasumi	TAKU	ARIMASEN	DESHITA

"I did not want to miss class."

3.4 NOTES

3.4.1 *Daihyooteki na geijutsu* means "representative art." *Daihyooteki* is an adjectival Nominative, and an adjectival Nominative plus *na* will be explained in Note 5.4.1.

Kyooto wa Nihon no daihyooteki na tokoro desu.   "Kyōto is the representative place of Japan."

3.4.2 *Nihon no daihyooteki na geijutsu no hitotsu* means "one of the representative arts of Japan." An expression like (Nominative)+*no hitotsu* always means "one of the plural."

Mori san wa watakushi no gakusei no hitori desu.   "Mr. Mori is one of my students."

3.4.3 *Irasshaimasu* is a polite equivalent of *imasu*. *Irasshaimasu* is used only to mean "someone else's being (in a place)," and the speaker can not use it for his own "being (in a place)." *Irasshaimasu* used as a polite equivalent of *ikimasu* and *kimasu* will be introduced in Lesson 14.

Yoshiko san wa irasshaimasu ka?   "Is Yoshiko there (at home, etc.)?"

Soko ni donata ga irasshaimashita ka?   "Who was there?"

3.4.4 *Watakushi desu ga . . . .* is often used in telephone conversation to mean "she (or he) is speaking," "this is she (he) speaking," or "this is she (he)."

Inoue san to hanashitai n desu ga, irasshaimasu ka?   "I'd like to talk with Mr. Inoue, but is he there?"

(Inoue wa) boku desu ga . . .   "This is he."
Watakushi desu ga . . .

3.4.5 In conversation, Relationals, such as *wa, o,* etc., are sometimes dropped.

Watakushi, Yoshiko desu.   "I'm Yoshiko."

Boku, Inoue desu.   "I'm Inoue."

3.4.6 *Kin'yoobi* is a Nominative meaning "Friday." The days of the week are as follows:

nichiyoobi	日曜日	"Sunday"	*sun*
getsuyoobi	月曜日	"Monday"	*moon*
kayoobi	火曜日	"Tuesday"	*fire*
suiyoobi	水曜日	"Wednesday"	*water*
mokuyoobi	木曜日	"Thursday"	*wood (tree)*
kin'yoobi	金曜日	"Friday"	*gold*
doyoobi	土曜日	"Saturday"	*soil, dirt*

"What day of the week?" is *nan'yoobi*. In this series of words *-yoobi* may be shortened into *-yoo;* *nichiyoo, getsuyoo,* etc. These days of the week are usually followed by the time Relational *ni*, but they may sometimes occur without *ni*.

Nichiyoobi ni Tookyoo e ikimashita.	"I went to Tōkyō on Sunday."
Raishuu no kayoobi, kabuki o mitai desu.	"Next Tuesday, I want to see *kabuki*."
Kayoo to mokuyoo ni nihon'go no jugyoo ga arimasu.	"I have Japanese lessons on Tuesdays and Thursdays."

3.4.7 *Aimasu* is a Verb meaning "meet." As this Verb is an intransitive Verb, "the person seen" is not followed by *o* but the Relational *ni*.

Anata ni aimashita ka?	"Did he meet you?"
Eki de dare ni aimasu ka?	"Whom are you going to meet at the station?"

3.4.8 *Aitakatta* means "wanted to meet," and is the combination of the Stem form (or Pre-Masu form) (see 1.4.19) of the Verb *aimasu* "meet" and the TA form of the adjectival Derivative *-tai* "want to," or "would like to." Like Adjectives, *-tai* is followed by the Copula *desu* or *n desu* in normal style, and conjugates in the following manner:

(ai)tai (n) desu	"want to (meet)"
(ai)taku arimasen	"do not want to (meet)"
(ai)takatta (n) desu	"wanted to (meet)"
(ai)taku arimasen deshita	"did not want to (meet)"

The *-tai desu* normally represents the speaker's desire to do such and such, and, when used as the second person's desire or the third person's, there is limitation in use. When the Verb before *-tai* requires a direct object, the Relational *o* following the direct object may be replaced by the Relational *ga*. At this stage, however, try to use *o*.

$$\text{(Predicate Modifier)} + \left\{ \begin{array}{l} \textbf{Verb (Stem form)} \\ \textit{"} \ \textbf{\textit{(-te)}} + \textbf{\textit{i}} \\ \textit{"} \ \textbf{\textit{(-te)}} + \textbf{\textit{mi}} \end{array} \right\} + \textbf{\textit{-tai (n) desu}}$$

Ashita no asa wa rokuji ni okitai n desu.	"I'd like to get up at six tomorrow morning."
Kibun ga warui (desu) kara, ichinichijuu nete itai desu. (See 3.4.13 on *nete imasu*.)	"I want to be in bed all day long because I feel sick."
Nani o misetakatta n desu ka?	"What did you want to show me?"
Sukiyaki wa tabetaku arimasen.	"I don't want to eat *sukiyaki*."

Such expressions of invitation as "Would you like to do such and such?" or "Do you want to do such and such?" normally should not be expressed by using the *-tai desu ka*? These connotations are expressed in negation as follows:

Issho ni kabuki o mimasen ka?	"Would you like to see *kabuki* with me?"

As explained in Note 1.4.5, the clause Relational *ga* is often used with the pattern of "would like to (do)," to soften the directness of the desire.

Uchi e kaeritai n desu ga . . .	"I want to go home, but may I?"
Koohii o nomitai n desu ga . . .	"I would like to have some coffee."

"I would like to do such and such, but will that be all right with you?" or "I want to do this, but do you mind it?" is the idea of using *ga*.

3.4.9 In the place of the direction Relational *e, ni* is often used, in the same meaning, with such Verbs as *ikimasu, kimasu, kaerimasu, hairimasu, iremasu,* etc.

Gakkoo ni kimasen deshita ne ?	"You didn't come to school, did you?"
Doko ni ikitai desu ka ?	"Where do you want to go?"

3.4.10 *Yasumimasu* is "miss (class)," or "take leave." Since *yasumimasu* is a transitive Verb, the Relational *o* precedes *yasumimasu*. The Nominative that precedes *o* can be a place or an event.

gakkoo	"do not go to school"
jimusho	"do not go to the office to work" or "take (a day) off"
daigaku	"do not go to the university"
——— } o yasumimasu	———
jugyoo	"miss class" or "do not go to class"
shigoto	"take (a day) off from work" or "do not (go to) work"
ben'kyoo	"do not (go to) study"

When *yasumimasu* is used as an intransitive Verb, it means "rest."

Yamamoto san wa kinoo shigoto o yasumimashita.	"Mr. Yamamoto took a day off yesterday."
Chotto sono hen de yasumimashoo.	"Let's take a rest around there for a while."

3.4.11 *Kaze de* means "because of a cold." *De* is a Relational meaning "cause."

Kinoo jugyoo o yasumimashita ne ?	"You missed class yesterday, didn't you?"
Ee, kinoo wa byooki de nete imashita.	"Yes, I was sick in bed yesterday."
Shigoto de Doitsu e ikimashita.	"I went to Germany on business."

3.4.12 *Ichinichijuu* means "all day long," and is the combination of *ichinichi* "a day" and a dependent Nominative *-juu* that means "throughout," or "all (day) long." More examples are *ichinen'juu* "all year around," *fuyujuu* "throughout the winter," etc. This expression is usually used with the pattern *-te imasu,* when the Predicate is a Verb.

Kinoo wa ichinichijuu nete imashita.	"I was in bed all day long yesterday."

| Hawai wa ichinen'juu atatakai desu. | "Hawaii is warm throughout the year." |
| Natsujuu arubaito o shite imashita. | "I was working all the summer." |

3.4.13 The Verb *nemasu* can mean "go to bed," "lie (down)," or "sleep." When there is a necessity to distinguish "go to bed" from "sleep," *nemurimasu* may be used in the meaning of actually being asleep. The Verb meaning "get up" is *okimasu*.

Kinoo no yoru nan'ji ni nemashita ka ?	"What time did you go to bed last night?"
San'jippun gurai nete imashita.	"I was sleeping for about thirty minutes."
Maiasa nan'ji ni okimasu ka ?	"What time do you get up every morning?"

3.4.14 *Raishuu* means "next week." Here are more words of this group:

kon'shuu	"this week"
sen'shuu	"last week"
raishuu	"next week"

Like *kotoshi* "this year," *kyonen* "last year," and *rainen* "next year," these time Nominatives are used without the time Relational following.

Raishuu no doyoobi ni kabuki o mitaku arimasen ka ?	"Don't you want to see *kabuki* on Saturday of next week?"
Kon'shuu gakkoo o yasumimashita.	"I did not go to school this week."
Sen'shuu wa byooki de nemashita.	"I was in bed last week because of sickness."

3.4.15 *Gogo* means "p.m." as in "5:15 p.m.," or "in the afternoon" when used by itself. Likewise, *gozen* is used in the meaning of "a.m.," but *gozen* is not normally used to mean "in the morning"; *asa* is used instead.

Kinoo wa gogo yoji ni nemashita.	"I went to bed at four p.m. yesterday."
Ashita no gogo ukagaimasu.	"I will visit you tomorrow afternoon."
Jugyoo wa gozen kujihan ni hajimarimasu.	"Class will start at 9:30 a.m."

3.4.16 *Juugofun* is "fifteen minutes." The *-fun* is a counter for "minute(s)." Depending upon the numeral that precedes *-fun*, *-fun* sometimes changes into *-pun*.

1	ippun	5	gofun	9	kyuufun
2	nifun	6	roppun	10	jippun; juppun
3	san'pun	7	nanafun; shichifun		
4	yon'pun	8	happun; hachifun		

"How many minutes?" is *nan'pun*.

In telling time, "o'clock" is always said first and then "minutes."

Yoji juugofun ni owarimasu.   "It will be over at 4:15."

Juuniji yon'juppun goro aimashoo.   "Let's meet at about twelve-forty."

Nan'pun hanashite imashita ka?   "How many minutes were you talking?"

San'jippun gurai hanashite imashita.   "I was talking about thirty minutes."

3.4.17 *Tomodachi o tsurete ikimasu* means "I'll take a friend with me," or literally it means "I'll go accompanying a friend." *Tsurete* is the TE form of the Verb *tsuremasu* meaning "accompany" or "lead." When someone leads someone else to a certain place, one of the Extenders *ikimasu, kimasu,* and *kaerimasu* will be used after the TE form of *tsuremasu,* depending upon where the speaker is. *Tsurete ikimasu* is equivalent to "take a person (or an animal) with one (to a place)," *tsurete kimasu* is "bring a person with one (to a place)," and *tsurete kaerimasu* "take or bring a person back with one."

Nominative + o + tsurete + { *ikimasu / kimasu / kaerimasu* }
(animate)

otooto, tomodachi, kodomo, otoko no ko, inu } o tsurete { ikimasu "take" / kimasu "bring" / kaerimasu "take (bring) back" } { my younger brother / my friend / a child / a boy / a dog } (with me)"

Uchi e tomodachi o tsurete ikimashoo.   "I think I'll take a friend of mine with me to my house."

Otooto wa inu o tsurete kaerimashita.   "My younger brother brought a dog back with him."

When a thing is taken or brought with someone, *motte* "hold" is used in the place of *tsurete.*

Nominative + o + motte + { *ikimasu / kimasu / kaerimasu* }
(inanimate)

kippu, okane, miyage } o motte { ikimasu "take" / kimasu "bring" / kaerimasu "take (bring) back" } { a ticket / some money / souvenier } (with me)"

Gakkoo e jisho o motte ikimasen deshita.   "I did not take a dictionary with me to school."

Sono hako o motte kite kudasai.   "Please bring that box to me."

Suzuki san wa Amerika kara jidoosha o motte kaerimashita.   "Mr. Suzuki brought a car back from the States."

gurai – about (quantity)
goro – about (time)

3.5 VOCABULARY

Presentation

かぶき	kabuki	......	N	*kabuki* performance (performed only by men)
はじまりました	hajimarimashita	......	V	began (intransitive Verb) (TA form of *hajimarimasu* ← *hajimaru*)
(その)ころ	(sono)-koro	......	Nd	(those) days; (that) time
しょみん	shomin	......	N	common people; populace
ごらく	goraku	......	N	amusement
だいひょう的	daihyooteki	......	Na	representative
な	na	......	C	(see 3.4.1 and 5.4.1)
芸術	geijutsu	......	N	art

Dialog

井上	Inoue	......	N	family name
もしもし	moshi moshi	......	SI	hello (regularly used in telephone conversation)
森	Mori	......	N	family name
(お)たく	(o)taku	......	N	house; home (polite equivalent of *uchi*) (regularly used in telephone conversation, to ask if it is Mr. So-and-so's residence)
よし子	Yoshiko	......	N	girl's first name
いらっしゃいます	irasshaimasu	......	V	exist; is (normal form of *irassharu*; polite equivalent of *imasu*)
あら	ara	......	SI	oh; ah (used only by women)
金曜日	kin'yoobi	......	N	Friday (see 3.4.6)
あい	ai	......	V	Stem form of *aimasu* ← *au* – meet (see 3.4.7)
たかった	-takatta	......	Da	wanted to (do) (TA form of *-tai*) (see 3.4.8)
に	ni	......	R	to (a place) (see 3.4.9)
びょうき	byooki	......	N	illness
じゅぎょう	jugyoo	......	N	class; instruction
やすみ	yasumi	......	V	Stem form of *yasumimasu* ← *yasumu* – be absent (from class); take leave (see 3.4.10)
たく	-taku	......	Da	KU form of *-tai* – want to (see 3.4.8)
かぜ	kaze	......	N	a cold
で	de	......	R	because of (see 3.4.11)
きぶん	kibun	......	N	feeling (cf. feel sick, feel fine)
一日中	ichinichijuu	......	N	all day long (see 3.4.12)
ねて	nete	......	V	TE form of *nemasu* ← *neru* – go to bed; sleep (see 3.4.13)

だいじょうぶ	daijoobu	......	Na	all right; safe (this word is used to allay fear or doubt)
じつは	jitsu wa	......	SI	the fact is; the reason why (I've called you) is
らいしゅう	raishuu	......	N	next week (see 3.4.14)
土曜日	doyoobi	......	N	Saturday
たい	-tai	......	Da	want to (do) (see 3.4.8)
ごご	gogo	......	N	p.m.; in the afternoon (see 3.4.15)
分	-fun	......	Nd	minute (see 3.4.16)
かぶきざ	Kabukiza	......	N	*Kabuki* Theater
あいましょう	aimashoo	......	V	let us meet (OO form of *aimasu* ← *au*)
つれて	tsurete	......	V	TE form of *tsuremasu* ← *tsureru* – take (with); bring (with); accompany (see 3.4.17)
いきます	ikimasu	......	E	go (~ing) (see 3.4.17)

Notes

日曜日	nichiyoobi	......	N	Sunday
月曜日	getsuyoobi	......	N	Monday
火曜日	kayoobi	......	N	Tuesday
水曜日	suiyoobi	......	N	Wednesday
木曜日	mokuyoobi	......	N	Thursday
曜(日)	-yoo(bi)	......	Nd	day of the week
おき(たい)	oki(tai)	......	V	Stem form of *okimasu* ← *okiru* – get up (intransitive Verb)
すきやき	sukiyaki	......	N	*sukiyaki;* beef cooked with vegetables
中	-juu	......	Nd	throughout
こんしゅう	kon'shuu	......	N	this week
せんしゅう	sen'shuu	......	N	last week
ごぜん	gozen	......	N	a.m.
おわります	owarimasu	......	V	end; finish (intransitive Verb) (normal form of *owaru*)
きます	kimasu	......	E	come (~ing) (see 3.4.17)
かえります	kaerimasu	......	E	go (come) back (~ing)
みやげ	miyage	......	N	souvenir; gift

Drills

バス	basu	......	N	bus

3.6 KANJI

3.6.1 子 (1) *ko* (2) child (3) forms the classifier 子 (4) フ　了　子

(5) 子ども、よし子、女の子

3.6.2 金 (1) KIN (2) gold (3) forms the classifier 金

(4) ノ　ハ　人　今　全　宇　余　金 (5) 金曜日、金ぱつ [blond]

^{2.6.5}

日 (1) *bi* (5) 金曜日、日曜日、たんじょう日 [birthday]

3.6.3 来 (1) *ki(masu)* (2) come (3) classifier 一 (4) 一　ー　つ　ユ　平　来　来

(5) 来ます、来てください

3.6.4 土 (1) DO (2) earth; soil (3) forms the classifier 土 (4) 一　十　土

(5) 土曜日

3.6.5 見 (1) *mi(masu)* (2) see; watch; look (3) forms the classifier 見

(4) 丨　冂　冂　月　目　尸　見 (5) 見ます、見ましょう、見せます

3.6.6 時 (1) JI (2) time; o'clock (3) classifier 日

(4) 丨　冂　冂　日　日一　日十　昨　昨　時　時 (5) 九時、十一時、なん時

3.6.7 分 (1) FUN [-PUN] (2) minute (3) classifier 刀 (4) ノ　八　分　分

(5) 二分、三分、十五分

^{2.6.7}

月 (1) GETSU (5) 月曜日、せん月、こん月、らい月、まい月

3.6.8 火 (1) KA (2) fire (3) forms the classifier 火 (4) 丶　丷　少　火

(5) 火曜日、火事 [a fire]

3.6.9 水 (1) SUI (2) water (3) forms the classifier 水 (4) 丨　才　水　水

(5) 水曜日

3.6.10 木 (1) MOKU (2) tree; wood (3) forms the classifier 木 (4) 一　十　才　木

(5) 木曜日

3.7 DRILLS

3.7.1 Pattern Drill

1. Kin'yoobi ni anata ni aitakatta n desu ga, gakkoo ni kimasen deshita ne?

2. Jugyoo o yasumitaku arimasen deshita ga, kaze de kibun ga warukatta n desu.

3. Yoshiko san wa kabuki o mitaku arimasen ka?

4. Ee, zehi mitai desu.

3.7.2 Transformation Drill

1. よし子さんに あいます。 ⟶ よし子さんに あいたいです。
2. おちゃを もう 一ぱい のみます。 ⟶ おちゃを もう 一ぱい のみたいです。
3. ごご えいがを 見ます。 ⟶ ごご えいがを 見たいです。
4. つぎの 月曜日に しごとを やすみます。 ⟶ つぎの 月曜日に しごとを やすみたいです。
5. なつやすみに アルバイトを します。 ⟶ なつやすみに アルバイトを したいです。
6. 東京に すみます。 ⟶ 東京に すみたいです。
7. おとこの くつを かいます。 ⟶ おとこの くつを かいたいです。
8. 日本の 芸術を べんきょうします。 ⟶ 日本の 芸術を べんきょうしたいです。
9. いもうとを つれていきます。 ⟶ いもうとを つれていきたいです。
10. みやげを もってかえります。 ⟶ みやげを もってかえりたいです。

3.7.3 Transformation Drill

1. かぶきへ いきたいんです。 ⟶ かぶきへ いきたかったんです。
2. 日本語を かきたいんです。 ⟶ 日本語を かきたかったんです。
3. 六時に おきたいんです。 ⟶ 六時に おきたかったんです。
4. 金曜日に 来たいんです。 ⟶ 金曜日に 来たかったんです。
5. デパートで はたらきたいんです。 ⟶ デパートで はたらきたかったんです。
6. えい語で はなしたいんです。 ⟶ えい語で はなしたかったんです。
7. おんがくを ききたいんです。 ⟶ おんがくを ききたかったんです。
8. きょうだいを つれていきたいんです。 ⟶ きょうだいを つれていきたかったんです。
9. じしょを もってきたいんです。 ⟶ じしょを もってきたかったんです。
10. 一日中 ねていたいんです。 ⟶ 一日中 ねていたかったんです。

3.7.4 Response Drill

1. かぶきを 見たいですか。 ⟶ いいえ、かぶきは 見たくありません。
2. じゅぎょうを やすみたいですか。 ⟶ いいえ、じゅぎょうは やすみたくありません。

3. らいしゅう　大阪へ　いきたいですか。　——→　いいえ、らいしゅう　大阪へは　いきたく
ありません。

4. てがみを　かきたいですか。　　　——→　いいえ、てがみは　かきたくありません。

5. コーヒーを　のみたいですか。　　——→　いいえ、コーヒーは　のみたくありません。

6. しんぶんを　よみたいですか。　　——→　いいえ、しんぶんは　よみたくありません。

7. ドイツ語を　ならいたいですか。　——→　いいえ、ドイツ語は　ならいたくありません。

8. ともだちに　あいたいですか。　　——→　いいえ、ともだちには　あいたくありません。

9. いぬを　つれていきたいですか。　——→　いいえ、いぬは　つれていきたくありません。

10. これを　学校へ　もってきたいですか。——→　いいえ、これは　学校へ　もってきたく
ありません。

3.7.5　Response Drill (short answer)

1. かぶきを　見たかったんですか。　　——→　いいえ、見たくありませんでした。

2. 火曜日に　いきたかったんですか。　——→　いいえ、いきたくありませんでした。

3. きょ年、日本へ　来たかったんですか。——→　いいえ、来たくありませんでした。

4. けい子さんに　あいたかったんですか。——→　いいえ、あいたくありませんでした。

5. 三月に　りょこうしたかったんですか。——→　いいえ、りょこうしたくありませんでした。

6. じゅぎょうを　やすみたかったん　　——→　いいえ、やすみたくありませんでした。
ですか。

7. 木曜日に　うちへ　かえりたかったん　——→　いいえ、かえりたくありませんでした。
ですか。

8. 東京を　けんぶつしたかったんですか。——→　いいえ、けんぶつしたくありませんでした。

9. おみやげを　かいたかったんですか。——→　いいえ、かいたくありませんでした。

10. うちへ　つれてかえりたかったん　　——→　いいえ、つれてかえりたくありませんでした。
ですか。

3.7.6　Transformation Drill

1. 東京へ　いきたいです。　　　　——→　東京へ　いってみたいです。

2. 井上さんに　あいたいです。　　——→　井上さんに　あってみたいです。

3. ここで　はたらきたいです。　　——→　ここで　はたらいてみたいです。

4. 日本語を　べんきょうしたいです。——→　日本語を　べんきょうしてみたいです。

5. あの　セーターを　きたいです。——→　あの　セーターを　きてみたいです。

6. すきやきを　たべたいです。　　——→　すきやきを　たべてみたいです。

7. ハワイに　すみたいです。　　　——→　ハワイに　すんでみたいです。

8. 一日中　ねたいです。　　　　——→　一日中　ねてみたいです。

3.7.7 Substitution Drill

かぜで　学校を　やすみました。

1. びょうき	……	びょうきで　学校を　やすみました。
2. 学校に　いきませんでした	……	びょうきで　学校に　いきませんでした。
3. ねていました	……	びょうきで　ねていました。
4. かぜ	……	かぜで　ねていました。
5. きぶんが　わるいです	……	かぜで　きぶんが　わるいです。
6. アルバイトしませんでした	……	かぜで　アルバイトしませんでした。
7. ゆき	……	ゆきで　アルバイトしませんでした。
8. バスが　来ませんでした	……	ゆきで　バスが　来ませんでした。
9. あめ	……	あめで　バスが　来ませんでした。
10. うみへ　いきませんでした	……	あめで　うみへ　いきませんでした。

3.7.8 Substitution Drill

A.　本を　もってきました。

1. ネクタイ	……	ネクタイを　もってきました。
2. こうちゃ	……	こうちゃを　もってきました。
3. はし	……	はしを　もってきました。
4. いきます	……	はしを　もっていきます。
5. いきましょう	……	はしを　もっていきましょう。
6. きてください	……	はしを　もってきてください。
7. くつ	……	くつを　もってきてください。
8. かえりました	……	くつを　もってかえりました。
9. みやげ	……	みやげを　もってかえりました。
10. かえりませんでした	……	みやげを　もってかえりませんでした。

B.　学生を　つれていきます。

1. いもうと	……	いもうとを　つれていきます。
2. いぬ	……	いぬを　つれていきます。
3. かえります	……	いぬを　つれてかえります。
4. きましょう	……	いぬを　つれてきましょう。
5. 女の　人	……	女の　人を　つれてきましょう。
6. きますか	……	女の　人を　つれてきますか。
7. 子ども	……	子どもを　つれてきますか。
8. いきません	……	子どもを　つれていきません。

9. きました   …… 子どもを　つれてきました。

10. いきませんでした   …… 子どもを　つれていきませんでした。

3.7.9　E-J Response Drill

1. いま　なん時ですか。
 six-thirty   …… 六時三十分です。

2. まい日、なん時に　大学へ　いきますか。
 eight-fifteen   …… 八時十五分に　いきます。

3. なん時に　あいたいですか。
 about three-twenty   …… 三時二十分ごろ(に)　あいたいです。

4. きょう、なん時に　おきましたか。
 five-thirty a.m.   …… ごぜん　五時三十分に　おきました。

5. かぶきは　なん時に　はじまりましたか。
 four-forty   …… 四時四十分に　はじまりました。

6. なん時ごろ、学校に　来たいですか。
 nine-ten   …… 九時十分に　来たいです。

7. じゅぎょうは　なん時ごろに　おわりますか。
 about four p.m.   …… ごご　四時ごろ(に)　おわります。

3.7.10　Response Drill

1. かぶきを　見たいですか。
 はい   …… はい、見たいです。
 いいえ   …… いいえ、見たくありません。

2. しごとを　やすみたいですか。
 はい   …… はい、やすみたいです。
 いいえ   …… いいえ、やすみたくありません。

3. レインコートを　かいたかったんですか。
 はい   …… はい、かいたかったんです。
 いいえ   …… いいえ、かいたくありませんでした。

4. 日本語で　はなしたかったんですか。
 はい   …… はい、はなしたかったんです。
 いいえ   …… いいえ、はなしたくありませんでした。

5. 水曜日に　かいものを　したいですか。
 はい   …… はい、したいです。
 いいえ   …… いいえ、したくありません。

6. 東京に　すみたかったんですか。
   はい　　　　　　　　　……　はい、すみたかったんです。
   いいえ　　　　　　　　……　いいえ、すみたくありませんでした。

3.8 EXERCISES

3.8.1 Make an appropriate question that fits each of the following answers:

1. かぶきを　見たいです。
2. いいえ、すきやきは　たべたくありません。
3. ええ、ゆっくり　はなしたかったです。
4. はい、アルバイトは　したくありませんでした。
5. いいえ、ここで　まっていたいんです。
6. いいえ、びょういんへは　いきたくありませんでした。

3.8.2 Insert an appropriate Relational in blank, if necessary:

1. 土曜日（　　）　よし子さん（　　）　あいます。
2. じゅぎょう（　　）　やすみたくありませんでした（　　）、かぜ（　　）　やすみました。
3. ごご（　　）　三時（　　）　学校（　　）　もっていきますよ。
4. 三月（　　）　東京（　　）　かえります。　そして、らい年（　　）　また　来ます。

3.8.3 Carry on the following conversation on a telephone in Japanese:

Mori:　　Hello, is this the Yamada home?

Kazuko:　Yes, it is.

Mori:　　Is Kazuko there?

Kazuko:　This is she speaking.

Mori:　　Good afternoon. This is Mori.

Kazuko:　Good afternoon.

Mori:　　I want to see you at school tomorrow. Are you going to school at about ten o'clock?

Kazuko:　Yes, I am.

Mori:　　Then please bring my Japanese language dictionary. I want to study Japanese tomorrow night.

Kazuko:　All right. I'll take it with me to school.

Mori:　　Then I'll meet you at school around ten o'clock.

54

Kazuko:　O.K.

Mori:　　Well, so long.

Kazuko:　Good-bye.

3.8.4　Answer the following questions in Japanese:

1.　日曜日は　なん時ごろ　おきますか。

2.　きのうは　なん時に　ねましたか。

3.　日本語の　じゅぎょうは　まいしゅう　なん曜日に　ありますか。

4.　きょう　学校へ　なにを　もってきましたか。

5.　土曜日に　どこへ　いきたいですか。

6.　せんしゅうの　月曜の　おてんきは　どうでしたか。

7.　この　へんの　えいがは　たいてい　なん時に　はじまりますか。

8.　じゅぎょうは　なん時ごろ　おわりますか。

3.8.5　Write the underlined *hiragana* in *kanji:*

1.　よしこさんは　きん曜びに　かぶきを　みます。

2.　ごじ　にじっぷんに　ともだちが　きます。それから、いっしょに　ほんやへ　いきます。

3.　にち曜び、　げつ曜び、　か曜び、　すい曜び、　もく曜び、　ど曜び

3.9　SITUATIONAL　CONVERSATION

3.9.1　Telephone conversation (1)

A boy telephones a girl friend's home.

The girl answers the phone.

Talking to the girl friend, the boy asks why she didn't come to school on Thursday.

She answers she was sick but has recovered now.

The boy wants to take her to a movie on Sunday.

She agrees to go.

They fix the place and time to meet on Sunday.

3.9.2　Telephone conversation (2)

Hello, is this the Yamadas' residence?

No, you have a wrong number. (lit. It's wrong.)

I'm sorry.

* * * * * *

Hello, is this the Yamadas' residence?

Yes, it is.

Is Ikuo there, please?

Ikuo is out now. He will be back around four o'clock.

Then I'll call back later.

3.9.3 Develop your own telephone conversation.

56

LESSON 4

— Review —

4.1 PREDICATES

4.1.1 TE form + *imasu*

a. "is doing"

くつを　うります	⟶　くつを　うって	
セーターを　かいます	⟶　セーターを　かって	
コーヒーを　のみます	⟶　コーヒーを　のんで	
ひるごはんを　たべます	⟶　ひるごはんを　たべて	
日本語を　かきます	⟶　日本語を　かいて	います
テレビを　見ます	⟶　テレビを　見て	いません
しんぶんを　よみます	⟶　しんぶんを　よんで	いました
東京で　はたらきます	⟶　東京で　はたらいて	いませんでした
大阪で　アルバイトします	⟶　大阪で　アルバイトして	
ぎんこうに　つとめます	⟶　ぎんこうに　つとめて	
しぶやに　すみます	⟶　しぶやに　すんで	
かぜで　ねます	⟶　かぜで　ねて	
じゅぎょうを　やすみます	⟶　じゅぎょうを　やすんで	

b. "is done" "has done"

これは　ちがいます	⟶　これは　ちがって	
森さんは　けっこんします	⟶　森さんは　けっこんして	
あの　人の　なまえを　わすれます	⟶　あの　人の　なまえを　わすれて	います
その　店に　はいります	⟶　その　店に　はいって、	いません
本を　かります	⟶　本を　かりて	いました
スポーツシャツを　きます	⟶　スポーツシャツを　きて	いませんでした
先生の　ところを　しります	⟶　先生の　ところを　しって	
日本語が　わかります	⟶　日本語が　わかって	
じどうしゃを　もちます	⟶　じどうしゃを　もって	

4.1.2   TE form + *kudasai* "please do"

うちへ　かえります	⟶	うちへ　かえって
あとで　来ます	⟶	あとで　来て
ぜひ　いきます	⟶	ぜひ　いって
六時に　おきます	⟶	六時に　おきて
お客^{きゃく}さまに　あいます	⟶	お客^{きゃく}さまに　あって
ゆっくり　はなします	⟶	ゆっくり　はなして
としょかんに　つとめます	⟶	としょかんに　つとめて
ぜんぶ　かいます	⟶	ぜんぶ　かって
その　カメラを　うります	⟶	その　カメラを　うって
かぶきを　見ます	⟶	かぶきを　見て
学生を　まちます	⟶	学生を　まって
これを　もちます	⟶	これを　もって
しごとを　やすみます	⟶	しごとを　やすんで
らいしゅう　見せます	⟶	らいしゅう　見せて
二かいで　ねます	⟶	二かいで　ねて
金曜^{よう}日に　はたらきます	⟶	金曜^{よう}日に　はたらいて
しょくどうで　アルバイトします	⟶	しょくどうで　アルバイトして
ごご　でんわします	⟶	ごご　でんわして
一ど　たべます	⟶	一ど　たべて
子どもたちを　つれてきます	⟶	子どもたちを　つれてきて
大阪^{おおさか}へ　つれていきます	⟶	大阪^{おおさか}へ　つれていって
いぬを　つれてかえります	⟶	いぬを　つれてかえって
はしを　もってきます	⟶	はしを　もってきて
みやげを　もってかえります	⟶	みやげを　もってかえって
そこへ　もっていきます	⟶	そこへ　もっていって

ください

4.1.3   TE form + *mimasu* "do and find out"

ちかへ　いきます	⟶	ちかへ　いって	みます
この　レインコートを　きます	⟶	この　レインコートを　きて	みません
日本の　カメラを　かいます	⟶	日本の　カメラを　かって	みました
すきやきを　たべます	⟶	すきやきを　たべて	みませんでした
ジャズを　ききます	⟶	ジャズを　きいて	みましょう
その　ざっしを　よみます	⟶	その　ざっしを　よんで	みてください

58

さけを　のみます	⟶　さけを　のんで	
一郎くんを　まちます	⟶　一郎くんを　まって	みます
林さんに　あいます	⟶　林さんに　あって	みません
五時に　おきます	⟶　五時に　おきて	みました
しょくどうで　はたらきます	⟶　しょくどうで　はたらいて	みませんでした
なつやすみに　アルバイトします	⟶　なつやすみに　アルバイトして	みましょう
ちちに　はなします	⟶　ちちに　はなして	みてください
ドイツ語で　いいます	⟶　ドイツ語で　いって	

4.1.4　Expression of desire　"want to do"

a.

おたくへ　うかがいます	⟶　おたくへ　うかがい	
東京へ　かえります	⟶　東京へ　かえり	
大学へ　いきます	⟶　大学へ　いき	
にっこうへ　でかけます	⟶　にっこうへ　でかけ	
てんぷらを　たべます	⟶　てんぷらを　たべ	
ゆっくり　けんぶつします	⟶　ゆっくり　けんぶつし	
たくさん　もっていきます	⟶　たくさん　もっていき	
日本語を　ならいます	⟶　日本語を　ならい	たい(ん)です
学校を　やすみます	⟶　学校を　やすみ	たくありません
大学生に　うります	⟶　大学生に　うり	たかった(ん)です
これを　いただきます	⟶　これを　いただき	たくありませんでした
みやげを　もってかえります	⟶　みやげを　もってかえり	たい(ん)でしょう
お客さんに　さしあげます	⟶　お客さんに　さしあげ	たかった(ん)でしょう
四時に　おきます	⟶　四時に　おき	
九時ごろ　おわります	⟶　九時ごろ　おわり	
三年生に　あいます	⟶　三年生に　あい	
デパートに　つとめます	⟶　デパートに　つとめ	
日本に　すみます	⟶　日本に　すみ	
東京で　はたらきます	⟶　東京で　はたらき	
きっさ店で　アルバイトします	⟶　きっさ店で　アルバイトし	
一年生を　つれてきます	⟶　一年生を　つれてき	

b.

しごとを　やすんでいます	⟶	しごとを　やすんで
ばんごはんを　たべています	⟶	ばんごはんを　たべて
テレビを　見ています	⟶	テレビを　見て
日本語を　べんきょうして　います	⟶	日本語を　べんきょう　して
ハワイに　すんでいます	⟶	ハワイに　すんで
ぎんこうに　つとめています	⟶	ぎんこうに　つとめて
一日中　はたらいています	⟶	一日中　はたらいて
としょかんで　よんでいます	⟶	としょかんで　よんで
クラシックを　きいています	⟶	クラシックを　きいて
あの　たてもので　まって　います	⟶	あの　たてもので　まって
女の　子と　はなしています	⟶	女の　子と　はなして

い

たい(ん)です
たくありません
たかった(ん)です
たくありませんでした
たい(ん)でしょう
たかった(ん)でしょう

c.

じんじゃへ　いってみます	⟶	じんじゃへ　いって
あの　店に　はいってみます	⟶	あの　店に　はいって
この　しごとを　してみます	⟶	この　しごとを　して
おさけを　のんでみます	⟶	おさけを　のんで
店員に　はなしてみます	⟶	店員に　はなして
スポーツシャツを　かって　みます	⟶	スポーツシャツを　かって
東京で　はたらいてみます	⟶	東京で　はたらいて
ともだちと　いっしょに　べんきょうしてみます	⟶	ともだちと　いっしょに　べんきょうして
本やで　アルバイトして　みます	⟶	本やで　アルバイトして
てんぷらを　たべてみます	⟶	てんぷらを　たべて
ラジオを　きいてみます	⟶	ラジオを　きいて
その　おとこの　子に　あってみます	⟶	その　おとこの　子に　あって

み

たい(ん)です
たくありません
たかった(ん)です
たくありませんでした
たい(ん)でしょう
たかった(ん)でしょう

4.1.5 "take" "bring"

a.

	を		
はは よし子さん ともだち いもうと 子ども 二年生 いぬ	を	つれて	いきます 来ます かえります
みやげ 日本の　ざっし セーターと　ネクタイ えいがの　きっぷ	を	もって	

b.

	へ		を		
うみ 大学 東京（とうきょう）		いもうと かない 子どもたち わたなべくん あなた 学生		つれて	いきます 来ます かえります
アメリカ くに	へ	日本語の　じしょ（ご）	を		
ともだちの　うち		みやげ			
二かい へや		レインコート コーヒー		もって	
おたく うち		しごと			

4.2 RELATIONALS

4.2.1 *de* "because of"

かぜ びょうき		じゅぎょうを　やすみました きぶんが　わるい(ん)です
あめ ゆき	で	にっこうを　けんぶつしませんでした でんしゃが　来ません
しごと アルバイト		アメリカへ　来ました いそがしかった(ん)です

なん	で	…………………………	か
どうして		…………………………	

4.2.2 time Relational *ni*

千九百四十六年 千九百六十五年四月		日本へ　来ました がいこくへ　いきました
九月		学校が　はじまります
日曜日 月曜日 火曜日 水曜日 木曜日 金曜日 土曜日	に ごろ(に)	えいがを　見ましょう すきやきを　たべました
ごぜん　五時 十一時十分 ごご　九時はん		おきます 大学で　あいましょう おわりました
なつやすみ やすみ	に	ハワイへ　いきます アルバイトを　しました

62

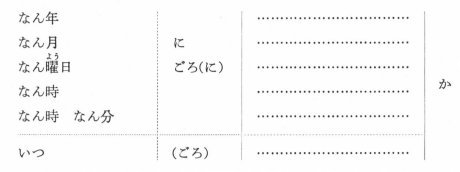

なん年		
なん月	に	
なん曜日	ごろ(に)	
なん時		か
なん時　なん分		
いつ	(ごろ)	

4.2.3　Relational of totalizing *de*

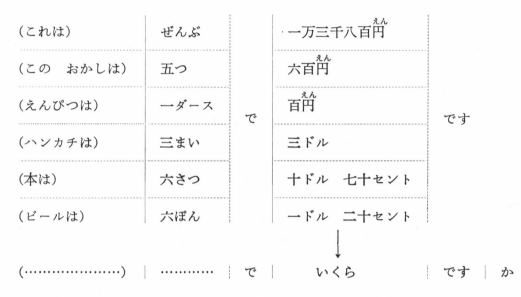

(これは)	ぜんぶ		一万三千八百円	
(この　おかしは)	五つ		六百円	
(えんぴつは)	一ダース	で	百円	です
(ハンカチは)	三まい		三ドル	
(本は)	六さつ		十ドル　七十セント	
(ビールは)	六ぽん		一ドル　二十セント	

(……………………)	…………	で	いくら	です	か

4.3　TIME NOMINATIVES

a.

こん月	大阪へ　いきたいんです
せん月	にっこうを　けんぶつしました
らい月	ほっかいどうで　はたらきます
こんしゅう	かぶきを　見たいんです
せんしゅう	日本の　カメラを　かってみました
らいしゅう	すきやきを　たべてみましょう
ごご	うちへ　来ました

いつ	………………………………………	か

b.

四年		東京に　います
三年	（ぐらい）	ハワイに　すんでいます
一年	（くらい）	日本語を　ならいたいんです
十分		よし子さんを　まちました
一年		レストランで　アルバイトしました
ふゆ	中	びょうきで　ねていました
一日		おんがくを　きいていたいです
↓		
なん年	（ぐらい）	‥‥‥‥‥‥‥‥‥‥‥‥‥‥‥‥‥‥
なん分	（くらい）	‥‥‥‥‥‥‥‥‥‥‥‥‥‥‥‥‥‥　か

4.4 COUNTERS

a.

いま	七百五十円		もっています
おかねが	十五ドル八セント		ありました
コカコーラを	六ぽん	（ぐらい）	ください
さけが	五はい	（くらい）	ほしいです
日本語の　本を	十さつ		かいました
かみを	二十まい		もらいました

‥‥‥‥‥‥‥	いくら
‥‥‥‥‥‥‥	なん円
‥‥‥‥‥‥‥	なんドル
‥‥‥‥‥‥‥	なんセント
‥‥‥‥‥‥‥	なんぼん
‥‥‥‥‥‥‥	なんばい
‥‥‥‥‥‥‥	なんさつ
‥‥‥‥‥‥‥	なんまい

（ぐらい）	‥‥‥‥‥‥
（くらい）	‥‥‥‥‥‥　か
	‥‥‥‥‥‥

64

b.

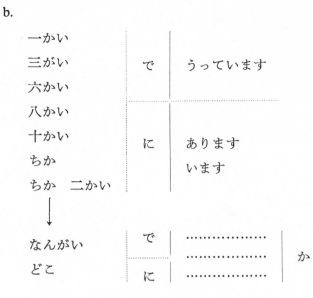

一かい
三がい
六かい　　で　｜　うっています
─────────
八かい
十かい　　に　｜　あります
ちか　　　　　｜　います
ちか　二かい
↓
なんがい　　で　｜　……………
　　　　　　　　｜　……………　か
どこ　　　　に　｜　……………

4.5　AURAL COMPREHENSION

a.

　　ぼくは　大学の　三年生です。　いま、　学校で　えい語を　べんきょうしていますが、

とても　むずかしいです。　きょ年の　なつやすみは　じむしょで　アルバイトを

しましたが、　ことしの　なつは、　デパートで　はたらきたいです。　そして、　あき、

ほっかいどうへ　いきたいです。

　　ちちは　せん月、　しごとで　アメリカへ　いきました。　ははを　いっしょに

つれていきたかったんですが、　ははは　びょうきで　いきませんでした。　ちちは、

アメリカから　みやげを　もってかえりました。　ぼくには　ジャズの　レコードを

くれました。　ぼくも　アメリカへ　いってみたいです。

b.

井上　「もしもし、　林さんの　おたくですか。」

林　　「はい、　そうです。」

井上　「ごしゅじんは　いらっしゃいますか。」

林　　「いま　ちょっと　るすですが、　どなたですか。」

井上　「井上です。」

林　　「ああ、　井上さんですか。　しばらくですねえ。」

井上　「おくさんですか。　おげんきですか。」

林　　「ええ、　おかげさまで。」

井上　「じつは、　あした　ごしゅじんに　あいたいんですが……。」

林　　「あしたは　土曜日ですね。　いま、　ちょっと　しゅじんの　あしたの　つごうは
　　　　わかりませんが……。」

井上　「じゃあ、　また　あとで　でんわを　してみます。」

林　　「ええ、　おねがいします。」

井上　「では、　また。」

LESSON 5

5.1 PRESENTATION

― 花　　見 ―

さくらは　ゆうめいな*1　日本の　花です。　だいたい　三月か　四月に　さきます。

日本の　人たちは、　よく　いろいろな*1　花を　見に*2　行きますが、　とくに　さくらが

好きです。

5.2 DIALOG

ジョージ　「みち子さん、　きょうは　すばらしい*3　天気ですね。　ごご、　さんぽに*2
　　　　　　行きませんか。」

みち子　　「ええ。」

ジョージ　「いい　所を　知っていますか。」

みち子　　「上野公園は　どうですか。　ちょうど　今、　さくらが　さいて
　　　　　　いますから*4、　お花見に　行きましょうか。」

ジョージ　「ああ、　花見ですね。　さくらは　好きな　花ですから、　ぜひ　見たい
　　　　　　ですね。　その　公園は　どんな*5　所ですか。」

みち子　　「そうですねえ……*6。　とても　大きい　公園です。　びじゅつかんや
　　　　　　どうぶつ園などが　あります。・だから、　おとなも　子どもも*7　大ぜい*8
　　　　　　あそびに*9　行きます。」

ジョージ　「じゃあ、　今は　花見の　きせつですから*4、　人が　とくに　おおい*10
　　　　　　でしょうね。」

みち子　　「ええ。　じゃあ、　ジョージさん、　こう　しましょう。　はじめに、
　　　　　　どうぶつ園へ　行きましょう。　そして、　ゆうがた　お花見を
　　　　　　しましょう。」

ジョージ　「それが　いいですね。　ゆうがたは　たぶん　人が　すくないでしょう
　　　　　　から*4、　ゆっくり　お花見が　できます*11ね。」

5.3 PATTERN SENTENCES

5.3.1

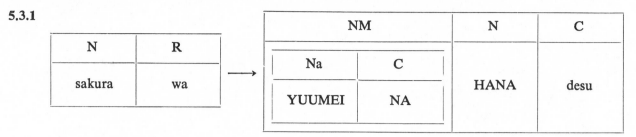

"Cherry blossoms are famous flowers."

5.3.2

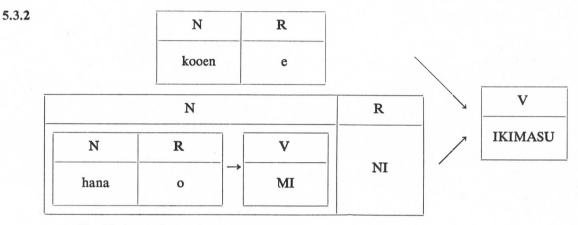

"I will go to the park to see flowers."

5.3.3

NM		N	C
Adv.	A	TEN'KI	desu
totemo →	II		

"It's a very nice day [weather]."

5.4 NOTES

5.4.1 *Yuumei na* means "(something) which is famous," and, together with *Nihon no,* modifies *hana; yuumei na Nihon no hana* "famous Japanese flower."

Yuumei "famous," *iroiro* "various," *kirei* "pretty," *shizuka* "quiet," etc., are adjectival Nominatives, and are normally used as equivalents of English adjectives. They behave like other ordinary Nominatives. However, when an adjectival Nominative is used as a Nominative Modifier, that is, before another Nominative, it can not occur as a Modifier of the Nominative by itself, but *na,* a conjugated form of the Copula — NA form, occurs immediately after the adjectival Nominative.

adjectival Nominative + *desu* ⟶ adjectival Nominative + *na* + Nominative

yuumei desu	"is famous"		yuumei		kooen	"famous park"
iroiro desu	"is various"		iroiro		hana	"various flowers"
hen desu	"is strange"		hen		ten'ki	"strange weather"
shitsurei desu	"is rude"	⟶	shitsurei	na	hito	"rude person"
teinei desu	"is polite"		teinei		kotoba	"polite speech"
daihyooteki desu	"is representative"		daihyooteki		geijutsu	"representative art"

Sakura wa yuumei na Nihon no
hana desu.　　　　　　　　　"Cherry blossoms are famous Japanese flowers."

Suki na supootsu wa nan desu ka?　　"What is your favorite sport?"

When there is also a Pre-Nominative modifying the Nominative, the Pre-Nominative normally precedes an adjectival Nominative.

Ano kirei na tatemono ni
hairimashoo.　　　　　　　"Let's go into that pretty building."

An Adverb or other Predicate Modifiers may modify an adjectival Nominative that precedes a Nominative.

Totemo shizuka na tokoro desu.　　"It is a very quiet place."

Chotto hen na ten'ki desu nee.　　"It's a little strange weather, isn't it?"

Jooji wa itsumo gen'ki na otoko no
ko desu.　　　　　　　　　"George is a boy who is always full of pep."

5.4.2　*Mi ni ikimasu* means "go to see." The Relational *ni* as in *mi ni ikimasu* denotes the purpose of action, normally that of motion Verbs, such as *ikimasu, kimasu, kaerimasu,* etc. *Ni* is used after the Stem form of a Verb, such as *mi(masu), ne(masu), san'po shi(masu).*

Stem form of Verb + *ni* + motion Verb

mi					"see"
kiki					"listen"
hanashi		ikimasu	"go		"talk"
hataraki	ni	kimasu	"come	to	"work"
ai		kaerimasu	"go back		"meet"
asobi		dekakemasu	"go out		"play"
yobi					"call"

Eiga o mi ni ikimasen ka?　　"Won't you go to see a movie?"

Ueno e on'gaku o kiki ni ikimashita.　　"I went to Ueno to listen to music."

Hirugohan o tabe ni kaerimashoo.　　"I think I'll go home to eat lunch."

When it is necessary to indicate a place where one goes, comes, etc., the place may precede either the phrase meaning "to see (it)," or be used immediately before the motion Verb, but the former case is more common.

Ueno Kooen e sakura o mi ni
ikimashoo.
　　　　　or　　　　　　　"Let's go to Ueno Park to see the cherry blossoms."
Sakura o mi ni Ueno Kooen e
ikimashoo.

In the above pattern, a Nominative may replace the Stem form of a Verb, if that Nominative should connote action, such as *san'po* "a walk," *ben'kyoo* "study," *ken'butsu* "sightseeing," *hanami* "flower viewing," etc., which is normally followed by *shimasu*.

san'po shimasu	san'po		ikimasu	"go	"for a walk"
ben'kyoo shimasu	ben'kyoo		kimasu	"come	to study"
ken'butsu shimasu →	ken'butsu	ni	kaerimasu	"go back	sightseeing"
hanami o shimasu	hanami		dekakemasu	"go out	flower viewing"
kaimono o shimasu	kaimono				shopping"
shokuji o shimasu	shokuji				for a meal"

Hiru wa uchi e shokuji ni kaerimasu.   "I go home for lunch."

Kinoo Mori san to issho ni Tookyoo e kaimono ni ikimashita.   "I went shopping with Mr. Mori yesterday."

Sumisu san wa sen'getsu Nihon e ben'kyoo ni kimashita.   "Mr. Smith came to Japan for study last month."

5.4.3   *Subarashii ten'ki* means "wonderful weather." As in English, an Adjective may precede a Nominative and modify it. As explained in Note 5.4.1, an Adverb or other Predicate Modifiers may modify the Adjective, and a Pre-Nominative may usually precede the Adjective when both the Pre-Nominative and the Adjective modify the following Nominative.

(Predicate Modifier) + **Adjective** + **Nominative**

(Pre-Nominative) + **Adjective** + **Nominative**

tsumetai mizu	"cold water"
subarashii tokoro	"wonderful place"
utsukushii hana	"beautiful flowers"
hoshii hon	"books I want"
kawaii on'na no ko	"cute girl"
furui tatemono	"old building"
atarashii sen'sei	"new teacher"

Totemo ii ten'ki desu nee.   "It's a very good day [weather], isn't it?"

Kono utsukushii hana wa nan desu ka?   "What is this beautiful flower?"

Kyooto ni wa furui tera ga takusan arimasu.   "There are many old temples in Kyōto."

5.4.4   *Kara* immediately after a Predicate is the clause Relational meaning "reason," or "cause," and is often translated as "so," "because," or "since." In normal spoken style, the Predicate occurring before the "reason" or "cause" Relational *kara* is either in normal forms or in plain forms. (Plain forms will be introduced later, and only the normal form, such as *desu, deshita, -masu, -mashita*, etc., will be drilled in this lesson.)

Note that when an Adjective occurs in the "reason" clause, the Copula *desu* may be omitted.

Sentence 1 }
Sentence 2 }   ⟶   Sentence 1 + *kara,* Sentence 2

Sakura ga saite imasu. ⎫ ⟶   Sakura ga saite imasu kara, ohanami ni
Ohanami ni ikimashoo. ⎭   ikimashoo.

  "Cherry blossoms are in bloom. Let's go   "Cherry blossoms are in bloom, so let's go
  cherry viewing."   cherry viewing."

Kibun ga warui (desu) kara, shigoto   "I don't feel well, so I won't go to work."
  o yasumimasu.

Ten'ki ga yokatta (desu) kara,   "Since the weather was good, we had a good time."
  totemo tanoshikatta desu.

Roshiago wa naraimasen deshita   "I haven't studied Russian, so I don't understand it."
  kara, wakarimasen.

San'po wa suki ja arimasen kara,   "As I don't like taking a walk, I will stay home."
  uchi ni imasu.

5.4.5 *Don'na* is a Pre-Nominative meaning "what sort of?" Like *kono, sono, ano,* and *dono,* here is
another group of Pre-Nominatives:

kon'na	"this sort of"
son'na	"that sort of"
an'na	"that sort of"
don'na	"what sort of?"

Sono kooen wa don'na tokoro desu   "What sort of place is that park?"
  ka ?

Totemo shizuka na tokoro desu.   "It is a very quiet place."

Yoshiko san wa don'na kata desu   "What sort of person is Yoshiko?"
  ka ?

Utsukushii kata desu yo.   "She is a beautiful lady."

5.4.6 *Soo desu nee* .... is an expression used in the meaning of "Let me see ....," or "What shall I
say?"

5.4.7 *Otona mo kodomo mo* means "both adults and children." When the Relational *mo* is repeated in
a sentence, it means "both .... and ....," or "either .... or ...." in negatives. It should be
noted that *mo* replaces *ga* and *o,* and it may also follow a phrase with Relationals such as *kara,*
e, ni, etc.

Nominative + *mo* + **Nominative** + *mo*   "both .... and ...."
                                                                  or
Nominative + **Relational** + *mo* + **Nominative** + **Relational** + *mo*   "(not) either .... or ...."

Otona mo kodomo mo asobi ni   "Both adults and children visit there."
  ikimasu.

Koohii mo koocha mo nomimasen.   "I don't drink either coffee or black tea."

Bijutsukan e mo doobutsuen e mo   "I went to the art museum as well as the zoo."
  ikimashita.

Ichiroo wa uchi ni mo gakkoo ni mo imasen.　　　"Ichirō is neither at home nor at school."

5.4.8　*Oozei* means "a lot (of people)." While *takusan* "many or much" may be used either for things or people, *oozei* is used only to mean "many people."

Hito ga oozei imasu.　　　"There are many people."

Hito ga oozei hataraite imasu.　　　"Many people are working."

Quantity Adverbs such as *oozei*, *takusan*, *sukoshi*, etc. may modify a Nominative, but when the Relational *no* occurs between it and a Nominative, *oozei*, *takusan*, etc. are classified as Nominatives.

oozei no otona	"many adults"
takusan no jidoosha	"a lot of cars"
sukoshi no ame	"a little rain"
san'mai no kami	"three sheets of paper"
gosatsu no jisho	"five dictionaries"

5.4.9　*Asobimasu* is a Verb that may be interpreted in various ways. The following are some of them:

(1)　"play"

Kodomotachi ga kooen de ason'de imasu.　　　"Children are playing in the park."

(2)　"enjoy oneself," "have a good time"

Ashita uchi e asobi ni kimasen ka?　　　"Won't you come to my house tomorrow (for chatting)?"

(3)　"do nothing"

Ima don'na shigoto o shite imasu ka?　　　"What sort of work are you doing now?"

Ason'de imasu.　　　"I have no job." "I am loafing."

Asobimasu can not be used for "play cards," "play tennis," or "play a musical instrument."

5.4.10　The Adjective *ooi* "are many; is much" or *sukunai* "is few; is little" may not occur as a Nominative Modifier. As explained in 5.4.8, a Nominative Modifier *takusan* or *oozei* plus *no* may be used instead.

$$\left.\begin{array}{l}\text{tatemono}\\\text{ame}\\\text{kodomo}\end{array}\right\} \text{ga ooi} \quad but \quad \begin{array}{l}\text{takusan no} \left\{\begin{array}{l}\text{tatemono}\\\text{ame}\end{array}\right.\\\text{oozei no} \left\{\begin{array}{l}\text{kodomo}\\\text{hito}\end{array}\right.\end{array}$$

$$\left.\begin{array}{l}\text{gakkoo}\\\text{hana}\\\text{otoko no ko}\end{array}\right\} \text{ga sukunai} \quad but \quad \text{sukoshi no} \left\{\begin{array}{l}\text{gakkoo}\\\text{hana}\\\text{otoko no ko}\end{array}\right.$$

5.4.11　The Verb *dekimasu* means "be able to (do)," "be possible," "can (do)," etc. The English equivalent may vary depending upon the words used in this expression. (e.g. *Ben'kyoo ga dekimasu* may mean either "can study" or "is good at one's studies.") The thing that one can do is followed by the Relational *ga,* and the one who can do it, if there is one, is followed by *wa.*

(Nominative + *wa*) + Nominative + *ga* + *dekimasu*

| watakushi wa
anata wa
Michiko san wa | suiei
tenisu
gorufu
boorin'gu
sukii
sukeeto
juudoo
karate

eigo
nihon'go
gaikokugo | ga dekimasu | "I
"you
"Michiko | can | swim"
play tennis"
play golf"
bowl"
ski"
skate"
do *jūdō*"
do *karate*"
speak English"
understand Japanese"
understand foreign languages" |

Michiko san wa sukii ga dekimasu.   "Michiko can ski."

Ichiroo kun wa karate ga dekimasu ka?   "Can Ichirō do *karate*?"

Ano kata wa eigo ga yoku dekimasu.   "That person has a good command of English."

5.5 VOCABULARY

Presentation

花見	hanami	....	N	flower viewing (usually cherry blossom viewing)
さくら	sakura	....	N	cherry (tree or blossoms)
ゆうめい	yuumei	....	Na	famous; noted
な	na	....	C	(see 5.4.1)
花	hana	....	N	flower; blossom
だいたい	daitai	....	Adv.	roughly speaking; mostly; approximately
さきます	sakimasu	....	V	bloom (normal form of *saku*)
いろいろ	iroiro	....	Na	various
に	ni	....	R	Relational of purpose (see 5.4.2)

Dialog

ジョージ	Jooji	....	N	George
みち子	Michiko	....	N	girl's first name
さんぽ	san'po	....	N	stroll; a walk
さんぽします	san'po shimasu	....	V	stroll; take a walk
上野	Ueno	....	N	a district of Tōkyō
公園	kooen	....	N	park; public garden

さいて	saite	 V	TE form of *sakimasu* ← *saku* – bloom
から	kara	.... Rc	because; since (see 5.4.4)
ああ	aa	.... SI	oh; ah
どんな	don'na	.... PN	what sort of? (see 5.4.5)
びじゅつかん	bijutsukan	.... N	art museum
どうぶつ園	doobutsuen	.... N	zoo
おとな	otona	.... N	adult; grown-ups
大ぜい	oozei	.... Adv.	many (people) (see 5.4.8)
あそび	asobi	 V	Stem form of *asobimasu* ← *asobu* – play (see 5.4.9)
きせつ	kisetsu	.... N	season
おおい	ooi	.... A	are many; is much (see 5.4.10)
こう	koo	.... Adv.	in this way
はじめ	hajime	.... N	beginning
ゆうがた	yuugata	.... N	late afternoon; early evening
すくない	sukunai	.... A	is few; is little (opposite of *ooi* – are many; is much)
できます	dekimasu	 V	is able to; can (do); is possible (see 5.4.11)

Notes

へん	hen	.... Na	strange; unusual; funny
しつれい	shitsurei	.... Na	rude
よび	yobi	 V	Stem form of *yobimasu* ← *yobu* – call (for)
しょくじ	shokuji	.... N	meal; dining
うつくしい	utsukushii	.... A	is beautiful
かわいい	kawaii	.... A	is cute
ふるい	furui	.... A	is old (thing)
あたらしい	atarashii	.... A	is new; is fresh
こんな	kon'na	.... PN	this sort of (see 5.4.5)
そんな	son'na	.... PN	that sort of
あんな	an'na	.... PN	that sort of
テニス	tenisu	.... N	tennis
ゴルフ	gorufu	.... N	golf
ボーリング	boorin'gu	.... N	bowling
スキー	sukii	.... N	ski
スケート	sukeeto	.... N	skate
じゅうどう	juudoo	.... N	*jūdō*; a Japanese art of self-defense
からて	karate	.... N	*karate*; an art of self-defense originated in the Ryūkyū Islands

5.6 KANJI

5.6.1 花 (1) *hana* (2) flower (3) classifier ⺾ "grass"
(4) 一 十 ⺾ 艹 艾 花 花 (5) 花見、花や、いけ花 [flower arrangement]

5.6.2 人 (1) *hito* (2) person (3) forms the classifier 人 (4) ノ 人
(5) あの人、日本の人たち、おとこの人

5.6.3 行 (1) *i(kimasu)* (2) go (3) forms the classifier 行
(4) ノ ク イ 行 行 行 (5) 行きました、行ってください

5.6.4 好 (1) *su(ki)* (2) like (3) classifier 女 (4) く タ 女 好 好
(5) 好きです、大好き

5.6.5 天 (1) TEN (2) sky; heaven (3) classifier 大 (4) 一 二 チ 天
(5) 天気、天こう [climate]、天皇 [Emperor]

5.6.6 気 (1) KI (2) spirit; mind; energy (3) classifier 气
(4) ノ 二 气 气 気 気 (5) 天気、気ぶん、げん気、びょう気

5.6.7 所 (1) *tokoro* (2) place; address (3) classifier 戸
(4) 一 ラ ヲ 戸 戸 所 所 所 (5) きれいな所、先生の所

5.6.8 知 (1) *shi(rimasu)* (2) know (3) classifier 矢
(4) ノ ト 上 チ 矢 知 知 知 (5) 知っています、知りません

5.6.9 今 (1) *ima* (2) now; present (3) classifier 个 (4) 人 个 今
(5) 今、なん時ですか

大 2.6.1 (1) *oo(kii)* (5) 大きいうち、大きい子ども、大ぜい

5.6.10 小 (1) *chii(sai)* (2) small (3) forms the classifier 小 (4) 亅 小 小
(5) 小さい公園

5.7 DRILLS

5.7.1 Pattern Drill

1. Sakura wa yuumei na Nihon no hana desu.

2. Nihon no hitotachi wa, yoku iroiro na hana o mi ni ikimasu.

3. Kyoo wa subarashii ten'ki desu ne.

4. Gogo, san'po ni ikimasen ka?

5. Ii tokoro o shitte imasu ka?

6. Ohanami ni ikimashoo ka?

7. Sakura wa suki na hana desu kara, zehi mitai desu ne.

8. Totemo ookii kooen desu.

9. Otona mo kodomo mo oozei asobi ni ikimasu.

5.7.2 Substitution Drill

A. それは　きれいな　花です。

1. ゆうめい	……	それは　ゆうめいな　花です。
2. うつくしい	……	それは　うつくしい　花です。
3. だいひょう的	……	それは　だいひょう的な　花です。
4. 大きい	……	それは　大きい　花です。
5. 好き	……	それは　好きな　花です。
6. たかい	……	それは　たかい　花です。
7. すばらしい	……	それは　すばらしい　花です。
8. きらい	……	それは　きらいな　花です。

B. あの　うつくしい　人は　わたしの　ともだちです。

1. かわいい	……	あの　かわいい　人は　わたしの　ともだちです。
2. しずか	……	あの　しずかな　人は　わたしの　ともだちです。
3. えらい	……	あの　えらい　人は　わたしの　ともだちです。
4. しつれい	……	あの　しつれいな　人は　わたしの　ともだちです。
5. 大きい	……	あの　大きい　人は　わたしの　ともだちです。
6. ていねい	……	あの　ていねいな　人は　わたしの　ともだちです。
7. きれい	……	あの　きれいな　人は　わたしの　ともだちです。
8. 小さい	……	あの　小さい　人は　わたしの　ともだちです。

C. そこは　とても　大きい　公園です。

1. しずか	……	そこは　とても　しずかな　公園です。

2. うつくしい   …… そこは とても うつくしい 公園<ruby>こうえん</ruby>です。

3. あたらしい   …… そこは とても あたらしい 公園<ruby>こうえん</ruby>です。

4. ゆうめい   …… そこは とても ゆうめいな 公園<ruby>こうえん</ruby>です。

5. きれい   …… そこは とても きれいな 公園<ruby>こうえん</ruby>です。

6. 小さい   …… そこは とても 小さい 公園<ruby>こうえん</ruby>です。

7. ふるい   …… そこは とても ふるい 公園<ruby>こうえん</ruby>です。

8. いい   …… そこは とても いい 公園<ruby>こうえん</ruby>です。

5.7.3 Substitution Drill

すばらしい 天気です。

1. いい   …… いい 天気です。

2. へん   …… へんな 天気です。

3. 女<ruby>おんな</ruby>の 人   …… へんな 女<ruby>おんな</ruby>の 人です。

4. げん気   …… げん気な 女<ruby>おんな</ruby>の 人です。

5. ゆうめい   …… ゆうめいな 女<ruby>おんな</ruby>の 人です。

6. 所   …… ゆうめいな 所です。

7. しずか   …… しずかな 所です。

8. きらい   …… きらいな 所です。

9. ことば   …… きらいな ことばです。

10. ていねい   …… ていねいな ことばです。

11. しつれい   …… しつれいな ことばです。

12. あたらしい   …… あたらしい ことばです。

13. 店<ruby>みせ</ruby>   …… あたらしい 店<ruby>みせ</ruby>です。

14. きたない   …… きたない 店<ruby>みせ</ruby>です。

15. うるさい   …… うるさい 店<ruby>みせ</ruby>です。

5.7.4 Transformation Drill

1. みち子さんは 女<ruby>おんな</ruby>の 人です。
   <u>きれいです。</u>   } ⟶ みち子さんは <u>きれいな</u> 女<ruby>おんな</ruby>の 人です。

2. ここは きっさ店<ruby>てん</ruby>です。
   しずかです。   } ⟶ ここは しずかな きっさ店<ruby>てん</ruby>です。

3. きのう えいがを 見ました。
   つまらないです。   } ⟶ きのう つまらない えいがを 見ました。

4. さくらは 日本の 花です。
   だいひょう的<ruby>てき</ruby>です。   } ⟶ さくらは 日本の だいひょう的<ruby>てき</ruby>な 花です。

78

78

5. 公園へ　行ってみました。
とても　とおいです。
⟶　とても　とおい　公園へ　行ってみました。

6. ジョージさんは　日本語を　はなします。
じょうずです。
⟶　ジョージさんは　じょうずな　日本語を
はなします。

7. まい日　おんがくを　ききます。
好きです。
⟶　まい日　好きな　おんがくを　ききます。

8. おてらを　けんぶつしました。
いろいろです。
⟶　いろいろな　おてらを　けんぶつしました。

5.7.5　Combination Drill

1. 上野へ　行きましょう。
花見に　行きましょう。
⟶　上野へ　花見に　行きましょう。

2. 日本へ　来ました。
けんぶつに　来ました。
⟶　日本へ　けんぶつに　来ました。

3. みち子さんと　いっしょに　でかけます。
かいものに　でかけます。
⟶　みち子さんと　いっしょに　かいものに
でかけます。

4. 先生の　所へ　うかがいたいんです。
べんきょうに　うかがいたいんです。
⟶　先生の　所へ　べんきょうに
うかがいたいんです。

5. らいしゅう　ヨーロッパへ　行きます。
りょこうに　行きます。
⟶　らいしゅう　ヨーロッパへ　りょこうに
行きます。

6. うちへ　かえりましたか。
しょくじに　かえりましたか。
⟶　うちへ　しょくじに　かえりましたか。

5.7.6　Combination Drill

1. さくらが　さいています。
見に　行きます。
⟶　さくらが　さいていますから、見に
行きます。

2. 花見の　きせつです。
たぶん　人が　おおいでしょう。
⟶　花見の　きせつですから、たぶん　人が
おおいでしょう。

3. しごとが　たくさん　あります。
いそがしいです。
⟶　しごとが　たくさん　ありますから、
いそがしいです。

4. 日本語を　ならいませんでした。
わかりません。
⟶　日本語を　ならいませんでしたから、
わかりません。

5. かぶきの　きっぷを　もらいました。
あなたに　さしあげましょう。
⟶　かぶきの　きっぷを　もらいましたから、
あなたに　さしあげましょう。

6. 気ぶんが わるいです。　　　　　　　　｝⟶　気ぶんが わるい(です)から、　やすみたい
　　やすみたいです。　　　　　　　　　　　　　　　です。

7. じどうしゃを もっていません。　　　　｝⟶　じどうしゃを もっていませんから、
　　でんしゃで かえりましょう。　　　　　　　　でんしゃで かえりましょう。

8. ハワイは あたたかいです。　　　　　　｝⟶　ハワイは あたたかい(です)から、　すみたい
　　すみたいです。　　　　　　　　　　　　　　　です。

5.7.7　Transformation Drill

1. ともだちと いっしょに くつを かいます。｝⟶　ともだちと いっしょに くつを かいに
　　行きました。　　　　　　　　　　　　　　　　　行きました。

2. 土曜日に よし子さんに あいます。　　　｝⟶　土曜日に よし子さんに あいに
　　行きましょう。　　　　　　　　　　　　　　　行きましょう。

3. 本やが じしょを うります。　　　　　　｝⟶　本やが じしょを うりに 学校へ 来ます。
　　学校へ 来ます。

4. らい月 はたらきます。　　　　　　　　　｝⟶　らい月 はたらきに 大阪へ 来てください。
　　大阪へ 来てください。

5. ゆうがた アルバイトを します。　　　　｝⟶　ゆうがた アルバイトを しに でかけます。
　　でかけます。

6. 大ぜいの 学生が 本を かります。　　　｝⟶　大ぜいの 学生が 本を かりに 来ます。
　　来ます。

7. きょういく学を べんきょうします。　　　｝⟶　きょういく学を べんきょうしに
　　アメリカへ かえりたいんです。　　　　　　　アメリカへ かえりたいんです。

8. いもうとを よびます。　　　　　　　　　｝⟶　いもうとを よびに へやへ 行きました。
　　へやへ 行きました。

5.7.8　Substitution Drill

A. 上野公園で 花見が できますか。
　　1. しょくじ　　　……　上野公園で しょくじが できますか。
　　2. さんぽ　　　　……　上野公園で さんぽが できますか。
　　3. かいもの　　　……　上野公園で かいものが できますか。
　　4. しごと　　　　……　上野公園で しごとが できますか。
　　5. アルバイト　　……　上野公園で アルバイトが できますか。
　　6. テニス　　　　……　上野公園で テニスが できますか。
　　7. ボーリング　　……　上野公園で ボーリングが できますか。

B. ジョージさんは　ゴルフが　できます。

   1.　すいえい　　　　　　…… ジョージさんは　すいえいが　できます。

   2.　日本語_ご　　　　　　…… ジョージさんは　日本語_ごが　できます。

   3.　べんきょう　　　　　…… ジョージさんは　べんきょうが　できます。

   4.　ピアノ　　　　　　　…… ジョージさんは　ピアノが　できます。

   5.　スケート　　　　　　…… ジョージさんは　スケートが　できます。

   6.　ドイツ語_ごの　かいわ …… ジョージさんは　ドイツ語_ごの　かいわが　できます。

5.7.9　Expansion Drill

1.　かいたいです。　　　　　…… かいたいです。

   花を　　　　　　　　　…… 花を　かいたいです。

   日本の　　　　　　　　…… 日本の　花を　かいたいです。

   だいひょう的_{てき}な　　…… だいひょう的_{てき}な　日本の　花を　かいたいです。

2.　だれですか。　　　　　　…… だれですか。

   女_{おんな}の　人は　　　　…… 女_{おんな}の　人は　だれですか。

   大きい　　　　　　　　…… 大きい　女_{おんな}の　人は　だれですか。

   あの　　　　　　　　　…… あの　大きい　女_{おんな}の　人は　だれですか。

3.　見に　行きました。　　　…… 見に　行きました。

   じんじゃや　おてらを　…… じんじゃや　おてらを　見に　行きました。

   いろいろな　　　　　　…… いろいろな　じんじゃや　おてらを　見に　行きました。

4.　ききました。　　　　　　…… ききました。

   おんがくを　　　　　　…… おんがくを　ききました。

   きっさ店_{てん}で　　　　…… きっさ店_{てん}で　おんがくを　ききました。

   きれいな　　　　　　　…… きれいな　きっさ店_{てん}で　おんがくを　ききました。

5.　よみました。　　　　　　…… よみました。

   ざっしを　　　　　　　…… ざっしを　よみました。

   おもしろい　　　　　　…… おもしろい　ざっしを　よみました。

   とても　　　　　　　　…… とても　おもしろい　ざっしを　よみました。

   きのう　　　　　　　　…… きのう　とても　おもしろい　ざっしを　よみました。

5.7.10　Transformation Drill

1.　おとなが　見に　来ます。　　　　　⎫
　　子どもが　見に　来ます。　　　　　⎬ ⟶　おとなも　子どもも　見に　来ます。

2.　びじゅつかんに　いませんでした。　⎫　　　　びじゅつかんにも　どうぶつ園_{えん}にも
　　どうぶつ園_{えん}に　いませんでした。⎬ ⟶　　　　いませんでした。

3. きのう　花見に　行きました。
   きょう　花見に　行きました。　　　⟶　きのうも　きょうも　花見に　行きました。

4. みち子さんに　レコードを　あげました。
   ジョージさんに　レコードを　あげました。　⟶　みち子さんにも　ジョージさんにも
   　　　　　　　　　　　　　　　　　　　　　　　　レコードを　あげました。

5. 月曜日に　じゅぎょうが　あります。
   木曜日に　じゅぎょうが　あります。　⟶　月曜日にも　木曜日にも　じゅぎょうが
   　　　　　　　　　　　　　　　　　　　　　　あります。

6. コーヒーは　ほしくありません。
   こうちゃは　ほしくありません。　⟶　コーヒーも　こうちゃも　ほしくありません。

7. ハンカチは　二かいで　うっています。
   ハンカチは　三がいで　うっています。　⟶　ハンカチは　二かいでも　三がいでも
   　　　　　　　　　　　　　　　　　　　　　　　うっています。

8. にっこうへ　りょこうしました。
   きょうとへ　りょこうしました。　⟶　にっこうへも　きょうとへも
   　　　　　　　　　　　　　　　　　　　　りょこうしました。

5.7.11　E-J Response Drill

1. ハワイは　どんな　所ですか。
   pretty place　　　　　　　　　……　きれいな　所です。

2. その　えいがは　どんな　えいがでしたか。
   very interesting movie　　　　……　とても　おもしろい　えいがでした。

3. どんな　はこが　ほしいですか。
   a big box　　　　　　　　　……　大きい　はこが　ほしいです。

4. どんな　本を　よみたいですか。
   a famous book　　　　　　　……　ゆうめいな　本を　よみたいです。

5. ほっかいどうは　どんな　天気でしたか。
   wonderful weather　　　　　……　すばらしい　天気でした。

6. あの　学生は　どんな　人ですか。
   a quiet man　　　　　　　　……　しずかな　人です。

7. どんな　うちに　すみたいですか。
   a new house　　　　　　　　……　あたらしい　うちに　すみたいです。

5.7.12　E-J Response Drill

1. きのう　どうして　しごとを　やすみましたか。
   I was sick　　　　　　　　……　びょう気でしたから、やすみました。

2. あなたは　どうして　日本語を　ならっていますか。
   I want to go to Japan　　　……　日本へ　行きたいから、ならっています。

3. どうして　知っていますか。
   I heard it from Yoshiko　　　　　……　よし子さんから　ききましたから、知っています。

4. どうして　ゆうがた　花見に　行きますか。
   there are few people　　　　　……　人が　すくないから、行きます。

5. せんしゅう　どうして　来ませんでしたか。
   I was busy　　　　　……　いそがしかったから、来ませんでした。

6. どうして　フランス語を　はなしませんでしたか。
   I am poor at it　　　　　……　へたですから、はなしませんでした。

7. どうして　森さんに　あいませんでしたか。
   I didn't have free time　　　　　……　ひまが　ありませんでしたから、あいませんでした。

5.8　EXERCISES

5.8.1　Transform the following sentences into ~ *ni ikimasu* ending:

1. あした　かず子さんと　よし子さんに　あいます。
2. かぶきの　きっぷを　もらいました。
3. 森先生を　よびます。
4. 日本語の　本を　かりました。
5. ちちも　わたしも　まい日　はたらきます。
6. さくらの　きせつですから、見ましょう。

5.8.2　Answer the following questions according to the instruction given:

1. どうして　ぎんざへ　あそびに　行きませんでしたか。
   because I was not free

2. ブラウンさんは　どんな　外国語が　できますか。
   Japanese and Chinese

3. きのう　どんな　所で　しょくじを　しましたか。
   a very pretty restaurant in Ginza

4. どうして　コーヒーを　のみませんか。
   because I don't like it

5. どんな　えいがを　見ましたか。
   an interesting American movie

5.8.3　Write the underlined *hiragana* in *kanji*:

1. いい　てんきですから、　はなみに　いきましょう。

2. あの おおきい ひとを しっていますか。

3. どんな ところが すきですか。

4. わたしは いま ちいさい うちに すんでいます。

5.8.4 Write in *katakana*:

1. tenisu
2. boorin'gu
3. gorufu
4. sukeeto
5. sukii
6. Jooji

5.9 SITUATIONAL CONVERSATION

5.9.1 Going to the park

Mr. A and Mr. B want to see the cherry blossoms.

Mr. A recommends that they go to a good park where the cherry blossoms are in bloom.

Mr. B asks about the park.

They decide to go to the park to see the cherry blossoms in the evening.

5.9.2 Talk about going somewhere to enjoy an evening.

5.9.3 Invite your friend to go to a famous spot you are familiar with and describe the place for your friend.

LESSON 6

6.1 PRESENTATION

― のりもの^{*1} ―

　東京から　大阪_{さか}まで^{*2}　五百五十六キロ　（三百四十六マイル）　ありますが、　むかしは、

たいてい　あるきましたから、　りょこうするのは^{*3}　たいへんでした。　今は、

ひこうきや　しんかん線_{せん}などの　はやい　のりもので　行くことが^{*4}　できます。

6.2 DIALOG

外国人　「ちょっと　うかがいますが、^{*5}　あれは　大阪行_{さかゆき}の^{*6}　急行_{きゅうこう}ですか。」

日本人　「さあ、　よく　わかりません。　あそこに　いる　駅員_{いん}に^{*7}　きいてみて^{*8}
　　　　　ください。」

外国人　「はい、　どうも　ありがとう。」

―――――――・―――――――

外国人　「あのう、^{*9}　大阪行_{さかゆき}の　急行_{きゅうこう}に　のりたいんですが、^{*10}　なん番線_{ばんせん}から^{*11}
　　　　　出ますか。」

駅　員_{いん}　「二十一時に　出る^{*7}　急行_{きゅうこう}ですね？　十四番線_{ばんせん}からです。^{*12}」

外国人　「大阪_{さか}まで　どのぐらい^{*13}　かかりますか。」

駅　員_{いん}　「よるは　ふつう急行_{きゅうこう}で　十時間半^{*14}_{はん}　かかります。　ですから、　急行_{きゅうこう}が^{*7}
　　　　　大阪_{さか}に　つく　時間は、　あしたの　あさ　七時二十八分です。」

外国人　「そうですか。　一等_{とう}の^{*15}　せきは　まだ　ありますか。」

駅　員_{いん}　「まどぐちには^{*16}　もう^{*17}　ないでしょう。　のってから、^{*18}　しゃしょうに
　　　　　きいてみてください。　たまに　のらない^{*19}　人や　すぐ　おりる^{*20}　人が
　　　　　いますから……。」

外国人　「じゃあ、　そう　します。　どうも　ありがとう。」

6.3 PATTERN SENTENCES

6.3.1

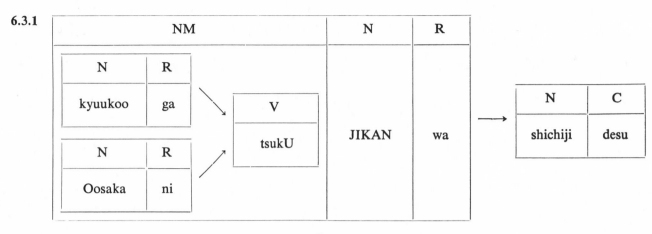

"The time when the express arrives at Ōsaka is seven o'clock."

6.3.2

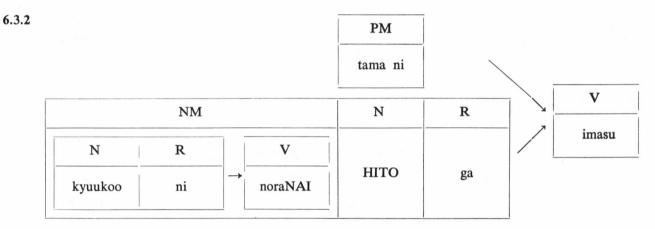

"There are occasionally some people who do not take an express."

6.3.3

NM			Nd	R		Na	C
N	R	V					
Oosaka	made	→ ikU	NO	wa	→	taihen	deshita

"It was very hard to travel to Ōsaka."

nom-imasu	⟶	nom-u	a-imasu	⟶	a-u
yasum-imasu	⟶	yasum-u	ka-imasu	⟶	ka-u
asob-imasu	⟶	asob-u	ma/t/-imasu	⟶	ma/t/-u
yob-imasu	⟶	yob-u	mo/t/-imasu	⟶	mo/t/-u
hana/s/-imasu	⟶	hanas-u			

(3) Irregular Verbs

| shimasu | ⟶ | suru |
| kimasu | ⟶ | kuru |

The *no* may be used in several patterns, but only the following use of *no* will be dealt with in this lesson:

(Predicate Modifier) + Dictionary form of Verb + *no* + {*wa* / *ga*} ......

Oosaka made ryokoo suru
issho ni iku
gaikokugo o narau
fune ni noru
no {*wa* / *ga*}
taihen desu
tanoshii desu
yasashii desu
suki desu

"it's {hard / pleasant / easy} / [I] like" to {travel to Ōsaka" / go together" / learn a foreign language" / take a ship"}

Maiasa aruku no wa tanoshii desu. "To walk every morning is pleasant."

Ima kyuukoo ni noru no wa muzukashii deshoo. "It must be difficult to catch an express now."

Nihon'go o ben'kyoo suru no wa taihen desu ga, omoshiroi desu yo. "It is hard to study Japanese, but it is interesting."

Suujii san wa nihon'go de hanasu no ga joozu desu. "Susie is good at speaking Japanese."

Boku wa kurashikku o kiku no ga suki desu. "I like to listen to classical music."

6.4.4 *Iku koto ga dekimasu* is "(we) can go," or literally means "going is possible." As already introduced in Note 5.4.11, *dekimasu* is an intransitive Verb meaning "is possible" or "can," and what one can do is followed by the subject Relational *ga*. The dependent Nominative or a nominalizer *koto* means "act," and is always preceded by a Nominative Modifier — the Dictionary form of a Verb precedes *koto* in this potential pattern ~ *koto ga dekimasu* "can do." Like *no* introduced in Note 6.4.3, *koto* preceded by the Dictionary form of a Verb behaves as a Nominative meaning "to (do)," or "(do)ing." Although *koto* and *no* are similar in their function and meaning and are sometimes interchangeable, *koto* can not be replaced by *no* in the pattern of ~ *koto ga dekimasu*.

(person + *wa*) + (Predicate Modifier) + Dictionary form of Verb + *koto* + *ga* + *dekimasu*

When it is necessary to mention who can do, the person is followed by the Relational *wa* and precedes ~ *koto ga*.

kau sen'sei ni au } koto ga dekimasu hikooki de kuru goji no kyuukoo ni noru	"[I] can buy it" "[you] can meet the teacher" "[I] can come by plane" "[he] can take the five o'clock express"

Ashita san'ji goro uchi ni kuru koto ga dekimasu ka?	"Can you come to my home at about three o'clock tomorrow?"
Iie, isogashii kara, iku koto wa dekimasen.	"No, I'm busy so I can't go."
Nihon'go de hanasu koto ga dekimasen ka?	"Can't you speak in Japanese?"
Ee, dekimasen.	"No, I can't."
Koko kara eki made hashiru koto ga dekimasu ka?	"Are you able to run from here to the station?"
Dekimasu yo!	"Yes, I am!"
Kan'ji o ikutsu kaku koto ga dekimasu ka?	"How many *kanji* can you write?"
San'juu gurai kaku koto ga dekimasu.	"I can write about thirty."

6.4.5 *Chotto ukagaimasu ga, ...* is used when the speaker needs some information and starts talking, usually with a stranger. This expression corresponds to "Excuse me, but may I ask you a question?" *Ukagaimasu* here is a polite equivalent of *kikimasu* "hear" or "inquire." (See 6.4.8.)

6.4.6 *Oosaka yuki no kyuukoo* means "express bound for Ōsaka." The *-yuki* is derived from *yuki(masu)*, that is an alternative form of *iki(masu)* "go." Sometimes, *-iki* is used instead of *-yuki*.

Nyuu Yooku yuki no hikooki	"airplane for New York"
Kono fune wa San Furan'shisuko yuki desu ka?	"Is this ship bound for San Francisco?"
Are wa doko yuki no basu desu ka?	"Where does that bus go?"

6.4.7 *Asoko ni iru ekiin* means "a station employee who is over there." When a Verb modifies or describes the following Nominative, the Verb is in the Dictionary form. The Dictionary forms of Verbs have been introduced in Notes 1.4.19 and 6.4.3. Depending upon what the Nominative modified by the preceding Predicate represents, the English equivalent will be "something which or that does such and such," "one who does such and such," "the time when one does such and such," etc. While a noun modifier in English may precede or follow the noun modified, the Nominative Modifier of Japanese always precedes the Nominative directly. Thus:

Nominative Modifier + Nominative

anata no		"your book"
kono		"this book"
omoshiroi	+ hon	"interesting book"
suki na		"favorite book" or "the book [I] like"
yomu		"the book that [I] read"

The verbal Nominative Modifier that precedes a Nominative can be a single Verb or have Predicate Modifiers:

(Predicate Modifier) + Verb (normal form) ⟶

        (Predicate Modifier) + Verb (plain form) + Nominative

asoko ni iru ekiin	"a station employee who is over there"
ryokoo suru hito	"a person who travels"
nijuu ichiji ni deru kyuukoo	"an express train that leaves at 2100"
Oosaka ni tsuku jikan	"the time when it arrives at Ōsaka"
sugu oriru hito	"a person who will get off soon"
mainichi kaimono o suru mise	"the store where I do some shopping every day"
yuki ga furu kisetsu	"the season when it snows"

Asoko ni iru on'na no gakusei wa dare desu ka?	"Who is the girl student over there?"
Watakushi wa rokuji ni deru kyuukoo ni norimasu.	"I will take an express train that leaves at six o'clock."
Hayashi san ga Oosaka ni tsuku jikan o shitte imasu ka?	"Do you know the time when Mr. Hayashi arrives at Ōsaka?"

When a sentence that modifies a Nominative includes the subject, the subject is followed either by the subject Relational *ga* or by *no*. *No* can replace *ga* in the Nominative Modifier. Note that the Relational *wa* never replaces *ga* in this case; in other words, when a sentence has *wa* following the subject, *wa* should be changed into *ga* or *no*.

Nominative + *ga* + Predicate
Nominative + *wa* + Predicate ⟶ **Nominative + *ga* / *no* + Predicate + Nominative**

kyuukoo ga tsukimasu	⟶ kyuukoo {ga/no} tsuku jikan
"an express arrives"	"time when an express arrives"
hana ga ooi desu	⟶ hana {ga/no} ooi kooen
"there are many flowers"	"a park where there are many flowers"
on'gaku ga suki desu	⟶ on'gaku {ga/no} suki na hito
"he likes music"	"a person who likes music"
Michiko san wa on'gaku ga suki desu	⟶ Michiko san {ga/no} suki na on'gaku
"Michiko likes music"	"the music which Michiko likes"

The following examples show how to form a Nominative Modifier plus a Nominative:

92

gakusei } *ga* { ikimasu / aruite imasu / nete imasu }   ⟶   { iku / aruite iru / nete iru } gakusei / kodomo
kodomo

"a student / "a child { goes" / is walking" / is sleeping" }   ⟶   "a student / "a child } who { goes" / is walking" / is sleeping"

jidoosha / kyuukoo } *ga* { kimasu / demasu / hashitte imasu }   ⟶   { kuru / deru / hashitte iru } jidoosha / kyuukoo

"a car / "an express { comes" / leaves" / is running" }   ⟶   "a car / "an express } that { comes" / leaves" / is running"

watakushi ga { tegami *o* kakimasu / zasshi *o* yomimasu / ben'kyoo *o* shite imasu }   ⟶   watakushi ga { kaku tegami / yomu zasshi / shite iru ben'kyoo }

"I { write a letter" / read a magazine" / am studying" }   ⟶   "a letter / "a magazine / "study } which I { write" / read" / am doing"

inu ga / shokudoo ga / basu ga } kooen *ni* { imasu / arimasu / tsukimasu }   ⟶   inu ga iru / shokudoo ga aru / basu ga tsuku } kooen

"a dog is / "an eating house is / "a bus arrives } in a park" (at)   ⟶   "a park where { there is a dog" / there is an eating house" / a bus arrives"

Sumisu san ga eki *de* { machimasu / hataraite imasu }   ⟶   Sumisu san ga { matsu / hataraite iru } eki

"Mr. Smith { waits / is working } at the station"   ⟶   "station where Mr. Smith { waits" / is working"

boku wa (ga) { mise *e* ikimasu / daigaku *e* kaerimasu / yuumei na tokoro *e* dekakemasu }   ⟶   boku ga { iku mise / kaeru daigaku / dekakeru yuumei na tokoro }

"I { go to the store" / return to the college" / go out to a famous place" }   ⟶   "the store / "the college / "a famous place } where { I go" / I return" / I go out"

Daigaku e iku gakusei wa nan'nin imasu ka?   "How many students are there going to the college?"

Sumisu san ga hataraite iru eki wa doko desu ka?   "Where is the station Mr. Smith is working at?"

Michiko san ga matte iru tokoro wa ano kissaten desu.   "The place where Michiko is waiting is that coffee shop."

6.4.8 The Verb *kikimasu* has another meaning, "inquire," in addition to "listen" or "hear." The person of whom one inquires is followed by the Relational *ni,* and what one inquires is followed by *o.*

Shashoo ni kiite mite kudasai.   "Please ask a conductor and find out."

Inoue san ni ano gakusei no namae   "I asked Mr. Inoue that student's name."
o kikimashita.

As already introduced in 6.4.5, *ukagaimasu* is a polite equivalent of *kikimasu.*

Sen'sei ni ukagaimashoo   "Let's ask the teacher about it."

6.4.9 *Anoo* is a Sentence Interjective meaning "Say," or "Er-r-r-r."

6.4.10 *Nori(masu)* is a Verb meaning "get on (a vehicle)" or "take (a train)." This Verb is an intransitive Verb, and what one gets on or takes is followed by the Relational *ni.*

Den'sha ni norimasu ka, basu ni   "Are you going to take a train or a bus?"
norimasu ka?

Shin'kan'sen ni norimashoo.   "Let's go by the New Tōkaidō Line."

6.4.11 *Nan'ban'sen* is "what track number?" The *-ban* is a counter for naming numbers in succession, and *sen* means "track" or "line." *Juuyon'ban'sen* is "track number fourteen."

Nan'ban'sen kara demasu ka?   "What track (number) does it leave from?"

Ichiban'sen kara demasu.   "It leaves from Track Number One."

6.4.12 *Juuyon'ban'sen kara desu* is a variation of *juuyon'ban'sen kara demasu.* A Predicate Modifier can be used alone as a short reply to a question. In this case, the Predicate Modifier is usually followed by the Copula *desu* in normal speech.

Kono kyuukoo wa doko made   "How far does this express go?"
ikimasu ka?

Oosaka made desu.   "It goes to Ōsaka."

6.4.13 *Dono gurai* (or *kurai*) means here "how long?" Depending upon the situation and the Predicate following it, *dono gurai* (*kurai*) may mean "how long?" "how far?" "how much?" etc. When the Verb following *dono gurai* is *kakarimasu* "require," *dono gurai* means "how long?" or "how much?" and *dono gurai* with *arimasu* means "how far?" or "how much?" *Desu* can be used in place of *arimasu* and *kakarimasu.*

Tookyoo kara Oosaka made dono   "How long does it take from Tōkyō to Ōsaka?"
gurai kakarimasu ka?

Juujikan gurai kakarimasu.   "It takes about ten hours."

Tookyoo kara Oosaka made dono gurai arimasu ka?	"How far is it from Tōkyō to Ōsaka?"
San'byaku yon'juu rokumairu arimasu.	"It is 346 miles."
Sumisu san wa dono gurai Nihon ni imashita ka?	"How long did Mr. Smith stay in Japan?"
San'nen gurai imashita.	"He stayed about three years."
Anata no sei wa dono gurai arimasu ka?	"How tall are you?"
Ichimeetoru hachijussen'chi gurai arimasu.	"I am about one meter and eighty centimeters tall."

6.4.14 *Jikan,* when used as an independent Nominative, means "hour" or "time."

shokuji ⎫ ben'kyoo ⎬ no jikan nihon'go ⎭	"time for ⎰a meal" ⎱study" Japanese"
gakkoo ⎰e iku ⎫ ⎱ni tsuku ⎬ jikan kara kaeru⎭	"time ⎰to go to ⎫ ⎱to arrive at ⎬ school" to return from⎭
Jikan ga kakarimasu.	"It takes time."

The *-jikan* preceded by numerals is a counter meaning "hour." *Nan'jikan* is "how many hours?"

Nan'jikan kakarimasu ka?	"How many hours does it take?"
Juujikan'han kakarimasu.	"It takes ten hours and a half."
Mainichi gojikan nihon'go o ben'kyoo shimasu. .	"I study Japanese five hours every day."

6.4.15 *Ittoo* means "first-class;" *nitoo* "second-class;" *san'too* "third-class." *Nan'too* is "what class?"

Ittoo no seki ga mada arimasu ka?	"Do you still have first-class seats [available]?"
Nitoo ni norimashoo.	"Let's go second-class."

6.4.16 When an Adverb *moo* is used with negation, it always means "(not) any more," or "(not) any longer." Note that *moo* in an affirmative sentence has the different meaning "already."

Moo ittoo no seki wa arimasen.	"There are no more first-class seats."
Moo ikitaku arimasen.	"I don't want to go there any longer."
Moo Tookyoo ni tsukimashita.	"We have already arrived at Tōkyō."

The Adverb *mada* "still" is often used in the question to ask if something is still so or if it is not so any more.

Minoru wa mada nete imasu ka?	"Is Minoru still sleeping?"
Iie, moo nete imasen.	"No, he is not sleeping any longer."

6.4.17 *Nai* is an Adjective meaning "nonexistent," and is an equivalent of *arimasen*. When the plain equivalent of *arimasen* is required, *nai* should be used. *Nai* inflects like other Adjectives. Only the following forms are considered at this stage.

arimasen   ⟶   nai (desu)
arimasen deshita ⟶   nakatta (desu)

Madoguchi ni wa nai deshoo.	"They may not have it at the window."
Kyoo, doitsugo no jugyoo wa nai desu.	"There is no German class today."
Mukashi wa, hayai norimono ga nakatta (n) desu.	"In the old days, there were no rapid transportation facilities."

6.4.18 *Notte kara* means "after getting on (a train)." This usage will be introduced in later volumes.

6.4.19 *Noranai hito* means "a person who does not get on (a train)." Like the pattern already introduced in 6.4.7, *hito* is described or modified by *noranai*. *Noranai* is the plain negative imperfect tense, and the plain equivalent of *norimasen*. The -*nai* form (-*nai* is the adjectival Derivative attached to the Pre-Nai form Verb) is formed as follows:

(1) When a Verb is a Vowel Verb, the Stem form (or the Pre-Nai form) plus -*nai*:

dekimasu	⟶	dekiru	⟶	deki-nai
imasu	⟶	iru	⟶	i-nai
mimasu	⟶	miru	⟶	mi-nai
tabemasu	⟶	taberu	⟶	tabe-nai

(2) When a Verb is a Consonant Verb, the Pre-Nai form (or the Base form plus -*a*) plus -*nai*:

ikimasu	⟶	iku	⟶	ika-nai
arukimasu	⟶	aruku	⟶	aruka-nai
tsukimasu	⟶	tsuku	⟶	tsuka-nai
norimasu	⟶	noru	⟶	nora-nai
kakarimasu	⟶	kakaru	⟶	kakara-nai
nomimasu	⟶	nomu	⟶	noma-nai
yasumimasu	⟶	yasumu	⟶	yasuma-nai
asobimasu	⟶	asobu	⟶	asoba-nai
hana/s/imasu	⟶	hanasu	⟶	hanasa-nai
aimasu	⟶	a(w)u	⟶	awa-nai
kaimasu	⟶	ka(w)u	⟶	kawa-nai
ma/t/imasu	⟶	ma/t/u	⟶	mata-nai
mo/t/imasu	⟶	mo/t/u	⟶	mota-nai

(3) Irregular Verbs:

shimasu	⟶	suru	⟶	shinai
kimasu	⟶	kuru	⟶	konai

The structural environment is the same as that of the affirmative form in Note 6.4.7.

kyuukoo ni $\begin{Bmatrix} noru \\ noranai \end{Bmatrix}$ hito "a person who $\begin{Bmatrix} \text{gets on} \\ \text{does not take} \end{Bmatrix}$ an express"

watakushi $\begin{Bmatrix} ga \\ no \end{Bmatrix}$ $\begin{Bmatrix} motte\ iru \\ motte\ inai \end{Bmatrix}$ hon "the book that I $\begin{Bmatrix} \text{have} \\ \text{do not have} \end{Bmatrix}$"

watakushi $\begin{Bmatrix} ga \\ no \end{Bmatrix}$ $\begin{Bmatrix} oriru \\ orinai \end{Bmatrix}$ eki "a station where $\begin{Bmatrix} \text{I get off} \\ \text{I don't get off} \end{Bmatrix}$"

ame ga $\begin{Bmatrix} furu \\ furanai \end{Bmatrix}$ kisetsu "the season when $\begin{Bmatrix} \text{it rains} \\ \text{it doesn't rain} \end{Bmatrix}$"

Takushii ni noru hito ga san'nin imasu. "There are three persons who take a taxi."

Den'sha ni noranai hito wa imasen. "There are no persons who do not get on (ride) a train."

Chichi ga ima yon'de iru shin'bun wa Asahi Shin'bun desu. "The newspaper my father is reading now is the Asahi Newspaper."

Chichi ga ima yon'de inai shin'bun wa Asahi Shin'bun desu. "The newspaper my father is not reading now is the Asahi Newspaper."

6.4.20 The opposite of *norimasu* is *orimasu* "get off," and what one gets off is followed by the Relational *kara*.

Oosaka de kyuukoo kara orimashita. "I got off an express at Ōsaka."

Hikooki kara orimashita. Soshite, sugu takushii ni norimashita. "I got off the airplane, and I took a taxi right away."

6.5 VOCABULARY

Presentation

のりもの	norimono	....	N	transportation facilities; vehicle (see 6.4.1)
まで	made	....	R	as far as; until (see 6.4.2)
キロ	-kiro	....	Nd	short form of *kiromeetoru* – kilometer
マイル	-mairu	....	Nd	mile
むかし	mukashi	....	N	old times
あるきました	arukimashita	....	V	walked (TA form of *arukimasu* ← *aruku*)
りょこうする	ryokoo suru	....	V	travel (Dictionary form)
の	no	....	Nd	nominalizer (see 6.4.3)
たいへん	taihen	....	Na	awful; hard; terrible; trouble
しんかん線	Shin'kan'sen	....	N	New Tōkaidō Line
はやい	hayai	....	A	is fast; is rapid; is early

行く	iku	....	V	go (Dictionary form)
こと	koto	....	Nd	act; fact (see 6.4.4)

Dialog

外国人	gaikokujin	....	N	foreigner
うかがいます	ukagaimasu	....	V	hear; inquire (normal form of *ukagau*)
行	-yuki	....	Nd	bound for; for (see 6.4.6)
急行	kyuukoo	....	N	express
日本人	nihon'jin	....	N	Japanese person
さあ	saa	....	SI	well (hesitance)
よく	yoku	....	Adv.	well; much
いる	iru	....	V	is; exist (Dictionary form)
駅員	ekiin	....	N	station employee
きいて	kiite	....	V	TE form of *kikimasu* ← *kiku* – inquire (see 6.4.8)
あのう	anoo	....	SI	say; well; er-r-r-r (see 6.4.9)
のり	nori	....	V	Stem form of *norimasu* ← *noru* – get on; ride (see 6.4.10)
なん番線	nan'ban'sen	....	Ni	what track number? (see 6.4.11)
出ます	demasu	....	V	go out; leave (normal form of *deru*)
出る	deru	....	V	go out; leave (Dictionary form)
どのぐらい（どのくらい）	dono gurai (dono kurai)	....	Ni	how long?; how far?; how much? (see 6.4.13)
かかります	kakarimasu	....	V	require; take (normal form of *kakaru*)
ふつう	futsuu	....	N	ordinary; usual; average
時間	-jikan	....	Nd	hour(s) (see 6.4.14)
ですから	desukara	....	SI	therefore; so (formal form of *dakara*)
つく	tsuku	....	V	arrive (Dictionary form)
時間	jikan	....	N	time; hour
一等	ittoo	....	N	first class (see 6.4.15)
せき	seki	....	N	seat
まどぐち	madoguchi	....	N	ticket window
もう	moo	....	Adv.	(not) any more; (not) any longer (see 6.4.16)
ない	nai	....	A	is nonexistent (see 6.4.17)
のってから	notte kara	....	V+R	after getting on (see 6.4.18)
しゃしょう	shashoo	....	N	conductor
たまに	tama ni	....	PM	occasionally; once in a while
のら（ない）	nora(nai)	....	V	Pre-Nai form of *norimasu* ← *noru* – get on; ride (see 6.4.19)

ない	-nai	....	Da	negative Derivative (see 6.4.19)
おりる	oriru	....	V	get off (Dictionary form) (see 6.4.20)

Notes

タクシー	takushii	....	N	taxi
はしって	hashitte	....	V	TE form of *hashirimasu* ← *hashiru* – run
たべもの	tabemono	....	N	food
のみもの	nomimono	....	N	a drink; a beverage
かんじ	kan'ji	....	N	Chinese character
ニューヨーク	Nyuu Yooku	....	N	New York
サンフランシスコ	San Furan'shisuko	....	N	San Francisco
番	-ban	....	Nd	counter for naming numbers in succession
線	sen	....	N	track; line
せい	sei	....	N	height; stature
メートル	-meetoru	....	Nd	meter
センチ	-sen'chi	....	Nd	centimeter
等	-too	....	Nd	~ class
なかった	nakatta	....	A	was nonexistent (TA form of *nai*)
の	no	....	R	*no* substituting *ga* (see 6.4.7)

6.6 KANJI

6.6.1 東 (1) TOO (2) east (3) classifier 木

(4) 一 ｢ 厂 戸 両 東 東 東 (5) 東京、東部 [eastern part]

6.6.2 京 (1) KYOO (2) capital (3) classifier 亠

(4) ` 亠 宀 方 亨 亨 京 京 (5) 東京、京都

6.6.3 外 (1) GAI (2) foreign; outside (3) classifier 夕

(4) ﾉ ク 夕 列 外 (5) 外国人、外人 [foreigner]

6.6.4 国 (1) KOKU [-GOKU] (2) country (3) classifier 囗

(4) 丨 冂 冂 冃 用 国 国 国 (5) 外国、中国

5.6.2
人 (1) JIN (5) 日本人、外国人、アメリカ人

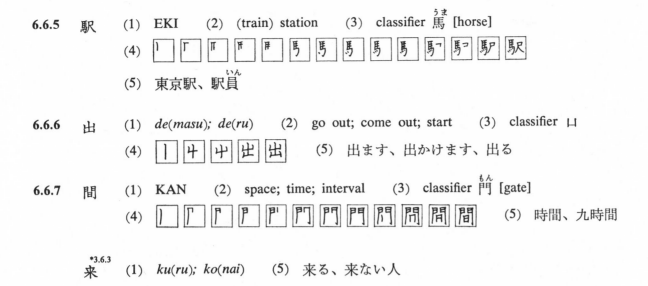

6.6.5 駅 (1) EKI (2) (train) station (3) classifier 馬 [horse]

(4) 丨 厂 﨤 厈 厈 馬 馬 馬 馬 馬 馬 馿 馿 駅 駅

(5) 東京駅、駅員

6.6.6 出 (1) *de(masu); de(ru)* (2) go out; come out; start (3) classifier 凵

(4) 丨 屮 屮 出 出 (5) 出ます、出かけます、出る

6.6.7 間 (1) KAN (2) space; time; interval (3) classifier 門 [gate]

(4) 丨 﨧 﨨 﨩 飯 門 門 門 門 間 間 間 (5) 時間、九時間

*3.6.3

来 (1) *ku(ru); ko(nai)* (5) 来る、来ない人

6.7 DRILLS

6.7.1 Pattern Drill

1. Tookyoo kara Oosaka made gohyaku gojuu rokkiro arimasu.

2. Mukashi wa, ryokoo suru no wa taihen deshita.

3. Hayai norimono de iku koto ga dekimasu.

4. Asoko ni iru ekiin ni kiite mite kudasai.

5. Nijuu ichiji ni deru kyuukoo desu ne?

6. Oosaka made dono gurai kakarimasu ka?

7. Kyuukoo ga Oosaka ni tsuku jikan wa, ashita no asa shichiji nijuu happun desu.

8. Tama ni noranai hito ya sugu oriru hito ga imasu kara.

6.7.2 Transformation Drill

1. 行きます	⟶	行く	9. すみます	⟶	すむ
2. 来ます	⟶	来る	10. はしります	⟶	はしる
3. あいます	⟶	あう	11. おります	⟶	おりる
4. べんきょうします	⟶	べんきょうする	12. 出ます	⟶	出る
5. のります	⟶	のる	13. つきます	⟶	つく
6. あるきます	⟶	あるく	14. かかります	⟶	かかる
7. います	⟶	いる	15. はなします	⟶	はなす
8. ききます	⟶	きく	16. よびます	⟶	よぶ

100

6.7.3 Transformation Drill

1. のりません	⟶	のらない	9. はしりません	⟶	はしらない
2. ならいません	⟶	ならわない	10. 知りません	⟶	知らない
3. おりません	⟶	おりない	11. あるきません	⟶	あるかない
4. わすれません	⟶	わすれない	12. ききません	⟶	きかない
5. かかりません	⟶	かからない	13. 来ません	⟶	来ない
6. 出ません	⟶	出ない	14. りょこうしません	⟶	りょこうしない
7. まちません	⟶	またない	15. いません	⟶	いない
8. つきません	⟶	つかない	16. ありません *Exception	⟶	ない

6.7.4 Transformation Drill

1. あそぶ	⟶	あそばない	9. つく	⟶	つかない
2. きく	⟶	きかない	10. かかる	⟶	かからない
3. 行く	⟶	行かない	11. もつ	⟶	もたない
4. ちがう	⟶	ちがわない	12. のる	⟶	のらない
5. おりる	⟶	おりない	13. はしる	⟶	はしらない
6. もらう	⟶	もらわない	14. つとめる	⟶	つとめない
7. はなす	⟶	はなさない	15. おりる	⟶	おりない
8. 出る	⟶	出ない			

6.7.5 Substitution Drill

1. あれは あたらしい でんしゃです。

    とても はやい …… あれは とても はやい でんしゃです。
    たいへん ふるい …… あれは たいへん ふるい でんしゃです。
    十時に 出る …… あれは 十時に 出る でんしゃです。
    大阪へ 行く …… あれは 大阪へ 行く でんしゃです。
    東京へ 行かない …… あれは 東京へ 行かない でんしゃです。

2. あの かわいい 子どもは スージーです。

    せいが たかい …… あの せいが たかい 子どもは スージーです。
    日本語が じょうずな …… あの 日本語が じょうずな 子どもは スージーです。
    にわで あそんでいる …… あの にわで あそんでいる 子どもは スージーです。
    おかしを たべている …… あの おかしを たべている 子どもは スージーです。
    でんしゃに のらない …… あの でんしゃに のらない 子どもは スージーです。

3. そこは いい 店です。

    きれいな …… そこは きれいな 店です。

レインコートを　うっている　　……　そこは　レインコートを　うっている　店です。

レコードを　うっていない　　　……　そこは　レコードを　うっていない　店です。

店員が　あまり　いない　　　　……　そこは　店員が　あまり　いない　店です。

子どもの　くつが　ない　　　　……　そこは　子どもの　くつが　ない　店です。

4. おもしろい　本を　よみたいです。

むずかしい　　　　　　　　　　……　むずかしい　本を　よみたいです。

いろいろな　　　　　　　　　　……　いろいろな　本を　よみたいです。

みち子さんが　もっている　　　……　みち子さんが　もっている　本を　よみたいです。

図書館に　ある　　　　　　　　……　図書館に　ある　本を　よみたいです。

先生が　知らない　　　　　　　……　先生が　知らない　本を　よみたいです。

5. 急行に　のる　時間を　知っていますか。

じゅぎょうが　はじまる　　　　……　じゅぎょうが　はじまる　時間を　知っていますか。

大阪に　つく　　　　　　　　　……　大阪に　つく　時間を　知っていますか。

東京行が　出る　　　　　　　　……　東京行が　出る　時間を　知っていますか。

スージーさんが　みち子さんに　……　スージーさんが　みち子さんに　あう　時間を
　あう　　　　　　　　　　　　　　　　知っていますか。

この　えいがが　おわる　　　　……　この　えいがが　おわる　時間を　知っていますか。

6. スージーさんが　たべない　たべものは　なんですか。

あなたの　知らない　　　　　　……　あなたの　知らない　たべものは　なんですか。

日本人が　たべている　　　　　……　日本人が　たべている　たべものは　なんですか。

あそこで　うっている　　　　　……　あそこで　うっている　たべものは　なんですか。

デパートで　うっている　　　　……　デパートで　うっている　たべものは　なんですか。

あの　子どもが　もっている　　……　あの　子どもが　もっている　たべものは　なんですか。

日本に　ない　　　　　　　　　……　日本に　ない　たべものは　なんですか。

6.7.6 Combination Drill

1. 本は　これです。
　　わたしが　よみたい　　　　}⟶　わたしが　よみたい　本は　これです。

2. 公園は　上野公園です。
　　いもうとが　行きたい　　　}⟶　いもうとが　行きたい　公園は　上野公園です。

3. バスは　三時に　つきます。
　　みち子さんが　のりたい　　}⟶　みち子さんが　のりたい　バスは　三時に
　　　　　　　　　　　　　　　　　　つきます。

4. 駅は　どこですか。
　　あなたが　おりたい　　　　}⟶　あなたが　おりたい　駅は　どこですか。

5. えいがは　どんな　えいがでしたか。⎫　　あなたが　見たかった　えいがは　どんな
　　あなたが　見たかった　　　　　　　⎬⟶　　　　　　　　　　　えいがでしたか。

6.7.7　Expansion Drill

1. きいてください。　　　　　…… きいてください。
　　駅員に　　　　　　　　　…… 駅員に　きいてください。
　　あそこに　いる　　　　　…… あそこに　いる　駅員に　きいてください。

2. かしてください。　　　　　…… かしてください。
　　本を　　　　　　　　　　…… 本を　かしてください。
　　よまない　　　　　　　　…… よまない　本を　かしてください。
　　あなたが　　　　　　　　…… あなたが　よまない　本を　かしてください。

3. 知っていますか。　　　　　…… 知っていますか。
　　時間を　　　　　　　　　…… 時間を　知っていますか。
　　つく　　　　　　　　　　…… つく　時間を　知っていますか。
　　大阪に　　　　　　　　　…… 大阪に　つく　時間を　知っていますか。
　　急行が　　　　　　　　　…… 急行が　大阪に　つく　時間を　知っていますか。

4. なん時ですか。　　　　　　…… なん時ですか。
　　時間は　　　　　　　　　…… 時間は　なん時ですか。
　　行く　　　　　　　　　　…… 行く　時間は　なん時ですか。
　　じむしょへ　　　　　　　…… じむしょへ　行く　時間は　なん時ですか。
　　ブラウンさんが　　　　　…… ブラウンさんが　じむしょへ　行く　時間は
　　　　　　　　　　　　　　　　　　なん時ですか。

5. います。　　　　　　　　　…… います。
　　大ぜい　　　　　　　　　…… 大ぜい　います。
　　お客さんが　　　　　　　…… お客さんが　大ぜい　います。
　　のらない　　　　　　　　…… のらない　お客さんが　大ぜい　います。
　　一等に　　　　　　　　　…… 一等に　のらない　お客さんが　大ぜい　います。

6. なんですか。　　　　　　　…… なんですか。
　　花は　　　　　　　　　　…… 花は　なんですか。
　　さく　　　　　　　　　　…… さく　花は　なんですか。
　　四月に　　　　　　　　　…… 四月に　さく　花は　なんですか。
　　日本で　　　　　　　　　…… 日本で　四月に　さく　花は　なんですか。

7. だれですか。　　　　　　　…… だれですか。
　　人は　　　　　　　　　　…… 人は　だれですか。
　　行かない　　　　　　　　…… 行かない　人は　だれですか。

見に	……	見に 行かない 人は だれですか。
えいがを	……	えいがを 見に 行かない 人は だれですか。
あした	……	あした えいがを 見に 行かない 人は だれですか。

6.7.8 Substitution Drill

1. <u>大阪へ 行く 急行は どれですか。</u>

九時に 出ます	……	九時に 出る 急行は どれですか。
あなたが のります	……	あなたが のる 急行は どれですか。
ごご 三時に つきます	……	ごご 三時に つく 急行は どれですか。
かとう先生が のっています	……	かとう先生が のっている 急行は どれですか。
しょくどうが あります	……	しょくどうが ある 急行は どれですか。

2. <u>京都へ 行く 学生は だれですか。</u>

くにへ かえります	……	くにへ かえる 学生は だれですか。
アルバイトを します	……	アルバイトを する 学生は だれですか。
日本語が できます	……	日本語が できる 学生は だれですか。
九月に けっこんします	……	九月に けっこんする 学生は だれですか。
あそこに います	……	あそこに いる 学生は だれですか。
日本語を ならっています	……	日本語を ならっている 学生は だれですか。
今 はなしています	……	今 はなしている 学生は だれですか。

3. <u>あした けんぶつする 所は どこですか。</u>

みずを のみます	……	みずを のむ 所は どこですか。
きっぷを かいます	……	きっぷを かう 所は どこですか。
しんかん線が つきます	……	しんかん線が つく 所は どこですか。
大阪行が 出ます	……	大阪行が 出る 所は どこですか。
先生が おります	……	先生が おりる 所は どこですか。
子どもたちが あそんでいます	……	子どもたちが あそんでいる 所は どこですか。
今、 さくらが さいています	……	今、 さくらが さいている 所は どこですか。

4. <u>これは わたしの もっていない</u> 本です。

図書館に ありません	……	これは 図書館に ない 本です。
本やで うっていません	……	これは 本やで うっていない 本です。
ぼくは 知りません	……	これは ぼくが 知らない 本です。
今、 よんでいません	……	これは 今、 よんでいない 本です。

104

6.7.9 Substitution Drill

A. わたしは　はしるのが　好きです。

　　1.　学校まで　あるきます　　　……　わたしは　<u>学校</u>まで　あるくのが　好きです。

　　2.　スキーを　します　　　　　　……　わたしは　スキーを　するのが　好きです。

　　3.　えいがを　見ます　　　　　　……　わたしは　えいがを　見るのが　好きです。

　　4.　ともだちに　あいます　　　　……　わたしは　ともだちに　あうのが　好きです。

　　5.　ジャズを　ききます　　　　　……　わたしは　ジャズを　きくのが　好きです。

　　6.　急行に　のります　　　　　　……　わたしは　急行に　のるのが　好きです。

　　7.　こうちゃを　のみます　　　　……　わたしは　こうちゃを　のむのが　好きです。

　　8.　かいものを　します　　　　　……　わたしは　かいものを　するのが　好きです。

B. タクシーで　けんぶつするのは　好きじゃありません。

　　1.　しごとを　します　　　　　　……　しごとを　するのは　好きじゃありません。

　　2.　すしを　たべます　　　　　　……　すしを　たべるのは　好きじゃありません。

　　3.　ボーリングを　します　　　　……　ボーリングを　するのは　好きじゃありません。

　　4.　花見に　行きます　　　　　　……　花見に　行くのは　好きじゃありません。

　　5.　バスに　のります　　　　　　……　バスに　のるのは　好きじゃありません。

　　6.　しょくどうで　はたらきます　……　しょくどうで　はたらくのは　好きじゃありません。

　　7.　セーターを　きます　　　　　……　セーターを　きるのは　好きじゃありません。

　　8.　じゅぎょうを　やすみます　　……　じゅぎょうを　やすむのは　好きじゃありません。

C. 日本語を　べんきょうするのは　たいへんです。

　　1.　日本語の　しんぶんを　よみます　……　日本語の　しんぶんを　よむのは　たいへんです。

　　2.　日本語で　はなします　　　　……　日本語で　はなすのは　たいへんです。

　　3.　あそこで　はたらきます　　　……　あそこで　はたらくのは　たいへんです。

　　4.　六時に　おきます　　　　　　……　六時に　おきるのは　たいへんです。

　　5.　子どもを　つれていきます　　……　子どもを　つれていくのは　たいへんです。

　　6.　ふゆやすみに　アルバイトします　……　ふゆやすみに　アルバイトするのは　たいへんです。

　　7.　バイオリンを　ならいます　　……　バイオリンを　ならうのは　たいへんです。

D. しんじゅくへ　行くのは　おもしろくありません。

　　1.　えいがを　見ます　　　　　　……　えいがを　見るのは　おもしろくありません。

　　2.　ふねに　のります　　　　　　……　ふねに　のるのは　おもしろくありません。

　　3.　ギターを　ひきます　　　　　……　ギターを　ひくのは　おもしろくありません。

　　4.　うちに　います　　　　　　　……　うちに　いるのは　おもしろくありません。

　　5.　デパートで　はたらきます　　……　デパートで　はたらくのは　おもしろくありません。

　　6.　テニスを　します　　　　　　……　テニスを　するのは　おもしろくありません。

　　7.　アルバイトを　します　　　　……　アルバイトを　するのは　おもしろくありません。

6.7.10 E-J Response Drill

1. どの　学生が　スミスさんですか。
   the student who is over there　　　　　……　あそこに　いる　学生が　スミスさんです。

2. どの　本を　よみたいですか。
   the book you have　　　　　　　　　　……　あなたが　もっている　本を　よみたいです。

3. どこを　けんぶつしたいですか。
   the place where there are temples　　　……　おてらが　ある　所を　けんぶつしたいです。

4. だれに　あいましたか。
   a person who is studying at Tōkyō University　……　東京大学で　べんきょうしている　人に
   　　　　　　　　　　　　　　　　　　　　　　　　　　あいました。

5. これは　どこへ　行く　急行ですか。
   the express that goes to Ōsaka　　　　　……　これは　大阪へ　行く　急行です。

6. なにを　ききましたか。
   the time when a train leaves　　　　　　……　でんしゃが　出る　時間を　ききました。

6.7.11　Substitution Drill

テニスを　することが　できますか。

1. ボーリングを　します　　　　　　　　　……　ボーリングを　することが　できますか。
2. なつやすみに　デパートで　はたらきます　……　なつやすみに　デパートで　はたらくことが
   　　　　　　　　　　　　　　　　　　　　　　　　　　できますか。
3. ドイツ語を　かきます　　　　　　　　　……　ドイツ語を　かくことが　できますか。
4. らい月　にっこうへ　行きます　　　　　……　らい月　にっこうへ　行くことが　できますか。
5. あの　きっさ店で　おんがくを　ききます　……　あの　きっさ店で　おんがくを　きくことが
   　　　　　　　　　　　　　　　　　　　　　　　　　　できますか。
6. 学校で　みち子さんに　あいます　　　　……　学校で　みち子さんに　あうことが
   　　　　　　　　　　　　　　　　　　　　　　　　　　できますか。
7. フランス語で　はなします　　　　　　　……　フランス語で　はなすことが　できますか。
8. アメリカで　日本語を　ならいます　　　……　アメリカで　日本語を　ならうことが
   　　　　　　　　　　　　　　　　　　　　　　　　　　できますか。
9. ピアノを　ひきます　　　　　　　　　　……　ピアノを　ひくことが　できますか。
10. あさ　三時に　おきます　　　　　　　　……　あさ　三時に　おきることが　できますか。

6.7.12　E-J Response Drill

1. あなたは　外国語を　はなしますか。
   no, I can't speak　　　　　　　　　　　……　いいえ、　はなすことが　できません。

2. ピアノを　ひきますか。

   no, I can't play　　　　　　　　　…… いいえ、　ひくことが　できません。

3. きのう　スージーさんに　学校で　あいましたか。

   no, I couldn't meet　　　　　　　…… いいえ、　あうことが　できませんでした。

4. ポールさんは　はしで　たべますか。

   no, I can't eat with chopsticks　…… いいえ、　はしで　たべることが　できません。

5. アメリカで　日本語を　ならいましたか。

   no, I couldn't study　　　　　　…… いいえ、　ならうことが　できませんでした。

6. 急行に　のりましたか。

   no, I couldn't get on　　　　　　…… いいえ、　のることが　できませんでした。

6.7.13　Substitution Drill

東京から　大阪まで　十時間半　かかります。

1. 三百マイルぐらい　あります　　　…… 東京から　大阪まで　三百マイルぐらい　あります。
2. どのぐらい　かかりますか　　　　…… 東京から　大阪まで　どのぐらい　かかりますか。
3. どのぐらい　ありますか　　　　　…… 東京から　大阪まで　どのぐらい　ありますか。
4. ひこうきで　一時間ぐらいです　　…… 東京から　大阪まで　ひこうきで　一時間ぐらい
                                       です。
5. むかしは　たいてい　あるきました　…… 東京から　大阪まで　むかしは　たいてい
                                       あるきました。

6.7.14　E-J Response Drill

1. あなたの　うちから　学校まで　どのぐらい　かかりますか。

   fifteen minutes　　　　　　　　　…… 十五分　かかります。

2. ここから　図書館まで　どのぐらい　ありますか。

   about one mile　　　　　　　　　　…… 一マイルぐらい　あります。

3. どのぐらい　日本に　いましたか。

   from June to November　　　　　…… 六月から　十一月まで　いました。

4. 東京から　京都まで　どのぐらい　ありますか。

   about five hundred kilometers　　…… 五百キロぐらい　あります。

5. まい日　どのぐらい　べんきょうしますか。

   six hours　　　　　　　　　　　　…… 六時間　べんきょうします。

6. 大学から　駅まで　どのぐらい　かかりますか。

   thirteen minutes　　　　　　　　　…… 十三分　かかります。

7. きみの　せいは　どのぐらいですか。

about a hundred eighty centimeters　　……　百八十センチぐらいです。

6.7.15　Response Drill

1. あなたは　まだ　学生ですか。

   はい　　　　　　　　　　　　　……　はい、　まだ　学生です。

   いいえ　　　　　　　　　　　　……　いいえ、　もう　学生ではありません。

2. やまださんは　まだ　アメリカに　いますか。

   はい　　　　　　　　　　　　　……　はい、　まだ　います。

   いいえ　　　　　　　　　　　　……　いいえ、　もう　いません。

3. まだ　なつやすみですか。

   はい　　　　　　　　　　　　　……　はい、　まだ　なつやすみです。

   いいえ　　　　　　　　　　　　……　いいえ、　もう　なつやすみではありません。

4. コーヒーを　まだ　のみたいんですか。

   はい　　　　　　　　　　　　　……　はい、　まだ　のみたいです。

   いいえ　　　　　　　　　　　　……　いいえ、　もう　のみたくありません。

5. みち子さんは　まだ　おんがくを　きいていますか。

   はい　　　　　　　　　　　　　……　はい、　まだ　きいています。

   いいえ　　　　　　　　　　　　……　いいえ、　もう　きいていません。

6. デパートで　まだ　アルバイトを　していますか。

   はい　　　　　　　　　　　　　……　はい、　まだ　しています。

   いいえ　　　　　　　　　　　　……　いいえ、　もう　していません。

6.8　EXERCISES

6.8.1　Answer the following questions in Japanese:

1. 学校^{こう}から　あなたの　うちまで　どのぐらい　かかりますか。
2. この　きょうしつから　図書館^{としょかん}まで　どのぐらいですか。
3. ボーリングを　するのは　好きですか。
4. あなたは　ギターを　ひくことが　できますか。
5. 月曜^{よう}日に　学校^{こう}へ　来る　時間は　なん時ですか。
6. あなたが　よく　ひるごはんを　たべる　しょくどうは　どこですか。

6.8.2 Using the given Japanese, express the following ideas in Japanese:

1. ヨーロッパへ　行きます。

   Who is the one going to Europe next year?

2. さくらが　さいています。

   Let's go to the park where cherry blossoms are in bloom.

3. 日本語を　はなします。

   Can Paul speak Japanese?

4. 日本の　えいがを　見ます。

   It is interesting to see a Japanese movie.

5. 図書館で　はたらきます。

   I like to work at the library.

6. すしを　たべません。

   A person who does not eat *sushi* is Mr. Hayashi.

7. ピアノを　ひきません。

   I can not play a piano.

8. ドイツ語を　ならいます。

   It is not easy to learn German.

6.8.3 Insert an appropriate Relational in each blank:

1. 急行は　二番線（　　）　出ます。
2. この　でんしゃは　なん時（　　）　大阪（　　）　つきますか。
3. たまに　うち（　　）　駅（　　）　タクシー（　　）　のります。
4. しゃしょう（　　）　時間（　　）　きいてみましょう。
5. ハワイ（　　）　ひこうき（　　）　おりました。　そして、　すぐ　ふね（　　）　のりました。
6. 東京行（　　）　急行（　　）　つく　時間（　　）　六時ですよ。
7. 日本語（　　）　はなすこと（　　）　できますか。

6.8.4 Write the following underlined *hiragana* in *kanji*:

1. <u>とうきょう</u>から　ハワイまで　<u>ひこうき</u>で　<u>なんじかん</u>ぐらい　かかりますか。
2. <u>がいこくじん</u>も　<u>にほんじん</u>も　よく　<u>きょう</u>都を　けんぶつします。
3. あの　<u>えき</u>から　急行が　<u>で</u>ますよ。

6.8.5 Write the following in *katakana*:

1. San Furan'shisuko
2. takushii
3. sen'chi
4. kiromeetoru

5. mairu
6. Nyuu Yooku
7. arubaito

6.9 SITUATIONAL CONVERSATION

6.9.1 At the station

A foreigner asks a man where he can catch an express for Tōkyō, the track number and the time when the train leaves.

The man tells the foreigner to ask either a station employee or a conductor.

6.9.2 At the ticket window

The foreigner wants to know the time when the express leaves, the time required to get to Tōkyō, the arrival time at Tōkyō, and whether there might still be any first-class tickets available.

6.9.3 Make a telephone call to the airport and find out about flight number and other information.

LESSON 7

7.1　PRESENTATION

－図書館－

　ひとりの　男の　学生が　図書館の　カードの　所で　本を　さがしています。*1

そこへ、　本を　二、三さつ*2　持った*3　女の　学生が　来ました。

7.2　DIALOG

けい子　「ポールさん。」

ポール　「あ、　けい子さん、　べんきょうですか。*4」

けい子　「ええ。　おととい*5　かりた*3　本を　かえしに　来ました。　それに、
　　　　　ちょっと　読みたい　本も　ありますから……。　ポールさんは？」

ポール　「けさの　日本文学の　時間に　わからなかった*6　もんだいを　しらべ
　　　　　たいんですが、　てきとうな　本が　見つかりません。*7」

けい子　「この　カードを　しらべてみましたか。」

ポール　「ええ、　しらべてみましたが、　ないんです。」

けい子　「図書館員に　聞いてみましたか。」

ポール　「いいえ、　まだです。*8」

けい子　「わたくしの　読んだ　さんこう書は　せつめいが*9　とても　くわしかった
　　　　　ですよ。　だいは　＜日本文学＞ですが、　読んだことが*10　ありますか。」

ポール　「いいえ、　ありません。　ここで　かりた　本ですか。」

けい子　「いいえ、　わたくしのです。　今、　つかっていませんから、　どうぞ。」

ポール　「じゃあ、　かしてください。　ゆうがた　かりに　行きますが、
　　　　　いいですか。*11」

けい子　「ええ、　かまいません。*11」

7.3 PATTERN SENTENCES

7.3.1

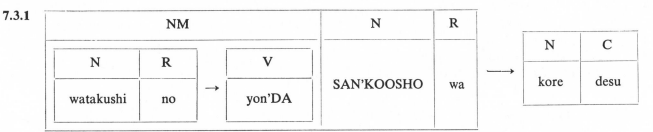

"The reference book that I read is this."

7.3.2

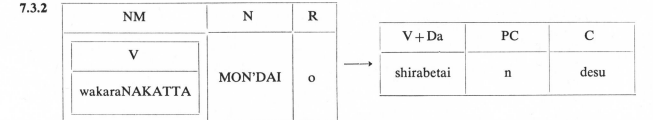

"I would like to check on the questions that I didn't understand."

7.3.3

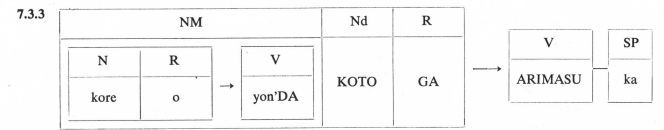

"Have you ever read this?"

7.4 NOTES

7.4.1 *Kaado no tokoro* means "where the cards are." In Japanese, a thing or a person usually cannot be followed directly by the Relationals concerning place, such as *e, ni, de,* etc. The Nominative *tokoro* is used in this case.

Hitori no gakusei ga watakushi no tokoro e kimashita.   "A student came to me."

Sen'sei wa doa ("door") no tokoro ni irasshaimashita.   "The teacher was at the door."

7.4.2 *Ni-san'satsu* means "two or three (books)." The numerals in succession may occur immediately before a counter and mean "one or two," "two or three," etc. *Ni-san'satsu* is similar in meaning to *nisatsu ka san'satsu*, but *nisatsu ka san'satsu* is said when the numbers referred to are to be more specified. Note that the first numeral to be used in succession is always a regular numeral such as *ichi, ni, san, shi,* etc.

ichi-nisatsu	san-yon'satsu	go-rokusatsu
ni-san'satsu	shi-gosatsu	etc.

7.4.3 *Hon o ni-san'satsu motta on'na no gakusei* means "a girl student who carried two or three books with her." *Motta* is the TA form or the plain perfect tense form of a Consonant Verb *mochimasu* ← *motsu*. The TA form of Verbs is formed in the same manner as the TE form is formed. (See Note 1.4.19.)

(1) Vowel Verb

imasu	⟶	iru	⟶	ita
mimasu	⟶	miru	⟶	mita
okimasu	⟶	okiru	⟶	okita
karimasu	⟶	kariru	⟶	karita
dekimasu	⟶	dekiru	⟶	dekita
demasu	⟶	deru	⟶	deta
shirabemasu	⟶	shiraberu	⟶	shirabeta

(2) Consonant Verb

arimasu	⟶	aru	⟶	atta
mitsukarimasu	⟶	mitsukaru	⟶	mitsukatta
ikimasu	⟶	iku	⟶	itta
kakimasu	⟶	kaku	⟶	kaita
hanashimasu	⟶	hanasu	⟶	hanashita
kashimasu	⟶	kasu	⟶	kashita
sagashimasu	⟶	sagasu	⟶	sagashita
kaeshimasu	⟶	kaesu	⟶	kaeshita
kaimasu	⟶	kau	⟶	katta
yomimasu	⟶	yomu	⟶	yon'da
asobimasu	⟶	asobu	⟶	ason'da

(3) Irregular Verb

kimasu	⟶	kuru	⟶	kita
shimasu	⟶	suru	⟶	shita

When a Predicate that modifies a Nominative is in the perfect tense, the plain TA form should be used. This form may occur in modifying or describing the following Nominative in the same structural environment as the Dictionary form occurs. (See Note 6.4.7.)

(Predicate Modifier) + Verb(*-ta*) + Nominative

The subject, if there is one, should be followed by the Relational *ga* or *no* in the Nominative Modifier. The Relational *wa* can not be used after the subject.

ototoi karimashita   ⟶   ototoi karita san'koosho

"borrowed it the day before yesterday"   "the reference book that [I] borrowed the day before yesterday" watakushi ga yomimashita   ⟶   watakushi { ga / no } yon'da hon

"I read (it)"   "the book I read"

itta / aruite ita / kippu o katta } hito "a person who" { went" / was walking" / bought tickets" }

kaeshita / karita / moratta / kashita / mitsukatta } okane "the money that [I]" { returned" / borrowed" / received" / lent" / could find" }

kono san'koosho o katta / boku no sun'de ita } tokoro "the place where" { [I] bought this reference book" / I used to live" }

boku ga ben'kyoo shita (no) / uchi ni ita } jikan "time when" { I studied" / [he] was home" }

Sumisu san wa boku no kashita hon o yon'de imasu. "Mr. Smith is reading the book I lent him."

Yamada san kara karita san'koosho wa totemo ii desu. "The reference book I borrowed from Mr. Yamada is very good."

Watakushi ga notta kyuukoo wa Oosaka yuki deshita. "The express I rode was bound for Ōsaka."

Shokudoo de anata to hanashite ita on'na no kata wa donata desu ka? "Who is the lady who was talking with you at the dining hall?"

7.4.4 *Ben'kyoo desu ka?* here is said to ask if one is studying or if one is going to study. *Ben'kyoo shite iru n desu ka?* or *ben'kyoo suru n desu ka?* is shortened this way.

7.4.5 *Ototoi* is a time Nominative meaning "the day before yesterday," and *asatte* is "the day after tomorrow."

ototoi   kinoo   kyoo   ashita   asatte

Ototoi wa taihen isogashikatta desu. "I was very busy the day before yesterday."

Asatte toshokan e karita hon o kaeshi ni ikimasu. "I am going to the library the day after tomorrow to return the book I borrowed."

7.4.6 *Wakaranakatta mon'dai* means "the problem that I couldn't solve," or "the question that I didn't understand." As the plain negative imperfect tense form of an adjectival Derivative, *-nai* occurs before a Nominative, forming a Nominative Modifier (see 6.4.19), its plain negative perfect tense form *-nakatta* occurs in the same manner. The *wakaranakatta* is the perfect tense form of *wakaranai,* and the adjectival Derivative *-nai* changes into *-nakatta.*

Pre-Nai form of Verb + *-nai* ——→ Pre-Nai form of Verb + *-nakatta*

(1) Vowel Verb

inai	——→	inakatta
minai	——→	minakatta
okinai	——→	okinakatta
agenai	——→	agenakatta
tabenai	——→	tabenakatta
dekinai	——→	dekinakatta
karinai	——→	karinakatta
shirabenai	——→	shirabenakatta

(2) Consonant Verb

kasanai	——→	kasanakatta
kaesanai	——→	kaesanakatta
owaranai	——→	owaranakatta
motanai	——→	motanakatta
nomanai	——→	nomanakatta
kakanai	——→	kakanakatta
tsukawanai	——→	tsukawanakatta

(3) Irregular Verb

konai	——→	konakatta
shinai	——→	shinakatta

(Predicate Modifier) + Verb(*-nakatta*) + Nominative

orinakatta
kikanakatta — hito "the person" who "didn't get off"
ben'kyoo shinakatta — gakusei "the student" "didn't ask"
soko ni sun'de inakatta "didn't study" "wasn't living there"

kawanakatta
yomanakatta — san'koosho "the reference book" that "[I] didn't buy"
tsukatte inakatta — jisho "the dictionary" "[I] didn't read" "[I] wasn't using"

watakushi ga ikanakatta
sakura no sakanakatta — tokoro "the place where" "I did not go" "the cherry blossoms did not bloom"

The subject in the Nominative Modifier should not be followed by the Relational *wa* but by *ga* or *no*.

Ototoi awanakatta tomodachi ni tegami o kakimasu. — "I'll write a letter to a friend whom I didn't see the day before yesterday."

Kinoo Mori san {ga/no} karinakatta hon wa nan desu ka? — "What is the book that Mr. Mori did not borrow yesterday?"

7.4.7 *Mitsukarimasu* means "something is found." This is an intransitive Verb. The thing one can find is the subject of *mitsukarimasu*, and is followed by the subject Relational *ga*.

Tekitoo na hon ga mitsukarimasen. "I cannot find any proper books."

Anata no nooto ga mitsukarimashita
ka? — "Did you find your notebook?"

7.4.8 *Mada desu* is an idiomatic expression meaning "not yet." *Mada* in the meaning of "(not) yet" will be drilled later.

Moo koohii o nomimashita ka? — "Have you already had coffee?"

Iie, mada desu. — "No, not yet."

Toshokan kara karita hon o
kaeshimashita ka? — "Have you returned the book you borrowed from the library?"

Mada desu ga, ashita kaeshimasu. — "Not yet, but I'll give it back tomorrow."

7.4.9 (*Watakushi no yon'da*) *san'koosho wa setsumei ga kuwashikatta desu* means "As for the reference book (I read), its explanation was in detail," or "The explanation of the reference book (I read) was in detail." When part of something or someone is described, that is, *A no B wa .... desu* "B of A is such and such," the same connotation may be expressed by the sentence structure *A wa B ga .... desu.*

N1 + *no* + N2 + *wa* + {Adjective / adjectival Nominative} + *desu* ⟶

N1 + *wa* + N2 + *ga* + {Adjective / adjectival Nominative} + *desu*

Kono san'koosho *no* setsumei *wa*
kuwashii desu.
Kono san'koosho *wa* setsumei *ga*
kuwashii desu. — "As for this reference book, the explanation is in detail."

Anata *no* me *wa* kirei desu.
Anata *wa* me *ga* kirei desu. — "Your eyes are pretty."

Anata *no* sei *wa* takai desu nee.
Anata *wa* sei *ga* takai desu nee. — "How tall you are!"

Ani *no* te to ashi *wa* ookii desu.
Ani *wa* te to ashi *ga* ookii desu. — "My older brother has big hands and feet."

7.4.10 *Yon'da koto ga arimasu ka*? means "Have you ever read it?," "Do you have an experience of reading it?" or "Do you have or is there the fact of having read it?" This pattern covers the experience of doing such and such, whereas mere occurrence in the past is covered by the perfect tense form *-mashita*, even though the English equivalents of both would be "have done," etc.

The Predicate Modifiers such as *ichido* "once," *nido* "twice," *mae* or *mae ni* "before" may be used in this pattern.

(person + *wa*) + (Predicate Modifier) + TA form of Verb + *koto ga* + {arimasu / arimasen / nai (n) desu}
(*wa*)

yon'da itta mita notta naratta oshieta sun'de ita tabete mita	koto ga (wa)	arimasu arimasen nai (n) desu	"[I] have (once) "[he] has never	read" been" seen" ridden" learned" taught" been living" tried (food)"

Sukiyaki o tabeta koto ga arimasu ka?	"Have you ever eaten *sukiyaki*?"
Hai, tabeta koto ga arimasu.	"Yes, I have eaten it (before)."
Keiko san wa hikooki ni notta koto ga arimasu ka?	"Has Keiko ever flown in an airplane?"
Iie, (notta koto wa) arimasen.	"No, she hasn't."
Nikkoo o ken'butsu shita koto ga arimasu ka?	"Have you had the experience of sightseeing in Nikkō?"
Hai, nido arimasu.	"Yes, I have twice."
Katoo sen'sei ni atta koto ga nai n desu ka?	"Haven't you ever met Prof. Katō?"
Ee, nai n desu.	"No, I haven't."

7.4.11 *Ii desu ka*? is used here in the meaning of "Is it all right?" asking for permission. On the other hand, a Verb *kamaimasen* means "I do not mind," and may be used to give mild permission. The affirmative form of *kamaimasen* is seldom used in Japanese. *Ii desu* and *kamaimasen* in the pattern of permission will be introduced in Lesson 9.

7.5 VOCABULARY

Presentation

カード	kaado	. . . .	N	card
持った	motta	. . . .	V	carried (TA form of *mochimasu* ← *motsu* – carry; have; hold) (see 7.4.3)

Dialog

ポール	Pooru	. . . .	N	Paul
おととい	ototoi	. . . .	N	the day before yesterday
かりた	karita	. . . .	V	borrowed; rented (TA form of *karimasu* ← *kariru*)
かえし	kaeshi	. . . .	V	Stem form of *kaeshimasu* ← *kaesu* – return; give back
文学	bun'gaku	. . . .	N	literature

わからなかった	wakaranakatta	...... V+Da	did not understand (Pre-Nai form of *wakarimasu* ← *wakaru* plus *-nakatta*) (see 7.4.6)
なかった	-nakatta	.... Da	TA form of *-nai* (see 7.4.6)
もんだい	mon'dai	.... N	problem; question
しらべ	shirabe	 V	make researches (on); check up; investigate (Stem form of *shirabemasu* ← *shiraberu*)
てきとう	tekitoo	.... Na	proper; adequate
見つかりません	mitsukarimasen	 V	is not found; can not find (negative of *mitsukarimasu* ← *mitsukaru*) (intransitive Verb) (see 7.4.7)
図書館員	toshokan'in	.... N	librarian; library clerk
まだ	mada	.... Adv.	(not) yet (see 7.4.8)
読んだ	yon'da	 V	read (TA form of *yomimasu* ← *yomu*) (see 7.4.3)
さんこう書	san'koosho	.... N	reference book
せつめい	setsumei	.... N	explanation
せつめいします	setsumei shimasu	 V	explain
くわしかった	kuwashikatta	.... A	was in detail (TA form of *kuwashii*)
だい	dai	.... N	title (of books, movies, etc.)
つかって	tsukatte	 V	TE form of *tsukaimasu* ← *tsukau* – use
かして	kashite	 V	TE form of *kashimasu* ← *kasu* – lend; rent
いい	ii	.... A	is all right (see 7.4.11)
かまいません	kamaimasen	 V	do not mind (see 7.4.11)

Notes

あさって	asatte	.... N	the day after tomorrow
ノート	nooto	.... N	notebook
め	me	.... N	eye
て	te	.... N	hand
あし	ashi	.... N	leg; foot

7.6 KANJI

7.6.1 男 (1) *otoko* (2) man; male (3) classifier 田 [field]; 力 [power]

(4) 丨 冂 冊 冊 田 男 男 (5) 男の学生、 男の子

7.6.2 持 (1) *mo(chimasu); mo(tsu)* (2) have; hold; carry (3) classifier 扌 [hand]

(4) 一 十 扌 扩 扩 扩 拌 持 持

(5) 持っています、 本を持った人、 持っていく、 持ってかえる

118

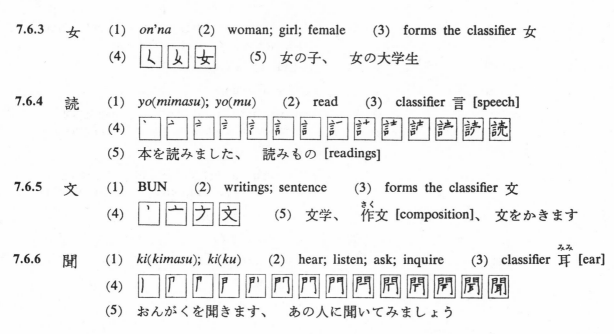

7.6.3 女 (1) *on'na* (2) woman; girl; female (3) forms the classifier 女

(4) ⟨stroke order boxes⟩ (5) 女の子、 女の大学生

7.6.4 読 (1) *yo(mimasu)*; *yo(mu)* (2) read (3) classifier 言 [speech]

(4) ⟨stroke order boxes⟩ (5) 本を読みました、 読みもの [readings]

7.6.5 文 (1) BUN (2) writings; sentence (3) forms the classifier 文

(4) ⟨stroke order boxes⟩ (5) 文学、 作文 [composition]、 文をかきます

7.6.6 聞 (1) *ki(kimasu)*; *ki(ku)* (2) hear; listen; ask; inquire (3) classifier 耳 [ear]

(4) ⟨stroke order boxes⟩ (5) おんがくを聞きます、 あの人に聞いてみましょう

7.7 DRILLS

7.7.1 Pattern Drill

1. Hon o ni-san'satsu motta on'na no gakusei ga kimashita.

2. Ototoi karita hon o kaeshi ni kimashita.

3. Kesa no Nihon bun'gaku no jikan ni wakaranakatta mon'dai o shirabetai n desu ga, tekitoo na hon ga mitsukarimasen.

4. Watakushi no yon'da san'koosho wa, setsumei ga totemo kuwashikatta desu yo.

5. Dai wa "Nihon Bun'gaku" desu ga, yon'da koto ga arimasu ka?

6. Koko de karita hon desu ka?

7.7.2 Transformation Drill

1. さがしました   ⟶ さがした
2. 行きました   ⟶ 行った
3. かりました   ⟶ かりた
4. しらべました   ⟶ しらべた
5. つかいました   ⟶ つかった
6. かしました   ⟶ かした
7. 出ました   ⟶ 出た
8. かえしました   ⟶ かえした

9. のりました	⟶	のった
10. 持ちました	⟶	持った
11. 見つかりました	⟶	見つかった
12. りょこうしました	⟶	りょこうした

7.7.3 Transformation Drill

1. わかりませんでした	⟶	わからなかった
2. かしませんでした	⟶	かさなかった
3. おりませんでした	⟶	おりなかった
4. さがしませんでした	⟶	さがさなかった
5. 見つかりませんでした	⟶	見つからなかった
6. しらべませんでした	⟶	しらべなかった
7. つかいませんでした	⟶	つかわなかった
8. 聞きませんでした	⟶	聞かなかった
9. かえしませんでした	⟶	かえさなかった
10. はしりませんでした	⟶	はしらなかった
11. かりませんでした	⟶	かりなかった
12. あいませんでした	⟶	あわなかった
13. 知りませんでした	⟶	知らなかった

7.7.4 Transformation Drill

1. 図書館に かえす 本	⟶	図書館に かえした 本
2. 学校で つかう さんこう書	⟶	学校で つかった さんこう書
3. けい子さんの はたらく じむしょ	⟶	けい子さんの はたらいた じむしょ
4. ともだちから かりる ノート	⟶	ともだちから かりた ノート
5. しょくどうに いる 時間	⟶	しょくどうに いた 時間
6. いもうとに かす セーター	⟶	いもうとに かした セーター
7. 十時に 出る 急行	⟶	十時に 出た 急行
8. ポールさんが はなす 日本語	⟶	ポールさんが はなした 日本語
9. にわで あそんでいる 子ども	⟶	にわで あそんでいた 子ども
10. 駅員に 聞いている 外国人	⟶	駅員に 聞いていた 外国人
11. ピアノを ひいている 女の子	⟶	ピアノを ひいていた 女の子
12. わたくしが しらべる もんだい	⟶	わたくしが しらべた もんだい

120

7.7.5 Transformation Drill

1. わたしが わからない もんだい   ⟶   わたしが わからなかった もんだい
2. 先生の 知らない 学生   ⟶   先生の 知らなかった 学生
3. 学校で ならわない ことば   ⟶   学校で ならわなかった ことば
4. くにへ かえらない 人   ⟶   くにへ かえらなかった 人
5. 図書館で 見つからない 本   ⟶   図書館で 見つからなかった 本
6. ポールさんが 行かない 公園   ⟶   ポールさんが 行かなかった 公園
7. あめが ふっていない 所   ⟶   あめが ふっていなかった 所
8. じゅぎょうに 来ない ともだち   ⟶   じゅぎょうに 来なかった ともだち
9. ひらがなを かくことが できない 人   ⟶   ひらがなを かくことが できなかった 人
10. ぼくの 持っていない さんこう書   ⟶   ぼくの 持っていなかった さんこう書

7.7.6 Transformation Drill

1. 日本文学を 読みました。   ⟶   日本文学を 読んだことが あります。
2. てんぷらを たべました。   ⟶   てんぷらを たべたことが あります。
3. 外国語を ならいました。   ⟶   外国語を ならったことが あります。
4. ぎんこうに つとめました。   ⟶   ぎんこうに つとめたことが あります。
5. 一郎くんに おかねを かしました。   ⟶   一郎くんに おかねを かしたことが あります。
6. あなたの おとうさんに あいました。   ⟶   あなたの おとうさんに あったことが あります。
7. その さんこう書を つかいました。   ⟶   その さんこう書を つかったことが あります。
8. 学校へ いぬを つれてきました。   ⟶   学校へ いぬを つれてきたことが あります。
9. 図書館で しらべました。   ⟶   図書館で しらべたことが あります。
10. しんかん線に のりました。   ⟶   しんかん線に のったことが あります。
11. さけを のみました。   ⟶   さけを のんだことが あります。
12. ハワイへ 一ど 行きました。   ⟶   ハワイへ 一ど 行ったことが あります。

7.7.7 Transformation Drill

1. ドイツ語を べんきょうしませんでした。   ⟶   ドイツ語を べんきょうしたことが ありません。
2. なつやすみに アルバイトを しませんでした。   ⟶   なつやすみに アルバイトを したことが ありません。

3. 辞書を　つかいませんでした。　　　　　　⟶　辞書を　つかったことが　ありません。

4. 日本の　おんがくを　聞きませんでした。　⟶　日本の　おんがくを　聞いたことが
　　　　　　　　　　　　　　　　　　　　　　　　　ありません。

5. 林先生に　あいませんでした。　　　　　　⟶　林先生に　あったことが　ありません。

6. 日曜日に　うちに　いませんでした。　　　⟶　日曜日に　うちに　いたことが　ありません。

7. しんじゅくで　かいものを　しませんでした。⟶　しんじゅくで　かいものを　したことが
　　　　　　　　　　　　　　　　　　　　　　　　　ありません。

8. ふゆやすみに　くにへ　かえりませんでした。⟶　ふゆやすみに　くにへ　かえったことが
　　　　　　　　　　　　　　　　　　　　　　　　　ありません。

9. じゅぎょうを　やすみませんでした。　　　⟶　じゅぎょうを　やすんだことが
　　　　　　　　　　　　　　　　　　　　　　　　　ありません。

10. ゴルフを　しませんでした。　　　　　　　⟶　ゴルフを　したことが　ありません。

7.7.8 Expansion Drill

1. さんこう書を　かえしに　行きました。

　　かりた　　　　　……　かりた　さんこう書を　かえしに　行きました。

　　おととい　　　　……　おととい　かりた　さんこう書を　かえしに　行きました。

　　図書館へ　　　　……　図書館へ　おととい　かりた　さんこう書を　かえしに　行きました。

2. 駅員が　持っています。

　　あそこに　いる　……　あそこに　いる　駅員が　持っています。

　　きっぷは　　　　……　きっぷは　あそこに　いる　駅員が　持っています。

3. 本は　むずかしいです。

　　いただいた　　　　……　いただいた　本は　むずかしいです。

　　けい子さんから　　……　けい子さんから　いただいた　本は　むずかしいです。

　　月曜日に　　　　　……　月曜日に　けい子さんから　いただいた　本は　むずかしいです。

4. 学生が　二、三人　いました。

　　来なかった　　　　……　来なかった　学生が　二、三人　いました。

　　じゅぎょうに　　　……　じゅぎょうに　来なかった　学生が　二、三人　いました。

　　日本語の　　　　　……　日本語の　じゅぎょうに　来なかった　学生が　二、三人　いました。

5. もんだいを　聞いてください。

　　わからなかった　　……　わからなかった　もんだいを　聞いてください。

　　よく　　　　　　　……　よく　わからなかった　もんだいを　聞いてください。

　　あなたが　　　　　……　あなたが　よく　わからなかった　もんだいを　聞いてください。

122

7.7.9 Transformation Drill

1. その 本の せつめいは よくありません
   でした。 　　　　　　　　　　⟶ その 本は せつめいが よくありません
   　　　　　　　　　　　　　　　　　でした。
2. あの 外国人の 日本語は じょうずです。 ⟶ あの 外国人は 日本語が じょうずです。
3. ブラウンさんの めは とても 大きい
   ですね。 　　　　　　　　　　⟶ ブラウンさんは めが とても 大きい
   　　　　　　　　　　　　　　　　　ですね。
4. きのう 行った きっさ店の コーヒーは
   おいしくありません。 　　　　　⟶ きのう 行った きっさ店は コーヒーが
   　　　　　　　　　　　　　　　　　おいしくありません。
5. デパートの 店員の ことばは ていねい
   です。 　　　　　　　　　　　⟶ デパートの 店員は ことばが ていねい
   　　　　　　　　　　　　　　　　　です。
6. 上野の さくらは きれいです。 　　⟶ 上野は さくらが きれいです。
7. あの 子どもの せいは たかいです。 ⟶ あの 子どもは せいが たかいです。
8. あなたの ては 大きいですね。 　　⟶ あなたは てが 大きいですね。

7.7.10 Transformation Drill

1. あにが のった でんしゃは もう
   出ました。 　　　　　　　　　⟶ あにの のった でんしゃは もう
   　　　　　　　　　　　　　　　　　出ました。
2. わたしが 行かなかった 所は にっこう
   です。 　　　　　　　　　　　⟶ わたしの 行かなかった 所は にっこう
   　　　　　　　　　　　　　　　　　です。
3. みち子さんが かく 日本語は へたです。 ⟶ みち子さんの かく 日本語は へたです。
4. あの せいが たかい 男の 人は
   だれですか。 　　　　　　　　⟶ あの せいの たかい 男の 人は
   　　　　　　　　　　　　　　　　　だれですか。
5. あなたが しらべている もんだいを
   はなしてください。 　　　　　　⟶ あなたの しらべている もんだいを
   　　　　　　　　　　　　　　　　　はなしてください。
6. あさって すきやきが おいしい
   レストランへ 行きます。 　　　　⟶ あさって すきやきの おいしい
   　　　　　　　　　　　　　　　　　レストランへ 行きます。

7.7.11 Response Drill

1. なにを さがしていますか。
   おととい かった さんこう書 …… おととい かった さんこう書を さがしています。
2. なにを しらべていますか。
   わからなかった もんだい …… わからなかった もんだいを しらべています。
3. なにを かえしましたか。
   あの 人から かりた ノート …… あの 人から かりた ノートを かえしました。
4. なにが 見つかりませんか。
   けさ 読んでいた しんぶん …… けさ 読んでいた しんぶんが 見つかりません。

5. どこへ　行きたいですか。

　　きょ年　けんぶつしなかった　所　……　きょ年　けんぶつしなかった　所へ　行きたいです。

6. だれに　あげましたか。

　　にわで　あそんでいた　子ども　……　にわで　あそんでいた　子どもに　あげました。

7.7.12　Response Drill

1. 京都へ　行ったことが　ありますか。

　　はい　　　　　　　　　……　はい、　行ったことが　あります。

　　いいえ　　　　　　　　……　いいえ、　行ったことは　ありません。
　　　　　　　　　　　　　　　　　　　　　　　　　(or が)

2. 日本の　えいがを　見たことが　ありますか。

　　はい　　　　　　　　　……　はい、　見たことが　あります。

　　いいえ　　　　　　　　……　いいえ、　見たことは　ありません。

3. ギターを　ひいたことが　ありますか。

　　はい　　　　　　　　　……　はい、　ひいたことが　あります。

　　いいえ　　　　　　　　……　いいえ、　ひいたことは　ありません。

4. 東京に　すんだことが　ありますか。

　　はい　　　　　　　　　……　はい、　すんだことが　あります。

　　いいえ　　　　　　　　……　いいえ、　すんだことは　ありません。

5. アルバイトを　したことが　ありますか。

　　はい　　　　　　　　　……　はい、　したことが　あります。

　　いいえ　　　　　　　　……　いいえ、　したことは　ありません。

6. 先生の　辞書を　つかったことが　ありますか。

　　はい　　　　　　　　　……　はい、　つかったことが　あります。

　　いいえ　　　　　　　　……　いいえ、　つかったことは　ありません。

7. 日本語を　べんきょうしたことが　ありますか。

　　はい　　　　　　　　　……　はい、　べんきょうしたことが　あります。

　　いいえ　　　　　　　　……　いいえ、　べんきょうしたことは　ありません。

8. はしで　たべたことが　ありますか。

　　はい　　　　　　　　　……　はい、　たべたことが　あります。

　　いいえ　　　　　　　　……　いいえ、　たべたことは　ありません。

9. スミス先生に　あったことが　ありますか。

　　はい　　　　　　　　　……　はい、　あったことが　あります。

　　いいえ　　　　　　　　……　いいえ、　あったことは　ありません。

124

10. あさひしんぶんを　読んだことが　ありますか。
　　はい　　　　　　　　　……　はい、　読んだことが　あります。
　　いいえ　　　　　　　……　いいえ、　読んだことは　ありません。

7.8　EXERCISES

7.8.1　Express the following ideas in Japanese:

1. The movie I saw the day before yesterday was dull.

2. The reference book I bought at Kanda was very inexpensive.

3. Who is the person you were talking with?

4. I want to ask my teacher about the problem I didn't understand.

5. Please give me the dictionary that you did not use.

6. Have you ever been to Kyōto?

7. I have never met Mr. Brown.

7.8.2　Insert an appropriate Relational into each of the following blanks:

1. 図書館(　　) てきとうな　さんこう書(　　) さがしてみましょう。
2. おととい　かりた　ざっし(　　) ともだち(　　) かえし(　　) 行きます。
3. 一郎くんは　森さん(　　) 外国文学(　　) 本(　　) もらいました。
4. この　辞書(　　) せつめい(　　) とても　くわしいですよ。
5. なに(　　) 見つかりましたか。
6. あなた(　　) 持っている　カメラ(　　) わたし(　　) かしてください。
7. かぶき(　　) 見たこと(　　) ありますか。

7.8.3　Make a complete sentence using each of the following expressions as a Nominative Modifier:

Example: 図書館で　かりました。　⟶　きのう　図書館で　かりた　本は　なんですか。

1. わたくしが　かえしました。
2. 大学で　しらべました。
3. あそこに　いました。
4. つかいませんでした。
5. なつやすみに　はたらきました。
6. わたしは　読みませんでした。
7. きみは　持っていませんでした。

7.8.4 Write the following underlined *hiragana* in *kanji*:

1. おんな<u>が</u><u>く</u><u>せ</u>いが もっていた ほんの だいは <u>が</u>い<u>こ</u>く<u>ぶ</u>ん<u>が</u>くです。

2. <u>し</u>んぶんを <u>よ</u>んでいる <u>おとこ</u>の <u>ひと</u>に <u>き</u>いてみてください。

7.8.5 Write the following in *katakana*:

1. kaado   2. Pooru   3. nooto

7.9 SITUATIONAL CONVERSATION

7.9.1 At the library

A male college student and a female college student meet in the library.
They ask each other why they are there.
The male student is looking for some reference books in vain.
The female student recommends some good reference books she bought.
She agrees to lend them to the male student.

7.9.2 Carry on a conversation about the books you have read, or about the libraries that you have visited and the reasons why you want to read books, etc.

LESSON 8

— Review —

8.1 CONJUGATION

8.1.1 Verbs of plain form

a. Vowel Verb

見せ		見せ	
いれ		いれ	
つとめ		つとめ	
き		き	
出かけ		出かけ	
くれ		くれ	
わすれ	る ⟶	わすれ	ない
かり		かり	
おり		おり	
出		出	
ね		ね	
おき		おき	
しらべ		しらべ	
い		い	
でき		でき	

見せ		見せ	
いれ		いれ	
つとめ		つとめ	
き		き	
出かけ		出かけ	
くれ		くれ	
わすれ	た ⟶	わすれ	なかった
かり		かり	
おり		おり	
出		出	
ね		ね	

おき
しらべ
い
でき ｜ る ⟶ おき
しらべ
い
でき ｜ た

b. Consonant Verb

知 はし かか の くださ 見つか わか	る		知 はし かか の くださ 見つか わか	らない
か 聞 はたら つ さ ひ	く		か 聞 はたら つ さ ひ	かない
ま 持	つ	⟶	ま 持	たない
あ つか か	う		あ つか か	わない
か かえ さが はな	す		か かえ さが はな	さない
す や 読	む		す や 読	まない
あそ よ	ぶ		あそ よ	ばない

128

知
はし
かか
の
くださ
見つか
わか　　った

か
聞
はたら
つ
さ
ひ　　いた

ま
持　　った

あ
つか
か　　った

か
かえ
さが
はな　　した

す
やす
読　　んだ

あそ
よ　　んだ

⟶

知
はし
かか
の
くださ
見つか
わか　　らなかった

か
聞
はたら
つ
さ
ひ　　かなかった

ま
持　　たなかった

あ
つか
か　　わなかった

か
かえ
さが
はな　　さなかった

す
やす
読　　まなかった

あそ
よ　　ばなかった

c. *Kuru* and *Suru*

来る		来ない
する		しない
けんぶつする		けんぶつしない
けっこんする		けっこんしない
りょこうする	⟶	りょこうしない
べんきょうする		べんきょうしない

```
さんぽする              さんぽしない
せつめいする            せつめいしない
   │                      │
   ↓                      ↓
来た                  来なかった
した                  しなかった
けんぶつした            けんぶつしなかった
けっこんした      ⟶    けっこんしなかった
りょこうした            りょこうしなかった
べんきょうした          べんきょうしなかった
さんぽした              さんぽしなかった
せつめいした            せつめいしなかった
```

8.2 NOMINATIVE MODIFIER

8.2.1 Adjectival Nominative

しずか		しずか	店
きれい		きれい	しょくどう
いろいろ		いろいろ	所
ゆうめい		ゆうめい	学校
げん気		げん気	ともだち
しつれい		しつれい	駅員
ていねい		ていねい	しゃしょう
ひま	です ⟶	ひま	な 学生
だめ		だめ	さんこう書
だいひょう的		だいひょう的	たべもの
好き		好き	セーター
きらい		きらい	しごと
へん		へん	えいが
てきとう		てきとう	ことば
じょうず		じょうず	日本語
へた		へた	かいわ
たいへん		たいへん	アルバイト

130

8.2.2 Adjective

あたらしい		あたらしい	図書館
きたない		きたない	たてもの
ふるい		ふるい	おてら
うつくしい		うつくしい	女の　人
大きい		大きい	じんじゃ
うるさい		うるさい	人
かわいい		かわいい	学生
いそがしい		いそがしい	店員
えらい	です　→	えらい	先生
はやい		はやい	のりもの
つまらない		つまらない	ざっし
まずい		まずい	しょくじ
おもしろい		おもしろい	しごと
むずかしい		むずかしい	もんだい
すばらしい		すばらしい	りょこう
わるい		わるい	ことば
くわしい		くわしい	せつめい
つめたい		つめたい	のみもの
ない		ない	おかね

8.2.3 Pre-Nominative and Predicate Modifier

a.

	ゆうめいな	
	しずかな	人
	しつれいな	学生
	うつくしい	ともだち
この		
その	へんな	
あの	おもしろい	所
	うるさい	店
	大きい	
	いい	

b.

とても	ゆうめいな	人
ちょっと	しずかな	学生
たいへん	しつれいな	ともだち
	うつくしい	
	へんな	所 みせ 店
	おもしろい	
	うるさい	
	大きい	
	いい	

c.

この	とても	ゆうめいな	人
その	ちょっと	しずかな	学生
あの	たいへん	しつれいな	ともだち
		うつくしい	
		へんな	所 みせ 店
		おもしろい	
		うるさい	
		大きい	
		いい	

d.

あし		小さい	人
て		大きい	子ども
め		かわいい	外国人
せい		たかい	ともだち
もんだい	が	ふるい	さんこう書（しょ）
せつめい	の	すくない	辞書（じしょ）
ことば		きれいな	え本
あめ		おおい	きせつ
ゆき		ない	ふゆ

のみもの		おいしい	所
てんぷら	が	ゆうめいな	店
たてもの	の	あたらしい	図書館

8.2.4 Verb

a.

これは	先生に　かえす	本です
	ポールさんに　あげる	さんこう書です
	わたくしが　かした	ノートです
	学校で　つかわない	
	スージーさんが　かった	
	きのう　さがしていた	
	ぼくの　読んでいる	

あの　店で　うっている	セーターは　　たかいです
図書館で　しらべていた	もんだいは　　なんですか
おととい　たべた	ひるごはんは　まずかったです
ぼくが　ならいたい	外国語は　日本語です
ジョージさんの　はなしている	ことばは　ていねいです

b.

あの　人は	日本語を　べんきょうしている	
あの　男の　子は	ハワイ大学へ　行った	学生です
	図書館に　いた	

あそこで　はたらいていた	
今　アルバイトしている	
じゅぎょうに　来なかった	人は　　だれですか
東京駅で　おりた	学生は　井上さんです

c.

ここは	ともだちが　つとめている	
	一郎くんが　はたらいている	じむしょです
	ぼくの　アルバイトした	
	まえ　すんでいた	
	いろいろな　かいものを　した	所です
	きょ年　花見に　来た	

あした　あそびに　行く 日本語を　べんきょうしている	所は　東京です

でんわが　ある あなたが　まっていた きのう　コーヒーを　のんだ いつも　ジャズを　聞く ともだちが　いる	店は　どこですか

d.

それは ごご　一時は	急行が　駅に　つく じゅぎょうの　おわる みち子さんが　うちへ　来る おとうとが　学校へ　出かけた わたくしが　うちに　いた	時間です

図書館で　しらべていた きのう　うちで　べんきょうした	時間は　六時から 　九時までです

東京から　大阪まで　かかる まい日　ぼくが　アルバイトする	時間は　三時間です

8.2.5 Nominative Modifier + *koto*

a. Potential

ぼく 林さん ともだち	は	日本語 ボーリング じゅうどうや　からて ピアノ		が (は)
		ドイツ語を　はなす フランス語を　読む バイオリンを　ひく 大阪へ　行く 日曜日に　来る あさ　三時に　おきる あした　四年生に　あう ふゆ　アルバイトする	こと	できます

駅で　タクシーを　よぶ		
あさって　しごとを　する		
きっさ店で　おんがくを　聞く	こと　が (は)	できます
まどぐちで　きっぷを　かう		
なつやすみに　はたらく		

b.　Experience

			アルバイトを　した		
			ピアノを　ひいた		
			てんぷらを　たべた		
			じゅぎょうを　やすんだ		
			しんかん線に　のった		
わたし			東京に　すんだ		あります
しゅ人	は	（まえ(に))	大阪に　いた	こと　が	ありません
あの　学生			にっこうへ　行った		ない（ん）です
			あの　子どもたちと　あそんだ		
			かぶきを　見た		
			ジャズを　聞いた		
			みち子さんに　あった		
			はたらいていた		
			この　辞書を　つかった		
			先生の　所へ　うかがった		

c.　Nominalizer *no*

ふねで　りょこうする			
ギターを　ならう			たのしいです
おんがくを　聞く			
公園まで　さんぽする			好きです
日本語を　べんきょうする			
かいものに　行く	の	は が	
あさ　五時に　おきる			たいへんです
あの　人と　いっしょに　はたらく			
じゅぎょうを　やすむ			きらいです
日曜日に　うちに　いる			

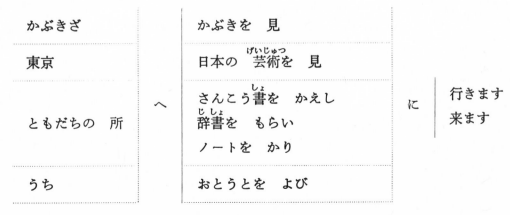

ピアノを　ひく
ドイツ語で　はなす
日本語の　しんぶんを　読む
ポールさんに　学校で　あう

の　は　むずかしいです
　　が　やさしいです

8.3　RELATIONALS

8.3.1　Purpose of a motion

a.　Nominative

大阪		アルバイト	
		しごと	
どうぶつ園		さんぽ	
公園		花見	
しょくどう		しょくじ	
そこ	へ	ゴルフ	に　行きます
デパート		かいもの	来ます
いろいろな　所		りょこう	
おもしろい　所		けんぶつ	
図書館		日本文学の　べんきょう	
大学		日本語の　じゅぎょう	
学校		もんだいを　せつめい	

b.　Verb

かぶきざ		かぶきを　見	
東京		日本の　芸術を　見	
ともだちの　所	へ	さんこう書を　かえし 辞書を　もらい ノートを　かり	に　行きます 　　来ます
うち		おとうとを　よび	

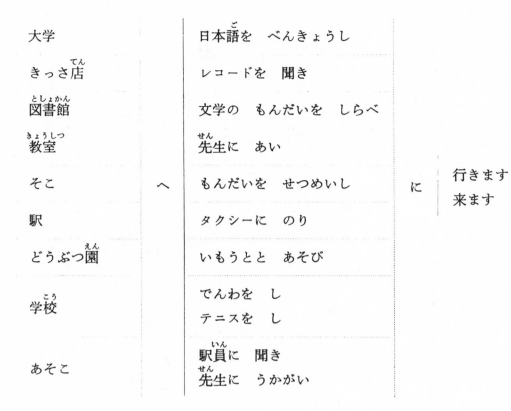

	へ		に	行きます
大学		日本語を　べんきょうし		来ます
きっさ店		レコードを　聞き		
図書館		文学の　もんだいを　しらべ		
教室		先生に　あい		
そこ	へ	もんだいを　せつめいし	に	
駅		タクシーに　のり		
どうぶつ園		いもうとと　あそび		
学校		でんわを　し テニスを　し		
あそこ		駅員に　聞き 先生に　うかがい		

8.3.2 Intransitive Verbs with Relational *ga*

	が	
さくら 花		さきます
じゅぎょう えいが かぶき しごと せつめい かいわ 学校	が	はじまります おわります
フランス語 日本人の　ことば この　もんだい 日本の　芸術 文学		わかります
日本語		できます

テニス		できます
さんこう書		
くつ		
しごと	が	見つかります
林さんの　おたく		
一等せき		
時間		かかります
おかね		

8.3.3　Relationals *ni, kara*

のりもの		
タクシー		
バス	に	のります
でんしゃ		
急行		
じどうしゃ		
ひこうき	から	おります
ふね		
おたく		
東京駅		
十八番線	に	つきます
あの　たてもの		
本やの　所		
ニューヨーク	から	出ます
うち		

8.3.4　Relational *made*

a.　"up to"

どうぶつ園		行きます
まどぐち	まで	来ます
東京		かえります
ちか		はしります

しんぶんや		本や		行きます
たばこや		わたしの うち		来ます
よし子さんの うち	から	駅	まで	かえります
あの たてもの		びじゅつ館		バスに のります
学校		しょくどう		あるきます
ちか		三がい		はしります

b. "from (a place) to (another)"

あの たてもの		パンや		一マイル	あります
ここ		学校		三キロ	
わたしの うち		ぎんこう		六百メートル	です
じむしょ	から	駅	まで		
先生の おたく		大学		四分ぐらい	かかります
どうぶつ園		びじゅつ館		十分	
神田		上野		十一時間半	です
ハワイ		東京			

……………………		……………			あります
……………………		……………		どのぐらい	かかります
……………………	から	……………	まで	（どのくらい）	
……………………		……………			です か

c. "until"

あき		います
ふゆやすみ		べんきょうしています
千九百六十八年		
きょ年		はたらきました
三月		すんでいました
先月	まで	うっていました
先しゅう		かかりました
おととい		
火曜日		
あさ		あそびましょう
ごご		まちましょうか
ゆうがた		さがしました
ごぜん 九時		

d. "from (time) to (another)"

むかし		今	あります
ふゆ		なつ	アルバイトします
千九百三十年		千九百五十年	いました
きょねん	から	ことし	まで すんでいました
四月		九月	
月曜日 きのう		金曜日 けさ	やすみました
ひる ごご　二時		ゆうがた 七時	あそびました はたらいています

8.3.5　～ *wa* ～ *ga* instead of ～ *no* ～ *wa*

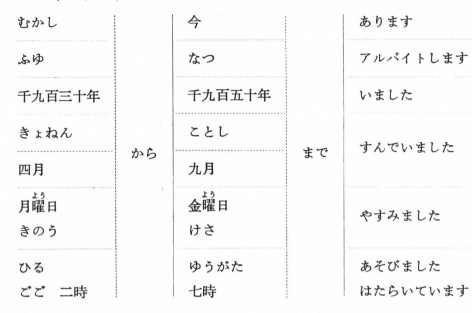

（この） （その） （あの）	駅員 しゃしょう 女の　人	の	しごと せい め	は	たいへん はやい いそがしい たかい 大きい かわいい
	ジョージ 外国人		日本語 かいわ		じょうず へん おもしろい
	店員		ことば		ていねい しつれい
	公園		さくら		うつくしい ゆうめい
	学校		たてもの		ふるい あたらしい
	しょくどう		コーヒー		まずい

です

	の		は		です
さんこう書		せつめい		へた / くわしい	
くつ		サイズ		小さい	

↓

		は		が		です
(この) (その) (あの)	駅員 しゃしょう 女の人		しごと		たいへん はやい いそがしい	
			せい		たかい	
			め		大きい かわいい	
	ジョージ 外国人		日本語 かいわ		じょうず へん おもしろい	
	店員		ことば		ていねい しつれい	
	公園		さくら		うつくしい ゆうめい	
	学校		たてもの		ふるい あたらしい	
	しょくどう		コーヒー		まずい	
	さんこう書		せつめい		へた くわしい	
	くつ		サイズ		小さい	

8.3.6 Clause Relational _kara_ "because"

花見の　きせつです	人が　おおいです
すきやきは　好きじゃありません	たべたくありません
あの　人は　ゆうめいでした	知っています
スケートは　じょうずではありませんでした	あまり　しませんでした
せつめいが　くわしい（です）	あの　さんこう書を　かいます
バスは　はやくありません	タクシーに　のりましょう
天気が　よかった（です）	さんぽに　行きました
気ぶんが　よくありませんでした	学校を　やすみました
日本語を　ならっています	ときどき　つかってみます
よく　わかりません	先生に　聞いてみてください
一日中　うちに　いました	子どもと　あそびました
あめが　ふっていました	出かけませんでした
てきとうな　本が　見つかりませんでした	しらべることが　できません

（から、）

8.4 INTERROGATIVE EXPRESSIONS

a. _don'na_ "what sort of?"

おもしろい あたらしい やさしい ゆうめいな	本が　ほしいです
すばらしい きれいな いろいろな	花を　もらいました
とおい たのしい しずかな	所へ　行きました

142

やすい だいひょう的な てきとうな	店で　かいましょう
大きい うつくしい 好きな きらいな	人に　あいました

↓

どんな	本が　ほしいです 花を　もらいました 所へ　行きました 店で　かいましょう 人に　あいました	か

b. *dono gurai* "how long?" "how much?" "how far?" etc.

みずを	三ばい		のみました
ネクタイを	二ほん		かいました
日本語を	四年		ならいました
かみを	二まい		ください
東京まで	六時間	（ぐらい）	かかります
うちから	四マイル	（くらい）	あります
ビールを	二、三ばい		のむことが　できます
京都に	五、六時間		いました
みち子さんを	二、三分		まちました
駅まで	四、五マイル		あるきました

↓

………	どのぐらい どのくらい	………	か

8.5 AURAL COMPREHENSION

先しゅうの　土曜日に　日光へ　あそびに　行きました。　いっしょに　行った　人は、
スミスさんと　林さんでした。　ブラウンさんは　かぜで　行くことが　できませんでした
から、　とても　ざんねんでした。

あさ、　上野から　急行に　のりました。　そして、　日光駅で　おりました。　上野から
日光まで、　二時間ぐらい　かかりました。　日光には、　見る　所が　たくさん
ありました。　とても　おもしろい　所でした。

みんな　京都へ　行ったことが　ありませんから、　らい月は　京都の　おてらも　見に
行きたいです。

LESSON 9

9.1 PRESENTATION

― 日本語の　教室 ―

教室の　中に、　先生が　ひとり、　学生が　八人　います。　先生は　黒板の　前に
たっています。　学生たちは、　いすに　すわっています。　つくえの　上には、　本や
ノートや　えんぴつなどが　あります。

9.2 DIALOG

先　　　生　「では、　これから、　きのう　習った　所の　しけんを　しましょう。
　　　　　　まず、　紙に　名前を　書いてください。」

学生（一）「先生。」

先　　　生　「はい、　なんですか。」

学生（一）「万年筆を　わすれました。　えんぴつで　書いてもいいですか。」

先　　　生　「ええ、　いいです。　でも、　これから　わすれないでくださいよ。」

学生（二）「辞書を　つかってもかまいませんか。」

先　　　生　「いいえ、　つかってはいけません。　辞書も　教科書も　つかわないで
　　　　　　ください。　では、　はじめましょう。　黒板に　もんだいを
　　　　　　書きますから、　今　わたした　紙に　こたえを　書いてください。」

学生（三）「先生、　こたえだけでいいんですか。」

先　　　生　「はい、　かまいません。」

学生（三）「それから、　ローマ字で　こたえてもいいですか。」

先　　　生　「いいえ、　かん字と　かなを　つかってください。　おそくても
　　　　　　かまいません。　わかりましたね？」

学生（三）「わかりました。」

9.3 PATTERN SENTENCES

9.3.1

A	(R)		V
osokuTE	MO	⟶	KAMAIMASEN

"I don't mind even if it takes time."

9.3.2

N	R	C	(R)		A	(PC)	C
kotae	dake	DE	MO	⟶	II	n	desu

"Only answers will be all right."

9.3.3

N	R		V	R		V
jisho	o	⟶	tsukatTE	WA	⟶	IKEMASEN

"You may not use a dictionary."

9.3.4

N	R		V+Da	E
jisho	o	⟶	tsukawaNAIDE	KUDASAI

"Please don't use a dictionary."

9.4 NOTES

9.4.1 *Naka* is a Nominative meaning "inside." In Japanese, certain Nominatives indicate place or location. They will be called "location Nominatives." Here are some of them.

naka	中	"inside"
soto	外	"outside"
mae	前	"front; before"
ushiro	うしろ	"back; behind"
ue	上	"topside"
shita	下	"under; below"
soba	そば	"vicinity; near"

These Nominatives may be used like other Nominatives and followed by Relationals. But they are often preceded by Nominative plus *no*.

$$(\sim no) + \begin{Bmatrix} naka \\ soto \\ mae \\ ushiro \\ ue \\ shita \\ soba \end{Bmatrix} + \begin{Bmatrix} ni \\ de \\ e \\ kara \\ made \\ \text{-----------} \\ ga \\ o \\ wa \end{Bmatrix}$$

Kyooshitsu no naka ni gakusei ga oozei imasu.	"There are many students in the classroom."
Soto e ikimashoo.	"Let's go outside."
Gin'koo no mae kara takushii de kimashita.	"I came by taxi from the front of the bank."
Tsukue no ue ga kitanai desu.	"The top of the desk is dirty."
Yamamoto san no ushiro ni suwarimashita.	"I sat behind Mr. Yamamoto."
Kinoo anata no uchi no soba made ikimashita.	"I went as far as the vicinity of your house yesterday."
Ki no shita de inu ga nete imasu.	"A dog is sleeping under the tree."

9.4.2 Verbs such as *tachimasu* "stand" and *suwarimasu* "sit" are used normally with the place Relational *ni* to indicate the place in which one gets to stand or on which one gets to sit. The Relational *ni* of existence is used because the result of action *tachimasu* or *suwarimasu* exists or remains in the place. "One sat on a chair" implies "one is on a chair." When it is necessary to mention the place where the action of standing up or of sitting down takes place, *de* may be used.

Kokuban no mae ni tatte imasu.	"He is standing in front of the blackboard."
Gakusei wa seki ni suwarimashita.	"Students sat on their seats."
Mise de ichinichijuu tatte imashita.	"I was standing all day long in the store."

Likewise, *kakimasu* "write" requires the Relational *ni* to state "on which one writes."

Kokuban ni ji o kaite kudasai.	"Please write characters on the blackboard."

9.4.3 *Kore kara* here means "from now on," or "after this time."

Kore kara shiken o hajimemashoo.	"Let's start the exam now."
Kore kara wasurenaide kudasai.	"Please don't forget after this time."

9.4.4 *Kaite mo ii desu ka?* means "May I write it?" or "Will it be all right to write it?" The verbal pattern of permission is formulated by the combination of the TE form of a Verb plus *mo* plus *ii (desu)* "all right," or *kamaimasen** "do not mind." The Relational *mo* in this pattern means "even," but it is optional. The literal translation of the Japanese pattern is "It is all right even if one does such and such," or "I do not mind even if one does such and such."

(Predicate Modifier) + Verb(-te) + (mo) + {*ii desu* / *kamaimasen}**

| kashite mite suwatte tsukatte | (mo) | ii desu kamaimasen | "it's all right" "I don't mind" | (even) if | [I] lend it" [you] see it" [you] sit" [he] uses it" |

* The affirmative form of *kamaimasen,* as previously noted (7.4.11), is seldom used in Japanese. When you DO MIND, another pattern "Please do not do such and such" (see Note 9.4.5) may be used instead.

An affirmative response to a question asking for permission can be made by repeating the whole sentence, or the Predicate. Sometimes *hai, doozo* is used as an affirmative answer.

En'pitsu de kaite mo ii desu ka? — "May I write it with pencil?"

Hai, (en'pitsu de kaite mo) ii desu. — "Yes, you may (write it with pencil)."

Hai, doozo. — "Yes, please go ahead."

Jisho o tsukatte mo kamaimasen ka? — "Don't you mind even if I use a dictionary?"

Ee, kamaimasen. — "No, I don't mind it."

9.4.5 *Wasurenaide kudasai* means "Please do not forget." The polite negative imperative "please do not do such and such" is expressed in Japanese as follows:

Pre-Nai form of Verb + adjectival Derivative *-naide + *kudasai*

| noranaide konaide shinaide misenaide | kudasai | "please don't" | get on" come" do it" show it" |

* The *-naide* is another form of *-nakute* — the TE form of the adjectival Derivative *-nai* (see 9.4.9). This form occurs in some patterns: the polite negative imperative is one of them.

Jisho mo kyookasho mo tsukawanaide kudasai. — "Please do not use either a dictionary or a textbook."

Asatte jugyoo o yasumanaide kudasai. — "Please do not miss class the day after tomorrow."

Roomaji de kakanaide kudasai. — "Please do not write it in Roman letters."

Shukudai o wasurenaide kudasai. — "Don't forget to bring in homework, please."

The pattern .... *-naide kudasai* is often used to give a mild negative answer to a question asking for permission.

Mado o akete mo ii desu ka? — "May I open the window?"

Samui kara, akenaide kudasai. — "Please don't open it, because it's cold."

Doa o shimenaide kudasai. — "Please don't close the door."

Note that an English expression "please don't BE such and such" is never applied to this pattern directly. The word that appears before *-naide kudasai* is always a Verb.

9.4.6 *Tsukatte wa ikemasen* means "You must not use it," or "You should not use it." The pattern of prohibition is formulated by the TE form of a Verb plus *wa* plus *ikemasen* "it won't do," or *dame desu* "is no good." The *wa* is mandatory in this pattern. The literal meaning of this pattern is "It is no good if you do such and such." This expression may be used as a strict negative answer to a question asking for permission ~ *-te (mo) ii desu ka*? The answer may be shortened into *ikemasen* or *dame desu*.

$$\textbf{(Predicate Modifier)} + \textbf{Verb}(\textit{-te}) + \textit{wa} + \begin{cases} \textit{ikemasen} \\ \textit{dame desu} \end{cases}$$

$$\left.\begin{matrix} \text{wasurete} \\ \text{yasun'de} \\ \text{tatte} \\ \text{kaite} \\ \text{motte ite} \end{matrix}\right\} \text{wa} \begin{cases} \text{ikemasen} \\ \text{dame desu} \end{cases} \begin{matrix} \text{"it won't do}\} \\ \text{"it's no good}\} \end{matrix} \text{if you} \begin{cases} \text{forget it"} \\ \text{take leave"} \\ \text{stand up"} \\ \text{write it"} \\ \text{have it"} \end{cases}$$

Eigo de kotaete mo ii desu ka?   "May I answer in English?"

Iie, (eigo de kotaete wa) ikemasen.   "No, you may not (answer in English)."

Kyuukoo ni notte wa dame desu yo.   "You must not take an express."

9.4.7 *Dake* is a Relational meaning "just," or "only," and functions to limit the reference only to the preceding Nominative. The Relational *dake* may take the place of such Relationals as *ga, o, wa,* or it may occur between a Nominative and *ga, o,* or *wa*. With other Relationals such as *ni, de, e, kara, to,* etc., the Relational *dake* may precede or follow another Relational.

$$\text{Nominative} + \begin{cases} \textit{ga} \\ \textit{o} \\ \textit{wa} \end{cases} + \text{Predicate} \longrightarrow \text{Nominative} + \textit{dake} + \begin{cases} (\textit{ga}) \\ (\textit{o}) \\ (\textit{wa}) \end{cases} + \text{Predicate}$$

$$\text{Nominative} + \begin{cases} \textit{ni} \\ \textit{de} \\ \cdots \\ \cdots \\ \textit{e} \\ \textit{kara} \\ \textit{to} \end{cases} + \text{Predicate} \longrightarrow \text{Nominative} + \textit{dake} + \begin{cases} \textit{ni} \\ \textit{de} \\ \cdots \\ \cdots \\ \textit{e} \\ \textit{kara} \\ \textit{to} \end{cases} + \text{Predicate}$$

$$\text{or Nominative} + \begin{cases} \textit{ni} \\ \textit{de} \\ \cdots \\ \cdots \\ \textit{e} \\ \textit{kara} \\ \textit{to} \end{cases} + \textit{dake} + \text{Predicate}$$

Kotae dake kaite kudasai.   "Please write only the answers."

Nan'nin kimashita ka?   "How many people came?"

San'nin dake kimashita.   "Only three came."

Pooru dake ni kyookasho o kaeshimashita.   "I returned the textbook only to Paul."

9.4.8 *Kotae dake de ii n desu ka?* means "Is it all right if (I write) only the answer?" *De* of the above sentence is the TE form of the Copula *desu*. The patterns of permission and prohibition that have been explained in Notes 9.4.4 and 9.4.6 are applicable to the copular Predicate.

$$\text{Nominative} + de + (mo) + \begin{cases} ii\ desu \\ kamaimasen \end{cases}$$

$$\text{Nominative} + de + wa^* + \begin{cases} ikemasen \\ dame\ desu \end{cases}$$
$$(ja)$$

* As already explained in Vol. I, 8.4.1, *de wa* may be shortened to *ja;* ~ *ja ikemasen* or ~ *ja dame desu*.

En'pitsu de mo ii desu ka?	"Is it all right with pencil?"
Heta de mo kamaimasen ka?	"Don't you mind if I am not good at it?"
Nomimono dake de ii desu ka?	"Is it all right with only drinks?"
Nihon'go de wa ikemasen.	"It must not be in Japanese."
Hiragana dake de wa dame desu.	"It's no good with only *hiragana*."

9.4.9 *Osokute* is the TE form of the Adjective *osoi* meaning "is slow; is late." The TE form of an Adjective is also used in the patterns of permission and prohibition, explained in Notes 9.4.4 and 9.4.6.

$$\text{TE form of Adjective} + (mo) + \begin{cases} ii\ desu \\ kamaimasen \end{cases}$$

$$\text{TE form of Adjective} + wa + \begin{cases} ikemasen \\ dame\ desu \end{cases}$$

The TE form of Adjectives is made by changing the final *-i* into *-kute*. Thus:

oso*i*	"is late; is slow"	⟶	oso*kute*
sukuna*i*	"is little; is few"	⟶	sukuna*kute*
oo*i*	"is much; are many"	⟶	oo*kute*
mijika*i*	"is short"	⟶	mijika*kute*
naga*i*	"is long"	⟶	naga*kute*
haya*i*	"is early; is fast"	⟶	haya*kute*
na*i*	"is nonexistent"	⟶	na*kute*

Takakute mo kamaimasen ka?	"Don't you mind if it's expensive?"
Kotae wa mijikakute wa ikemasen.	"Answers must not be short."
Heya no naka wa kitanakute wa dame desu.	"It's no good if the room is dirty."
Setsumei wa nagakute mo ii desu.	"It's all right if the explanation is long."

Note that the TE form of the plain negative of a Verb is also formulated as an Adjective is:

tsukawana*i*	⟶	tsukawana*kute*
tabena*i*	⟶	tabena*kute*

Tsukawanakute mo ii desu.   "It is all right if you don't use it."

Tabenakute mo kamaimasen.   "I don't mind if you do not eat it."

Sukoshi yasumanakute wa ikemasen   "You must rest for a while."
    yo.

9.5 VOCABULARY

Presentation

中	naka	....	N	inside (see 9.4.1)
黒板	kokuban	....	N	blackboard
前	mae	....	N	front; before (see 9.4.1)
たって	tatte	....	V	TE form of *tachimasu* ← *tatsu* – stand (see 9.4.2)
いす	isu	....	N	chair
すわって	suwatte	....	V	TE form of *suwarimasu* ← *suwaru* – sit (see 9.4.2)
つくえ	tsukue	....	N	desk
上	ue	....	N	top; topside (see 9.4.1)

Dialog

これから	kore kara	....	PM	from now on (see 9.4.3)
しけん	shiken	....	N	examination; test
まず	mazu	....	Adv.	first of all; to begin with
万年筆	man'nen'hitsu	....	N	fountain pen
も	mo	....	R	even (see 9.4.4)
ないで	-naide	....	Da	(see 9.4.5)
いけません	ikemasen	....	V	it won't do (see 9.4.6)
教科書	kyookasho	....	N	textbook
はじめましょう	hajimemashoo	....	V	let's begin (OO form of *hajimemasu* ← *hajimeru*) (transitive Verb) (cf. *Vi: hajimarimasu*)
わたした	watashita	....	V	handed (TA form of *watashimasu* ← *watasu*)
こたえ	kotae	....	N	answer
だけ	dake	....	R	only; just (see 9.4.7)
で	de	....	C	TE form of *desu* (see 9.4.8)
ローマ字	roomaji	....	N	Roman letters
こたえて	kotaete	....	V	TE form of *kotaemasu* ← *kotaeru* – answer; respond

かな	kana	....	N	Japanese syllabary
おそくて	osokute	....	A	TE form of *osoi* – is slow; is late (see 9.4.9)

Notes

外	soto	....	N	outside
うしろ	ushiro	....	N	behind; back (see 9.4.1)
下	shita	....	N	under; below
そば	soba	....	N	vicinity; near
木	ki	....	N	tree
字	ji	....	N	letter; character
しゅくだい	shukudai	....	N	homework
まど	mado	....	N	window
あけて	akete	....	V	TE form of *akemasu* ← *akeru* – open
あけない	akenai	....	V	do not open (plain negative of *akemasu* ← *akeru*)
ドア	doa	....	N	door
しめない	shimenai	....	V	do not shut; do not close (plain negative of *shimemasu* ← *shimeru*)
だめ	dame	....	Na	no good
みじかい	mijikai	....	A	is short
ながい	nagai	....	A	is long

Drills

やね	yane	....	N	roof
テーブル	teeburu	....	N	table

9.6 KANJI

9.6.1 語 (1) GO (2) language; word (3) classifier 言

(4)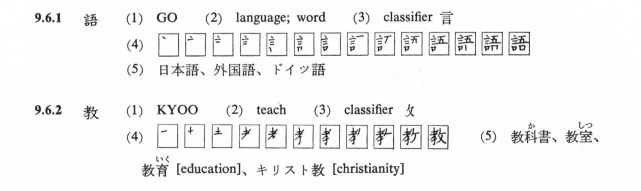

(5) 日本語、外国語、ドイツ語

9.6.2 教 (1) KYOO (2) teach (3) classifier 攵

(4) [strokes] (5) 教科書、教室、

教育 [education]、キリスト教 [christianity]

9.6.3 中 (1) *naka* (2) inside; within (3) classifier 丨 (4) 丶　冖　口　中
(5) 教室の中

9.6.4 先 (1) SEN (2) previous; ahead (3) classifier 儿
(4) 丿　亇　牛　生　失　先 (5) 先生、先月、先週

9.6.5 上 (1) *ue* (2) top; above; on (3) classifier 一 (4) 丨　卜　上
(5) 本の上、つくえの上

9.6.6 習 (1) *nara(imasu); nara(u)* (2) learn (3) classifier 羽
(4) 丁　习　习　刁　羽　羽　羽　習　習
(5) 日本語を習います、習った所

9.6.7 紙 (1) *kami [-gami]* (2) paper (3) classifier 糸 [thread; string]
(4) く　幺　幺　糸　糸　糸　紅　紅　絍　紙 (5) しけんの紙、手紙

9.6.8 名 (1) *na* (2) name (3) classifier 口 (4) 丿　ク　タ　タ　名　名
(5) 名前

9.6.9 書 (1) *ka(kimasu); ka(ku)* (2) write (3) classifier 日
(4) 丁　聿　聿　ヨ　言　聿　書　書　書 (5) 書く

9.6.9 書 (1) SHO (5) 教科書、辞書、さんこう書、図書館

9.6.10 字 (1) JI (2) letter; character (3) classifier 子
(4) 丶　宀　宀　宇　宁　字 (5) ローマ字、かん字

6.6.3 外 (1) *soto* (2) outside (5) 外へ出ましょう

9.6.11 下 (1) *shita* (2) under; beneath; below; bottom (3) classifier 一
(4) 一　丁　下 (5) つくえの下、くつ下 [socks; stockings]、木の下

9.7 DRILLS

9.7.1 Pattern Drill

1. En'pitsu de kaite mo ii desu ka?

2. Ee, ii desu.

3. Demo, kore kara wasurenaide kudasai yo.

4. Jisho o tsukatte mo kamaimasen ka?

5. Iie, tsukatte wa ikemasen.

6. Jisho mo kyookasho mo tsukawanaide kudasai.

7. Kotae dake de ii n desu ka?

8. Hai, kamaimasen.

9. Sore kara, roomaji de kotaete mo ii desu ka?

10. Osokute mo kamaimasen.

9.7.2 Transformation Drill

A. まどを　あけます。 ⟶ まどを　あけてもいいです。

  1. ドアを　しめます。 ⟶ ドアを　しめてもいいです。

  2. いすに　すわります。 ⟶ いすに　すわってもいいです。

  3. 日本語で　こたえます。 ⟶ 日本語で　こたえてもいいです。

  4. じゅぎょうを　やすみます。 ⟶ じゅぎょうを　やすんでもいいです。

  5. 東京駅で　おります。 ⟶ 東京駅で　おりてもいいです。

  6. よるまで　にわで　あそんでいます。 ⟶ よるまで　にわで　あそんでいてもいいです。

  7. ともだちから　かりてみます。 ⟶ ともだちから　かりてみてもいいです。

B. ハワイへ　行きます。 ⟶ ハワイへ　行ってもかまいません。

  1. しけんを　はじめます。 ⟶ しけんを　はじめてもかまいません。

  2. カードを　しらべます。 ⟶ カードを　しらべてもかまいません。

  3. 万年筆を　つかいます。 ⟶ 万年筆を　つかってもかまいません。

  4. タクシーに　のります。 ⟶ タクシーに　のってもかまいません。

  5. かず子さんに　かします。 ⟶ かず子さんに　かしてもかまいません。

  6. 黒板の　そばに　たっています。 ⟶ 黒板の　そばに　たっていてもかまいません。

  7. 先生に　はなしてみます。 ⟶ 先生に　はなしてみてもかまいません。

9.7.3 Transformation Drill

A. やすみは　すくないです。 ⟶ やすみは　すくなくてもいいです。

  1. 辞書は　たかいです。 ⟶ 辞書は　たかくてもいいです。

  2. もんだいは　ながいです。 ⟶ もんだいは　ながくてもいいです。

  3. ひるごはんは　おそいです。 ⟶ ひるごはんは　おそくてもいいです。

  4. しけんは　むずかしいです。 ⟶ しけんは　むずかしくてもいいです。

154

5. コーヒーは　つめたいです。　　　　　→　コーヒーは　つめたくてもいいです。

6. えいがは　つまらないです。　　　　　→　えいがは　つまらなくてもいいです。

B. しごとは　いそがしいです。　　　　　→　しごとは　いそがしくてもかまいません。

  1. レポートは　みじかいです。　　　　→　レポートは　みじかくてもかまいません。

  2. 学校は　とおいです。　　　　　　　→　学校は　とおくてもかまいません。

  3. へやは　さむいです。　　　　　　　→　へやは　さむくてもかまいません。

  4. 教科書は　ふるいです。　　　　　　→　教科書は　ふるくてもかまいません。

  5. セーターは　大きいです。　　　　　→　セーターは　大きくてもかまいません。

  6. 教室は　きたないです。　　　　　　→　教室は　きたなくてもかまいません。

9.7.4 Transformation Drill

A. やすい　アルバイトです。　　　　　　→　やすい　アルバイトでもいいです。

  1. 天気が　へんです。　　　　　　　　→　天気が　へんでもいいです。

  2. のる　でんしゃは　急行です。　　　→　のる　でんしゃは　急行でもいいです。

  3. あう　所は　おたくです。　　　　　→　あう　所は　おたくでもいいです。

  4. こたえは　ローマ字です。　　　　　→　こたえは　ローマ字でもいいです。

  5. きたない　字です。　　　　　　　　→　きたない　字でもいいです。

  6. えいがは　四百円です。　　　　　　→　えいがは　四百円でもいいです。

  7. むずかしい　もんだいです。　　　　→　むずかしい　もんだいでもいいです。

B. みやげは　万年筆です。　　　　　　　→　みやげは　万年筆でもかまいません。

  1. 日本語が　へたです。　　　　　　　→　日本語が　へたでもかまいません。

  2. りょこうが　きらいです。　　　　　→　りょこうが　きらいでもかまいません。

  3. 大学の　三年生です。　　　　　　　→　大学の　三年生でもかまいません。

  4. せきは　うしろです。　　　　　　　→　せきは　うしろでもかまいません。

  5. つまらない　しごとです。　　　　　→　つまらない　しごとでもかまいません。

  6. しけんは　あさってです。　　　　　→　しけんは　あさってでもかまいません。

  7. おとうとの　セーターです。　　　　→　おとうとの　セーターでもかまいません。

9.7.5 Transformation Drill

A. ジャズを　聞きます。　　　　　　　　→　ジャズを　聞いてはいけません。

  1. やねの　上で　あそびます。　　　　→　やねの　上で　あそんではいけません。

  2. まどを　あけます。　　　　　　　　→　まどを　あけてはいけません。

  3. わるい　ことばを　つかいます。　　→　わるい　ことばを　つかってはいけません。

  4. 万年筆を　わすれます。　　　　　　→　万年筆を　わすれてはいけません。

  5. カメラを　かいます。　　　　　　　→　カメラを　かってはいけません。

6. うちで　ねています。　　　　　　　⟶　うちで　ねていてはいけません。

7. ここに　すわっています。　　　　　⟶　ここに　すわっていてはいけません。

B. 学生に　わたします。　　　　　　　⟶　学生に　わたしてはだめです。

1. 黒板(こくばん)に　書きます。　　　⟶　黒板(こくばん)に　書いてはだめです。

2. 教科書(か)を　かります。　　　　　⟶　教科書(か)を　かりてはだめです。

3. バスに　のります。　　　　　　　　⟶　バスに　のってはだめです。

4. 子どもに　あげます。　　　　　　　⟶　子どもに　あげてはだめです。

5. えい語で　はなします。　　　　　　⟶　えい語で　はなしてはだめです。

6. つくえの　上に　すわります。　　　⟶　つくえの　上に　すわってはだめです。

7. そこに　たっています。　　　　　　⟶　そこに　たっていてはだめです。

9.7.6 Transformation Drill

A. へやが　さむいです。　　　　　　　⟶　へやが　さむくてはいけません。

1. くつが　大きいです。　　　　　　　⟶　くつが　大きくてはいけません。

2. せつめいが　みじかいです。　　　　⟶　せつめいが　みじかくてはいけません。

3. 教室(しつ)は　きたないです。　　　⟶　教室(しつ)は　きたなくてはいけません。

4. 辞書(じ)は　ふるいです。　　　　　⟶　辞書(じ)は　ふるくてはいけません。

5. レインコートは　小さいです。　　　⟶　レインコートは　小さくてはいけません。

6. しけんは　やさしいです。　　　　　⟶　しけんは　やさしくてはいけません。

7. 字が　きたないです。　　　　　　　⟶　字が　きたなくてはいけません。

B. こたえが　みじかいです。　　　　　⟶　こたえが　みじかくてはだめです。

1. さんこう書が　むずかしいです。　　⟶　さんこう書が　むずかしくてはだめです。

2. コーヒーが　つめたいです。　　　　⟶　コーヒーが　つめたくてはだめです。

3. 学校(こう)は　とおいです。　　　　⟶　学校(こう)は　とおくてはだめです。

4. 天気が　わるいです。　　　　　　　⟶　天気が　わるくてはだめです。

5. おちゃが　あついです。　　　　　　⟶　おちゃが　あつくてはだめです。

6. 男の　人が　おおいです。　　　　　⟶　男の　人が　おおくてはだめです。

7. しけんは　ながいです。　　　　　　⟶　しけんは　ながくてはだめです。

9.7.7 Transformation Drill

A. えい語の　辞書(じ)です。　　　　　⟶　えい語の　辞書(じ)ではいけません。
　　　　　　　　　　　　　　　　　　　　　　　　　　　　　（じゃ）

1. テーブルの　上です。　　　　　　　⟶　テーブルの　上ではいけません。

2. 学生が　大ぜいです。　　　　　　　⟶　学生が　大ぜいではいけません。

3. かん字が　へたです。　　　　　　　⟶　かん字が　へたではいけません。

4.　ふるい　さんこう書です。　　　　　——→　ふるい　さんこう書ではいけません。

5.　ながい　せつめいです。　　　　　　——→　ながい　せつめいではいけません。

6.　いすの　下です。　　　　　　　　　——→　いすの　下ではいけません。

7.　子どもです。　　　　　　　　　　　——→　子どもではいけません。

B.　べんきょうが　きらいです。　　　　——→　べんきょうが　きらいではだめです。

1.　教室の　外です。　　　　　　　　　——→　教室の　外ではだめです。

2.　フランス語の　教科書です。　　　　——→　フランス語の　教科書ではだめです。

3.　森さんの　うちです。　　　　　　　——→　森さんの　うちではだめです。

4.　りょこうは　らいしゅうです。　　　——→　りょこうは　らいしゅうではだめです。

5.　やすい　アルバイトです。　　　　　——→　やすい　アルバイトではだめです。

6.　のみものは　おちゃです。　　　　　——→　のみものは　おちゃではだめです。

7.　先生が　外国人です。　　　　　　　——→　先生が　外国人ではだめです。

9.7.8　Transformation Drill

1.　へやに　はいりません。　　——→　へやに　はいらないでください。

2.　こたえを　見ません。　　　——→　こたえを　見ないでください。

3.　ドアを　あけません。　　　——→　ドアを　あけないでください。

4.　図書館に　かえしません。　——→　図書館に　かえさないでください。

5.　しけんを　はじめません。　——→　しけんを　はじめないでください。

6.　黒板の　前に　たちません。——→　黒板の　前に　たたないでください。

7.　さんこう書を　かりません。——→　さんこう書を　かりないでください。

8.　えい語を　つかいません。　——→　えい語を　つかわないでください。

9.　名前を　書きません。　　　——→　名前を　書かないでください。

10.　紙を　わたしません。　　　——→　紙を　わたさないでください。

11.　ここに　すわりません。　　——→　ここに　すわらないでください。

12.　林さんを　よびません。　　——→　林さんを　よばないでください。

9.7.9　Response Drill

1.　えんぴつで　書いてもいいですか。

　　はい　　　　　　　　　　……　はい、えんぴつで　書いてもいいです。

　　いいえ、～いけません　　……　いいえ、えんぴつで　書いてはいけません。

　　いいえ、～ないでください　……　いいえ、えんぴつで　書かないでください。

2.　まどの　そばに　いてもいいですか。

　　はい　　　　　　　　　　……　はい、まどの　そばに　いてもいいです。

　　いいえ　　　　　　　　　……　いいえ、まどの　そばに　いてはいけません。

```
          いいえ                ……  いいえ、まどの　そばに　いないでください。
```

3. 教室の　中へ　はいってもいいですか。

```
    はい                    ……  はい、教室の　中へ　はいってもいいです。
    いいえ                ……  いいえ、教室の　中へ　はいってはいけません。
    いいえ                ……  いいえ、教室の　中へ　はいらないでください。
```

4. いすに　すわってもいいですか。

```
    はい                    ……  はい、いすに　すわってもいいです。
    いいえ                ……  いいえ、いすに　すわってはいけません。
    いいえ                ……  いいえ、いすに　すわらないでください。
```

5. 学生に　しけんを　わたしてもかまいませんか。

```
    はい                    ……  はい、学生に　しけんを　わたしてもかまいません。
    いいえ                ……  いいえ、学生に　しけんを　わたしてはいけません。
    いいえ                ……  いいえ、学生に　しけんを　わたさないでください。
```

6. じむしょの　前に　たっていてもかまいませんか。

```
    はい                    ……  はい、じむしょの　前に　たっていてもかまいません。
    いいえ                ……  いいえ、じむしょの　前に　たっていてはいけません。
    いいえ                ……  いいえ、じむしょの　前に　たっていないでください。
```

7. ポールさんから　さんこう書を　かりてもかまいませんか。

```
    はい                    ……  はい、ポールさんから　さんこう書を　かりてもかまいません。
    いいえ                ……  いいえ、ポールさんから　さんこう書を　かりてはいけません。
    いいえ                ……  いいえ、ポールさんから　さんこう書を　かりないでください。
```

8. あなたが　かった　本を　読んでもかまいませんか。

```
    はい                    ……  はい、わたくしが　かった　本を　読んでもかまいません。
    いいえ                ……  いいえ、わたくしが　かった　本を　読んではいけません。
    いいえ                ……  いいえ、わたくしが　かった　本を　読まないでください。
```

9.7.10 Response Drill

1. セーターは　大きくてもいいですか。

```
    はい                    ……  はい、セーターは　大きくてもいいです。
    いいえ                ……  いいえ、セーターは　大きくてはいけません。
```

2. もんだいは　ながくてもいいですか。

```
    はい                    ……  はい、もんだいは　ながくてもいいです。
    いいえ                ……  いいえ、もんだいは　ながくてはいけません。
```

3. しごとは　いそがしくてもいいですか。

はい	…… はい、しごとは　いそがしくてもいいです。
いいえ	…… いいえ、しごとは　いそがしくてはいけません。

4. こうちゃは　つめたくてもかまいませんか。

はい	…… はい、こうちゃは　つめたくてもかまいません。
いいえ	…… いいえ、こうちゃは　つめたくてはいけません。

5. 教室は　小さくてもかまいませんか。

はい	…… はい、教室は　小さくてもかまいません。
いいえ	…… いいえ、教室は　小さくてはいけません。

6. せつめいは　なくてもかまいませんか。

はい	…… はい、せつめいは　なくてもかまいません。
いいえ	…… いいえ、せつめいは　なくてはいけません。

7. べんきょうする　へやは　うるさくてもかまいませんか。

はい	…… はい、べんきょうする　へやは　うるさくてもかまいません。
いいえ	…… いいえ、べんきょうする　へやは　うるさくてはいけません。

9.7.11 Response Drill

1. かいわは　へたでもいいですか。

はい	…… はい、かいわは　へたでもいいです。
いいえ	…… いいえ、かいわは　へたではいけません。

2. 店員は　大ぜいでもいいですか。

はい	…… はい、店員は　大ぜいでもいいです。
いいえ	…… いいえ、店員は　大ぜいではいけません。

3. あの　まどぐちでもいいですか。

はい	…… はい、あの　まどぐちでもいいです。
いいえ	…… いいえ、あの　まどぐちではいけません。

4. かん字と　ひらがなでもかまいませんか。

はい	…… はい、かん字と　ひらがなでもかまいません。
いいえ	…… いいえ、かん字と　ひらがなではいけません。

5. わたしが　持っている　辞書でもかまいませんか。

はい	…… はい、あなたが　持っている　辞書でもかまいません。
いいえ	…… いいえ、あなたが　持っている　辞書ではいけません。

6. せつめいが　みじかい　さんこう書でもかまいませんか。

はい	…… はい、せつめいが　みじかい　さんこう書でもかまいません。
いいえ	…… いいえ、せつめいが　みじかい　さんこう書ではいけません。

9.7.12 Substitution Drill

1. 教室の　中に　ポールさんが　います。
   前　　　　　　…… 教室の　前に　ポールさんが　います。
   そば　　　　　…… 教室の　そばに　ポールさんが　います。
   外　　　　　　…… 教室の　外に　ポールさんが　います。

2. いすの　前に　でんわが　あります。
   上　　　　　　…… いすの　上に　でんわが　あります。
   うしろ　　　　…… いすの　うしろに　でんわが　あります。
   下　　　　　　…… いすの　下に　でんわが　あります。
   そば　　　　　…… いすの　そばに　でんわが　あります。

3. 図書館の　うしろで　かず子さんに　あいました。
   そば　　　　　…… 図書館の　そばで　かず子さんに　あいました。
   前　　　　　　…… 図書館の　前で　かず子さんに　あいました。
   中　　　　　　…… 図書館の　中で　かず子さんに　あいました。

4. つくえの　そばが　きたないです。
   上　　　　　　…… つくえの　上が　きたないです。
   下　　　　　　…… つくえの　下が　きたないです。
   前　　　　　　…… つくえの　前が　きたないです。
   中　　　　　　…… つくえの　中が　きたないです。

9.7.13 Response Drill

1. 万年筆は　どこに　ありましたか。
   つくえの　上　　　　　　…… つくえの　上に　ありました。

2. 子どもたちは　どこに　いましたか。
   公園の　中　　　　　　…… 公園の　中に　いました。

3. 東京行の　バスは　どこに　つきますか。
   あの　本やの　そば　　　…… あの　本やの　そばに　つきます。

4. どこに　すわりましょうか。
   黒板の　前　　　　　　…… 黒板の　前に　すわりましょう。

5. ノートは　どこに　ありますか。
   教科書の　下　　　　　…… 教科書の　下に　あります。

6. どこを　さがしましたか。
   つくえの　うしろ　　　…… つくえの　うしろを　さがしました。

7. どこで　タクシーに　のりましたか。

160

きっさ店の　そば　　　　　　　　……　きっさ店の　そばで　のりました。

8.　どこまで　はしりましたか。
うちの　前から　駅の　そばまで　……　うちの　前から　駅の　そばまで　はしりました。

9.　いぬは　どこに　いましたか。
木の　下　　　　　　　　　　　　……　木の　下に　いました。

9.7.14　E-J Transformation Drill

A.　まどを　あけます。

　1.　please don't　　　　　……　まどを　あけないでください。
　2.　may I　　　　　　　　……　まどを　あけてもいいですか。
　3.　don't you mind　　　　……　まどを　あけてもかまいませんか。
　4.　you may not　　　　　……　まどを　あけてはいけません。
　5.　I don't mind　　　　　……　まどを　あけもかまいません。
　6.　it is all right　　　　　……　まどを　あけてもいいです。

B.　黒板の　そばに　すわります。

　1.　please don't　　　　　……　黒板の　そばに　すわらないでください。
　2.　may I　　　　　　　　……　黒板の　そばに　すわってもいいですか。
　3.　don't you mind　　　　……　黒板の　そばに　すわってもかまいませんか。
　4.　you may not　　　　　……　黒板の　そばに　すわってはいけません。
　5.　it is no good　　　　　……　黒板の　そばに　すわってはだめです。
　6.　it is all right　　　　　……　黒板の　そばに　すわってもいいです。

C.　しけんの　もんだいが　ながいです。

　1.　is it all right　　　　　……　しけんの　もんだいが　ながくてもいいですか。
　2.　don't you mind　　　　……　しけんの　もんだいが　ながくてもかまいませんか。
　3.　it is not all right　　　……　しけんの　もんだいが　ながくてはいけません。
　4.　it is no good　　　　　……　しけんの　もんだいが　ながくてはだめです。

D.　天気が　わるいです。

　1.　is it all right　　　　　……　天気が　わるくてもいいですか。
　2.　don't you mind　　　　……　天気が　わるくてもかまいませんか。
　3.　it is not all right　　　……　天気が　わるくてはいけません。
　4.　it is no good　　　　　……　天気が　わるくてはだめです。

E.　この　万年筆です。

　1.　is it all right　　　　　……　この　万年筆でもいいですか。
　2.　don't you mind　　　　……　この　万年筆でもかまいませんか。

3. it is not all right ...... この 万年筆ではいけません。

4. I don't mind ...... この 万年筆でもかまいません。

F. ローマ字だけです。

1. is it all right ...... ローマ字だけでもいいですか。

2. don't you mind ...... ローマ字だけでもかまいませんか。

3. it is not all right ...... ローマ字だけではいけません。

4. it is no good ...... ローマ字だけではだめです。

5. I don't mind ...... ローマ字だけでもかまいません。

G. 日本語が へたです。

1. is it all right ...... 日本語が へたでもいいですか。

2. don't you mind ...... 日本語が へたでもかまいませんか。

3. it is not all right ...... 日本語が へたではいけません。

4. I don't mind ...... 日本語が へたでもかまいません。

5. it is all right ...... 日本語が へたでもいいです。

9.7.15 E-J Response Drill

1. 本と ノートは どこに ありますか。
   on the desk ...... 本と ノートは つくえの 上に あります。

2. えんぴつは どこに ありますか。
   under the chair ...... えんぴつは いすの 下に あります。

3. 先生は どこに たっていますか。
   in front of the blackboard ...... 先生は 黒板の 前に たっています。

4. スミスさんは どこに いますか。
   sitting near Mr. Brown ...... スミスさんは ブラウンさんの そばに すわっています。

5. ポールさんは どこに いますか。
   behind Mr. Smith ...... ポールさんは スミスさんの うしろに います。

6. ブラウンさんは なにを していますか。
   studying Japanese in the classroom ...... ブラウンさんは 教室の 中で 日本語を べんきょうしています。

7. 井上さんは どこに いましたか。
   outside the room ...... 井上さんは へやの 外に いました。

9.8 EXERCISES

9.8.1 Answer the following questions according to the pictures below:

Picture A

1. へやの　中に　なにが　ありますか。
2. テレビの　上に　なにが　ありますか。
3. テーブルの　上に　なにが　ありますか。
4. テレビは　どこに　ありますか。
5. 人が　なん人（にん）　いますか。
6. どこに　いますか。
7. その　人たちは　なにを　していますか。

Picture B

1. じどうしゃは　どこに　ありますか。
2. 女の　人は　なにを　していますか。
3. いぬは　どこに　いますか。
4. 木（き）は　どこに　ありますか。
5. とりは　やねの　上に　いますか。

9.8.2 Insert appropriate Relationals into the following blanks:

1. けい子さん（　）わたして（　）いけません。
2. しけんは　ながくて（　）いいです。
3. 黒板（こくばん）（　）前（まえ）の　いす（　）すわっている　人は　だれですか。
4. おそくて（　）だめです。
5. さんこう書（　）辞書（じ）（　）つかわないでください。
6. 紙（　）所（　）名前（まえ）（　）書いてください。
7. 図書館（と）（かん）（　）そば（　）ぎんこう（　）あるきました。
8. ノート（　）ローマ字や　えい語（　）書かないでください。

9.8.3 Write the Japanese equivalent:

1. May I go home at 9:30?

2. You must not speak English in the classroom.

3. I don't mind if it is bad weather tomorrow.

4. It is all right for you to study Japanese in my room.

5. Please don't stand by the blackboard.

6. The examination should not be easy.

9.8.4 Write the following underlined *hiragana* in *kanji*:

1. つくえの　うえに　にほんごの　きょう科しょが　あります。　つくえの　したには
かみが　あります。

2. へやの　なかに　がくせいが　います。　そして、　そとに　せんせいが　います。

3. ならった　かんじを　かいてください。

4. な前を　わすれないでください。

9.8.5 Write the following in *katakana*:

1. doa   2. teeburu   3. rooma(ji)

9.9 SITUATIONAL CONVERSATION

9.9.1 In the classroom

An instructor is about to give a quiz.
A student asks if he can use the textbook and a dictionary.
The instructor gives permission to use a dictionary, but not the textbook.
The student asks if he can write with pencil.
The instructor says that it is all right, but tells him not to forget to bring a pen in the future.
The student asks if he can write the answers in Roman letters, but the teacher says no.

9.9.2 In the classroom

A student wants to get his instructor's permission to be absent from his class on Friday.
The instructor asks why.
The student says that he wants to go to his home town since his mother is sick.
The instructor gives permission.

9.9.3 Carry on a conversation normally conducted in the Japanese language class.

LESSON 10

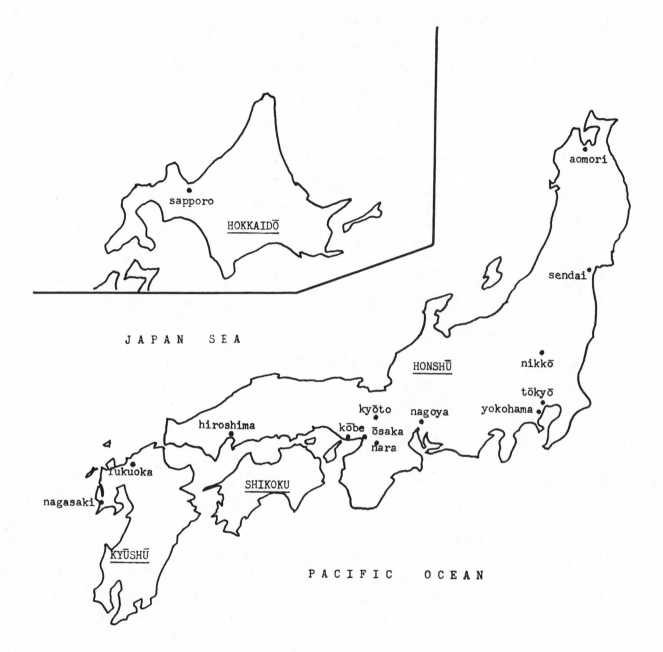

aomori

sapporo

HOKKAIDŌ

sendai

JAPAN SEA

HONSHŪ

nikkō

tōkyō

kyōto   nagoya   yokohama

hiroshima   kōbe   ōsaka

nara

fukuoka

SHIKOKU

nagasaki

KYŪSHŪ

PACIFIC OCEAN

10.1 PRESENTATION

ー 日本の　国 ー

日本は　四つの　島に　わかれています。　その　中で、　一番 [*1]　大きいのは [*1]　本州、[*2]

二番目は [*3]　北海道、　三番目は　九州、　一番　小さいのは　四国です。

10.2 DIALOG

青　木　「テーラーさん、　あなたの　お国は　どこですか。」

テーラー　「南カリフォルニアです。 [*4]」

青　木　「カリフォルニアは　北アメリカで　一番 [*1]　ゆたかな　州でしょう？」

テーラー　「ええ、　まあ　そうですね。　それに、　気候が　いいから、　いろいろな
　　　　　　くだ物が　一年中　あります。　ほかの　州より [*5]　うんどうも [*6]　さかん
　　　　　　ですね。　青木さんは　関西でしたね？」

青　木　「ええ、　京都です。」

テーラー　「京都と　東京と、 [*6]　どっちが [*6]　好きですか。」

青　木　「京都と　東京を　くらべるのは [*7]　むずかしいですけれど、 [*8]　気候は、
　　　　　　東京の　ほうが [*6]　いいですね。　京都は、　なつ　とても　むしあついん
　　　　　　です。」

テーラー　「でも、　町は　京都の　ほうが　きれいでしょう？」

青　木　「もちろん、　ずっと [*9]　きれいですよ。　それに、　東京ほど [*10]　うるさく
　　　　　　ありませんからねえ。」

10.3 PATTERN SENTENCES

10.3.1

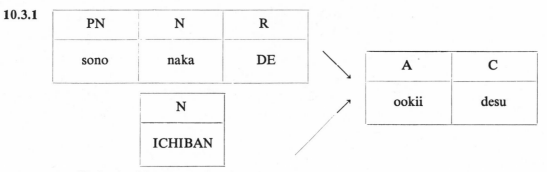

"It is the biggest among them."

10.3.2

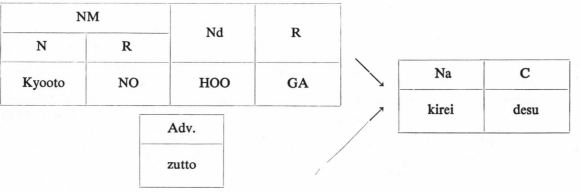

"Kyōto is far prettier."

10.3.3

N	R
Kariforunia	wa

N	R	N	R
hoka	no	shuu	YORI

Na	C
yutaka	desu

"California is richer than the other states."

10.3.4

N	R
Kyooto	wa

N	R
Tookyoo	HODO

A	E
urusaku	arimaSEN

"Kyōto is not as noisy as Tōkyō is."

10.4 NOTES

10.4.1 Unlike in English, an Adjective in Japanese does not have the superlative degree and the comparative degree such as "best," "better," etc. Instead, the superlative degree of an Adjective or of an adjectival Nominative is shown by using the Nominative *ichiban* that literally means "number one." To indicate items or persons to one of which the superlative description is true, phrases (*gakusei*) *no naka de, sono naka de, kono naka de*, etc. may be used. The *naka* here means "within a scope." The Relational *de* is also used to show a scope or an area to which the superlative description is applied.

$$\left.\begin{matrix} \sim \textit{no naka} \\ \textit{sono naka} \\ \cdots\cdots\cdots\cdots \\ \textbf{an area} \end{matrix}\right\} + \textit{de} + \textit{ichiban} + \left\{\begin{matrix} \textbf{Adjective} \\ \textbf{adjectival Nominative} \end{matrix}\right\} + \textit{desu}$$

The subject of the sentence or what is superlative may precede (~ *no*) *naka de* or may occur between ~ (*no*) *naka de* and *ichiban,* followed by the emphatic subject Relational *ga* or the topic Relational *wa* depending upon the emphasis. The superlative expressions of adjectival Nominatives and Adjectives may be used as Nominative Modifiers. (See Notes 5.4.1 and 5.4.3.)

$$\left.\begin{matrix} \sim \textit{wa} \\ \sim \textit{ga} \end{matrix}\right\} \left\{\begin{matrix} \left.\begin{matrix} \textrm{yottsu no shima} \\ \textrm{kodomotachi} \\ \textrm{yonen'sei} \\ \textrm{Nihon no geijutsu} \\ \textrm{Nihon no mono} \\ \textrm{sono naka} \end{matrix}\right\} \textrm{no naka} \\ \cdots\cdots\cdots\cdots\cdots\cdots\cdots \\ \textrm{sekai} \\ \textrm{Ajia} \\ \textrm{Afurika} \\ \textrm{kono machi} \end{matrix}\right\} \textrm{de ichiban} \left\{\begin{matrix} \textrm{ookii desu} \\ \textrm{kirei desu} \end{matrix}\right.$$

$$\begin{matrix} \textrm{``}\sim\textrm{ is the biggest} \\ \textrm{``}\sim\textrm{ is the prettiest} \end{matrix}\left\{\begin{matrix} \textrm{of the four islands''} \\ \textrm{among the children''} \\ \textrm{of the seniors''} \\ \textrm{of the Japanese arts''} \\ \textrm{of the Japanese things''} \\ \textrm{among them''} \\ \cdots\cdots\cdots\cdots\cdots \\ \textrm{in the world''} \\ \textrm{in Asia''} \\ \textrm{in Africa''} \\ \textrm{in this town''} \end{matrix}\right.$$

Norimono no naka de, hikooki ga ichiban hayai desu.	"Among transportation facilities, the airplane is the fastest."
Tookyoo wa sekai de ichiban hito ga ooi desu.	"Tōkyō has the greatest population in the world."
Gakusei no naka de, watakushi wa ichiban sei ga hikui desu.	"I am the shortest of the students."

When several items are given for choice, a question is formulated as follows:

Nominative 1 *to* **Nominative 2** *to*....**Nominative N** (*to*) *de* (*wa*),

$$\textit{dore ga ichiban} \left\{\begin{matrix} \textbf{Adjective} \\ \textbf{adjectival Nominative} \end{matrix}\right\} \textit{desu ka?}$$

The interrogative Nominative *dore* may be replaced by other interrogative Nominatives such as *nani, dare, doko, itsu*, etc., or *dono* plus Nominative depending upon the items being compared in the sentence. The answer to the above question is ~ *ga ichiban* ~ *desu*.

Suujii san to Pooru san to Jooji san to de wa, dare ga ichiban nihon'go ga joozu desu ka?	"Among Susie, Paul, and George, who is the most proficient in Japanese?"
Kyoo no shiken no naka de, dore ga ichiban muzukashikatta desu ka?	Which was the most difficult among the exams today?"
Nihon no kisetsu no naka de, itsu ga ichiban suki desu ka?	Of the Japanese seasons, which do you like the best?"
Ajia to Afurika to Kita Amerika de wa, doko ga ichiban hiroi desu ka?	'Of Asia, Africa, and North America, which is the largest?"

10.4.2 *Ichiban ookii no* means "the biggest one." The Nominative that is modified by an Adjective, an adjectival Nominative+*na,* or a Verb may be replaced by the dependent Nominative *no* "one(s)," when the Nominative is understood by both the speaker and the listener. The *no* may be followed by any Relational.

$$\left. \begin{array}{l} \text{Adjective} \\ \text{adjectival Nominative} + \textit{na} \\ \text{Verb} \end{array} \right\} + \text{Nominative} \longrightarrow \left. \begin{array}{l} \text{Adjective} \\ \text{adjectival Nominative} + \textit{na} \\ \text{Verb} \end{array} \right\} + \textit{no}$$

ookii shima	"big islands"	⟶	ookii no	"the big ones"
yutaka na shuu	"the rich state"	⟶	yutaka na no	"the rich one"
soko ni aru isu	"the chair that is there"	⟶	soko ni aru no	"the one that is there"
kinoo katta hon	"the books I bought yesterday"	⟶	kinoo katta no	"the ones I bought yesterday"

Amerika no shuu no naka de ichiban ookii no wa Arasuka desu.	"Of the states in the U.S.A., the largest one is Alaska."
Ichiban atarashii no o kudasai.	"Please give me the newest one."
Haha ga kureta no wa kore desu.	"This is the one my mother gave me."

When an object is already under discussion and one wants to mention the kind of object, the object may be followed by the topic Relational *wa* and a Nominative Modifier plus *no* may then follow *wa.*

$$\text{Nominative} + \textit{wa} + \left\{ \begin{array}{l} \textbf{Adjective} \\ \textbf{adjectival Nominative} \\ \textbf{Verb} \end{array} \right\} + \textit{no} + \left\{ \begin{array}{l} \textit{ga} \cdots \\ \textit{o} \cdots \end{array} \right.$$

"as for a Nominative, (the) ∼ one...."

| Koocha wa atsui no ga hoshii n desu ga ... | "As for tea, I would like to have it hot." |
| Nekutai wa takai no o kaimashita. | "As for a tie, I bought an expensive one." |

10.4.3 *Niban'me* and *futatsume* both mean "the second." The dependent Nominative *-me* is attached to a number to show a sequence.

| hitotsume | "the first (object)" |
| ninen'me | "the second year" |

san'nin'me	"the third person"
yon'haime	"the fourth cup (of ~)"
goban'me	"the fifth (object)"

Futatsume no mise wa tabakoya desu.	"The second store is a cigarette stand."
Koko kara yonin'me no gakusei wa Tanaka san desu.	"The fourth student from here is Mr. Tanaka."
Daigaku no ninen'me ni Nihon e kimashita.	"I came to Japan in my second year of college."
Goban'me no mon'dai wa totemo muzukashii desu.	"The fifth question is very difficult."

10.4.4 *Minami Kariforunia* is "Southern California." Here are words of this kind:

minami	南	"south"
kita	北	"north"
higashi	東	"east"
nishi	西	"west"

Minami Amerika	"South America"
Kita Afurika	"North Africa"
Higashi Yooroppa	"East Europe"
Nishi Nihon	"the western part of Japan"

10.4.5 The Nominative *hoka* is translated "other," "another," "different," "else," etc. The meaning of *hoka* is "(one or ones) excluding the particular one(s) that has been mentioned or is understood."

Hoka e ikimashoo.	"Let's go somewhere else."
Hoka de shokuji o shimashita.	"I had a meal somewhere else."
Hoka no mono o misete kudasai.	"Please show me other things."
Hoka no hito ni kikimashoo.	"I'll ask someone else."

10.4.6 *Yori* is a Relational meaning "(more) than." The comparative degree is expressed as follows when a sentence is a statement.

Nominative 1 + *wa* + Nominative 2 + *yori* + {Adjective / adjectival Nominative} + *desu*

"N1 is more ...... than N2"

| Nihon wa Kariforunia yori chiisai desu. | "Japan is smaller than California." |
| Koko no ten'in wa ano mise no ten'in yori kotoba ga teinei desu. | "The salesclerk here speaks more politely than the salesclerk in that store." |

A question of comparative degree is formulated as follows:

$$\text{Nominative } 1 + to + \text{Nominative } 2 + to + \begin{cases} (de), \\ (de\ wa), \end{cases}$$

$$\begin{cases} dochira\ (no\ hoo) \\ dotchi\ (no\ hoo) \end{cases} + ga + \begin{cases} \textbf{Adjective} \\ \textbf{adjectival Nominative} \end{cases} desu\ ka?$$

"which is more ......, N1 or N2?"

When the two items to be compared are understood, Nominative 1 *to* Nominative 2 *to* (*de wa*) may be omitted. Note that the interrogative Nominative *dochira* or an informal alternative *dotchi* meaning "which one of the two?" should be used in comparison of two items. The ~ *no hoo* may be attached to *dotchi* or *dochira*. *Hoo* is a dependent Nominative meaning "alternative," "side," etc. The interrogative Nominative *dore* can not be used in the above pattern as it means "which one of the three or more items?" *Dore* is used in the pattern of superlative degree.

Kono san'koosho to sono san'koosho to, dotchi ga yasui desu ka?	"Which is cheaper, this reference book or that reference book?"
Sukiyaki to ten'pura to de wa, dochira no hoo ga suki desu ka?	"Which do you like better, *sukiyaki* or *tempura*?"

A reply to the above question is made in one of the following ways:

~ *no hoo ga ... desu*
~ *no hoo ga* ~ *yori ... desu* or ~ *yori* ~ (*no hoo*) *ga ... desu*
~ *ga ... desu*

San Furan'shisuko to Hawai to de wa, dotchi ga atatakai desu ka?	"Which is warmer, San Francisco or Hawaii?"
Hawai no hoo ga atatakai desu.	"Hawaii is warmer."
Anata no uchi to Yoshiko san no uchi to de wa, dotchi ga tooi desu ka?	"Which is farther, your house or Yoshiko's?"
Watakushi no hoo ga tooi desu.	"Mine is farther (than Yoshiko's)."
Kinoo mita eiga to kyoo no to de wa, dotchi ga omoshirokatta desu ka?	"Which movie was more interesting, the one you saw yesterday or the one you saw today?"
Kyoo no hoo ga omoshirokatta desu.	"Today's was more interesting (than yesterday's)."

10.4.7 *Kuraberu* is a transitive Verb meaning "compare." Some Verbs or some Predicates whose function is equally related to two items or two persons occur in the following patterns:

$$\text{Nominative } 1\ to\ \text{Nominative } 2 \begin{cases} o\ kurabemasu \\ ga\ kekkon\ shimasu \\ wa\ chigaimasu \end{cases}$$

"compare N1 and (with) N2"
"N1 and N2 will get married"
"N1 and N2 are different"

or

Nominative 1 *o* Nominative 2 *to kurabemasu*   "compare N1 with N2"
Nominative 1 *ga* Nominative 2 *to kekkon shimasu*   "N1 will marry N2"
Nominative 1 *wa* Nominative 2 *to chigaimasu*   "N1 is different from N2"

Boku no katta san'koosho to anata
no o kurabemashita.

Boku no katta san'koosho o anata
no to kurabemashita.

"I compared a reference book I bought with yours."

10.4.8   *Keredo* is a clause Relational meaning "although." The clause followed by *keredo* is a subordinate clause meaning "although ...." *Keredo* is a shortened form of *keredomo,* and another shorter form is *kedo. Keredomo* occurs more frequently in writing than in conversation.
The Predicate before *keredo,* or *kedo* can be either in normal form or in plain form when the final clause is in normal form, while the Predicate before the clause Relational *ga* meaning "but" should always be identical in style with the final Predicate — that is, either both plain or both normal.

Kono kissaten wa kirei desu keredo,
urusai desu.

"Although this coffee shop is clean, it's noisy."

Kyoo wa nichiyoo desu keredo,
jimusho de hatarakimasu.

"It is Sunday today, but I'll work at the office."

Nihon'go wa muzukashii (desu) kedo,
narau no ga omoshiroi desu.

"The Japanese language is difficult, but it is interesting to learn it."

Toshokan de hoshii hon o
ichinichijuu sagashita kedo,
arimasen deshita.

"Although I looked all day in the library for a book I want, it wasn't there."

10.4.9   An Adverb *zutto* "by far" may occur in the comparison to mean "far (better)," "much (more)," etc.

Nyuu Yooku wa Kariforunia yori
zutto samui desu.

"New York is much colder than California."

Pooru san no hoo ga zutto atama
ga ii desu yo.

"Paul is much smarter."

Kono heya yori watakushi no heya
no hoo ga zutto semai desu.

"My room is much smaller than this room."

10.4.10   *Tookyoo hodo urusaku arimasen* means a negative comparison "~ is not as noisy as Tōkyō." The *hodo* is a Relational meaning "as much as," and when it is used with a negative Predicate it carries the meaning of negative comparison "is not as .... as," or "someone does not do so .... as someone else does," etc.

Nominative 1 + *wa* + Nominative 2 + *hodo* + negative Predicate

Hawai		Kariforunia		hiroku
nihon'jin		amerikajin		sei ga takaku
kamera	wa	rajio	hodo	hoshiku	arimasen
sukiyaki		ten'pura		suki ja
boku		kimi		gen'ki de wa

172

Japanese	Romaji	English
Kyooto wa Tookyoo hodo atsuku arimasen.		"Kyōto is not as hot as Tōkyō."
Basu wa takushii hodo hayaku arimasen.		"A bus is not as fast as a taxi."
Kono tatemono wa ano depaato hodo furuku arimasen.		"This building is not as old as that department store."
Koko wa asoko hodo kirei ja arimasen.		"This place is not as clean as that place."
Watakushi wa Pooru san hodo nihon'go ga joozu de wa arimasen yo.		"I am not as good as Paul is at Japanese."

10.5 VOCABULARY

Presentation

島	shima	....	N	island
に	ni	....	R	into
わかれて	wakarete	....	V	TE form of *wakaremasu* ← *wakareru* – is separated; is divided (intransitive Verb)
(その)中	(sono) naka	....	N	among (them) (see 10.4.1)
で	de	....	R	(see 10.4.1)
一番	ichiban	....	N	the most (see 10.4.1)
の	no	....	Nd	one(s) (see 10.4.2)
本州	Hon'shuu	....	N	the main island of Japan
目	-me	....	Nd	(see 10.4.3)
九州	Kyuushuu	....	N	Kyūshū Island
四国	Shikoku	....	N	Shikoku Island

Dialog

青木	Aoki	....	N	family name
テーラー	Teeraa	....	N	Taylor
南	minami	....	N	south (see 10.4.4)
北	kita	....	N	north
ゆたか	yutaka	....	Na	rich; abundant
州	shuu	....	N	state
まあ	maa	....	SI	you might say; roughly; well, I think (showing some hesitation)

気候	kikoo	....	N	climate
くだ物	kudamono	....	N	fruit
ほか	hoka	....	N	other; another; different; else (see 10.4.5)
より	yori	....	R	(more) than (see 10.4.6)
うんどう	un'doo	....	N	sport; physical exercises
さかん	sakan	....	Na	flourishing; prosperous; popular
関西	Kan'sai	....	N	a district including Ōsaka, Kyōto, Kōbe, etc. (cf. *Kan'too* "a district including Tōkyō, Yokohama, etc.")
どっち	dotchi	....	Ni	which (of the two)? (see 10.4.6)
くらべる	kuraberu	....	V	compare (Dictionary form) (see 10.4.7)
けれど	keredo	....	Rc	although (see 10.4.8)
ほう	hoo	....	Nd	alternative (see 10.4.6)
むしあつい	mushiatsui	....	A	is hot and humid
町	machi	....	N	town; city
もちろん	mochiron	....	SI	of course; certainly
ずっと	zutto	....	Adv.	by far; much (more) (see 10.4.9)
ほど	hodo	....	R	as much as (see 10.4.10)

Notes

物	mono	....	N	thing (tangible)
せかい	sekai	....	N	world
アジア	Ajia	....	N	Asia
アフリカ	Afurika	....	N	Africa
ひくい	hikui	....	A	is low; is short (stature)
ひろい	hiroi	....	A	is large; is wide; is spacious
アラスカ	Arasuka	....	N	Alaska
東	higashi	....	N	east
西	nishi	....	N	west
どちら	dochira	....	Ni	which (of the two)? (see 10.4.6)
けれども	keredomo	....	Rc	although (see 10.4.8)
けど	kedo	....	Rc	although (see 10.4.8)
あたま	atama	....	N	head
せまい	semai	....	A	is small; is narrow; is limited (in space)

10.6 KANJI

国 [6.6.4] (1) *kuni* (5) ぼくの国はドイツです

10.6.1 番 (1) BAN (2) number; order (3) classifier 田

(4)

(5) 一番、八番、三番線[せん]

10.6.2 目 (1) *me* (2) eye; ordinal suffix (3) forms the classifier 目

(4) (5) 目が大きい、三番目、五つ目

10.6.3 南 (1) *minami* (2) south (3) classifier 十

(4) (5) 南アメリカ、南日本、東京の南

10.6.4 北 (1) *kita* (2) north (3) classifier ヒ (4)

(5) 北九州[きゅうしゅう]、北アジア、北日本

中 [9.6.3] (1) -JUU (5) 一日中、一年中

10.6.5 町 (1) *machi* (2) town; city (3) classifier 田 (4)

(5) 町へ行く、町の東、町中 [throughout the town]

東 [*6.6.1] (1) *higashi* (5) 東ヨーロッパ、東ドイツ

10.6.6 西 [*] (1) *nishi* (2) west (3) forms the classifier 西

(4) (5) 西アジア、駅の西、西日本

10.7 DRILLS

10.7.1 Pattern Drill

1. Sono naka de, ichiban ookii no wa Hon'shuu, niban'me wa Hokkaidoo, san'ban'me wa Kyuushuu, ichiban chiisai no wa Shikoku desu.

2. Kariforunia wa Kita Amerika de ichiban yutaka na shuu deshoo?

3. Hoka no shuu yori un'doo mo sakan desu ne.

4. Kyooto to Tookyoo to, dotchi ga suki desu ka?

5. Kikoo wa, Tookyoo no hoo ga ii desu ne.

6. Demo, machi wa Kyooto no hoo ga kirei deshoo?

7. Mochiron, zutto kirei desu yo.

8. Tookyoo hodo urusaku arimasen kara nee.

10.7.2 Substitution Drill

A. 東京は 京都<ruby>京都<rt>と</rt></ruby>より ひろいです。

   1. アメリカ、日本 　　　　…… アメリカは 日本より ひろいです。

   2. ゆたかな 国 　　　　…… アメリカは 日本より ゆたかな 国です。

   3. 人が おおい 　　　　…… アメリカは 日本より 人が おおいです。

   4. ニューヨーク、サンフランシスコ …… ニューヨークは サンフランシスコより 人が おおいです。

   5. 大きい 町 　　　　…… ニューヨークは サンフランシスコより 大きい 町です。

   6. とおい 　　　　…… ニューヨークは サンフランシスコより とおい です。

   7. おもしろい 所 　　　　…… ニューヨークは サンフランシスコより おもしろい 所です。

B. テーラーさんは わたしより せいが たかいです。

   1. 日本語が じょうず 　　　　…… テーラーさんは わたしより 日本語が じょうずです。

   2. あの 人、ブラウンさん 　　　　…… あの 人は ブラウンさんより 日本語が じょうずです。

   3. ゆうめいな 学生 　　　　…… あの 人は ブラウンさんより ゆうめいな 学生です。

   4. げん気 　　　　…… あの 人は ブラウンさんより げん気です。

   5. ことばが ていねい 　　　　…… あの 人は ブラウンさんより ことばが ていねいです。

   6. 青木さん、林さん 　　　　…… 青木さんは 林さんより ことばが ていねい です。

   7. せいが ひくい 　　　　…… 青木さんは 林さんより せいが ひくいです。

   8. わたし、あなた 　　　　…… わたしは あなたより せいが ひくいです。

C. これは それより ずっと いいです。

   1. たかい 　　　　…… これは それより ずっと たかいです。

176

2. あなたの　くつ、わたしの　くつ　……　あなたの　くつは　わたしの　くつより　ずっと
　　　　　　　　　　　　　　　　　　　　　たかいです。

3. きれい　　　　　　　　　　　　……　あなたの　くつは　わたしの　くつより　ずっと
　　　　　　　　　　　　　　　　　　　　　きれいです。

4. いい　　　　　　　　　　　　　……　あなたの　くつは　わたしの　くつより　ずっと
　　　　　　　　　　　　　　　　　　　　　いいです。

5. コーヒー、こうちゃ　　　　　　……　コーヒーは　こうちゃより　ずっと　いいです。

6. 好き　　　　　　　　　　　　　……　コーヒーは　こうちゃより　ずっと　好きです。

7. 好きな　のみ物　　　　　　　　……　コーヒーは　こうちゃより　ずっと　好きな
　　　　　　　　　　　　　　　　　　　　　のみ物です。

10.7.3　Substitution Drill

ひこうきと　ふねと、どちらが　はやいですか。

1. タクシー、バス　　　　　　　……　タクシーと　バスと、どちらが　はやいですか。

2. おそい　　　　　　　　　　　……　タクシーと　バスと、どちらが　おそいですか。

3. 好き　　　　　　　　　　　　……　タクシーと　バスと、どちらが　好きですか。

4. みち子さん、よし子さん　　　……　みち子さんと　よし子さんと、どちらが　好きですか。

5. すきやき、てんぷら　　　　　……　すきやきと　てんぷらと、どちらが　好きですか。

6. カリフォルニア、ニューヨーク……　カリフォルニアと　ニューヨークと、どちらが　好き
　　　　　　　　　　　　　　　　　　　ですか。

7. あつい　　　　　　　　　　　……　カリフォルニアと　ニューヨークと、どちらが　あつい
　　　　　　　　　　　　　　　　　　　ですか。

8. せまい　　　　　　　　　　　……　カリフォルニアと　ニューヨークと、どちらが　せまい
　　　　　　　　　　　　　　　　　　　ですか。

10.7.4　Expansion Drill

1. しずかです。　　　……　しずかです。
　　ずっと　　　　　　……　ずっと　しずかです。
　　ここの　ほうが　　……　ここの　ほうが　ずっと　しずかです。
　　あの　店より　　　……　あの　店より　ここの　ほうが　ずっと　しずかです。

2. いそがしかったです。……　いそがしかったです。
　　ずっと　　　　　　……　ずっと　いそがしかったです。
　　月曜日より　　　　……　月曜日より　ずっと　いそがしかったです。
　　火曜日は　　　　　……　火曜日は　月曜日より　ずっと　いそがしかったです。

3. ゆたかです。　　　　……　ゆたかです。
　　南日本の　ほうが　……　南日本の　ほうが　ゆたかです。

北日本より	……	北日本より　南日本の　ほうが　ゆたかです。
くだ物は	……	くだ物は　北日本より　南日本の　ほうが　ゆたかです。

4. さかんでした。　　…… さかんでした。

ずっと　　　　　…… ずっと　さかんでした。

むかしの　ほうが　…… むかしの　ほうが　ずっと　さかんでした。

今より　　　　　…… 今より　むかしの　ほうが　ずっと　さかんでした。

かぶきは　　　　…… かぶきは　今より　むかしの　ほうが　ずっと　さかんでした。

5. 好きですか。　　…… 好きですか。

どちらが　　　　…… どちらが　好きですか。

あついのと　　　…… あついのと　つめたいのでは、どちらが　好きですか。
　つめたいのでは、

こうちゃは　　　…… こうちゃは　あついのと　つめたいのでは、どちらが　好きですか。

6. あたたかいです。　…… あたたかいです。

ことしの　ほうが　…… ことしの　ほうが　あたたかいです。

きょ年の　ふゆより　…… きょ年の　ふゆより　ことしの　ほうが　あたたかいです。

東京は　　　　　…… 東京は　きょ年の　ふゆより　ことしの　ほうが　あたたかいです。

10.7.5 Substitution Drill

のり物の　中で、なにが　一番　好きですか。

1. くだ物　　　…… くだ物の　中で、なにが　一番　好きですか。

2. たべ物　　　…… たべ物の　中で、なにが　一番　好きですか。

3. のみ物　　　…… のみ物の　中で、なにが　一番　好きですか。

4. ほしい　　　…… のみ物の　中で、なにが　一番　ほしいですか。

5. 日本の　物　…… 日本の　物の　中で、なにが　一番　ほしいですか。

6. ゆうめい　　…… 日本の　物の　中で、なにが　一番　ゆうめいですか。

7. 日本の　芸術　…… 日本の　芸術の　中で、なにが　一番　ゆうめいですか。

8. さかん　　　…… 日本の　芸術の　中で、なにが　一番　さかんですか。

10.7.6 Expansion Drill

1. むしあついです。　…… むしあついです。

一番　　　　　…… 一番　むしあついです。

一年中で　　　…… 一年中で、一番　むしあついです。

八月が　　　　…… 八月が　一年中で、一番　むしあついです。

2. くわしいです。　　…… くわしいです。

一番　　　　　…… 一番　くわしいです。

さんこう書の せつめいが	……	さんこう書の せつめいが 一番 くわしいです。
よし子さんの 持っている	……	よし子さんの 持っている さんこう書の せつめいが 一番 くわしいです。
この 中で	……	この 中で よし子さんの 持っている さんこう書の せつめいが 一番 くわしいです。

3. さかんですか。　　　…… さかんですか。

　一番　　　　　　　…… 一番 さかんですか。

　うんどうが　　　　…… うんどうが 一番 さかんですか。

　どの　　　　　　　…… どの うんどうが 一番 さかんですか。

　この 大学では　　…… この 大学では、どの うんどうが 一番 さかんですか。

4. どこですか。　　　…… どこですか。

　州は　　　　　　　…… 州は どこですか。

　大きい　　　　　　…… 大きい 州は どこですか。

　一番　　　　　　　…… 一番 大きい 州は どこですか。

　アメリカで　　　　…… アメリカで、一番 大きい 州は どこですか。

5. 青木さんです。　　…… 青木さんです。

　学生は　　　　　　…… 学生は 青木さんです。

　フランス語の
じょうずな　　　…… フランス語の じょうずな 学生は 青木さんです。

　一番　　　　　　　…… 一番 フランス語の じょうずな 学生は 青木さんです。

　四年生の 中で　　…… 四年生の 中で、 一番 フランス語の じょうずな 学生は
青木さんです。

10.7.7 Transformation Drill

1. 一番 ながい 島は 本州です。　　　⟶ 一番 ながいのは 本州です。

2. 一番 ひまな 人は だれですか。　　⟶ 一番 ひまなのは だれですか。

3. くだ物が ゆたかな 州は
　カリフォルニアです。　　　　　　⟶ くだ物が ゆたかなのは カリフォルニアです。

4. あそこに いる 男の 子は ぼくの
　おとうとです。　　　　　　　　　⟶ あそこに いるのは ぼくの おとうとです。

5. きみが 習った 外国語は 日本語
　ですか。　　　　　　　　　　　　⟶ きみが 習ったのは 日本語ですか。

6. 青木さんが 読みたい 本は ここで
　うっています。　　　　　　　　　⟶ 青木さんが 読みたいのは ここで うって
　　　　　　　　　　　　　　　　　　います。

7. きのう 来なかった 学生は
　テーラーさんです。　　　　　　　⟶ きのう 来なかったのは テーラーさんです。

10.7.8　Substitution Drill

A.　この　本の　中で、むずかしいのは　どれですか。
   1.　だいひょう的な　　　……　この　本の　中で、だいひょう的なのは　どれですか。
   2.　ほしい　　　　　　　……　この　本の　中で、ほしいのは　どれですか。
   3.　たかかった　　　　　……　この　本の　中で、たかかったのは　どれですか。
   4.　つまらなかった　　　……　この　本の　中で、つまらなかったのは　どれですか。
   5.　読みたかった　　　　……　この　本の　中で、読みたかったのは　どれですか。
   6.　読んだ　　　　　　　……　この　本の　中で、読んだのは　どれですか。

B.　うんどうの　中で、好きなのは　なんですか。
   1.　むずかしい　　　　　……　うんどうの　中で、むずかしいのは　なんですか。
   2.　さかんな　　　　　　……　うんどうの　中で、さかんなのは　なんですか。
   3.　あたらしい　　　　　……　うんどうの　中で、あたらしいのは　なんですか。
   4.　じょうずな　　　　　……　うんどうの　中で、じょうずなのは　なんですか。
   5.　大好きな　　　　　　……　うんどうの　中で、大好きなのは　なんですか。
   6.　きらいな　　　　　　……　うんどうの　中で、きらいなのは　なんですか。

C.　あなたの　ともだちの　中で、げん気なのは　だれですか。
   1.　来なかった　　　……　あなたの　ともだちの　中で、来なかったのは　だれですか。
   2.　やすんだ　　　　……　あなたの　ともだちの　中で、やすんだのは　だれですか。
   3.　アルバイト　　　……　あなたの　ともだちの　中で、アルバイトしているのは
      している　　　　　　　　　　だれですか。
   4.　ぎんこうに　　　……　あなたの　ともだちの　中で、ぎんこうに　つとめているのは
      つとめている　　　　　　　　だれですか。
   5.　日本文学を　　　……　あなたの　ともだちの　中で、日本文学を　習ったのは
      習った　　　　　　　　　　　だれですか。

D.　この　中で、一番　ちかいのは　どこですか。
   1.　すずしい　　　　　　……　この　中で、一番　すずしいのは　どこですか。
   2.　ゆうめい　　　　　　……　この　中で、一番　ゆうめいなのは　どこですか。
   3.　おもしろかった　　　……　この　中で、一番　おもしろかったのは　どこですか。
   4.　行きたい　　　　　　……　この　中で、一番　行きたいのは　どこですか。

10.7.9　Response Drill

 1.　一年生の　中で、だれが　一番
   　せいが　たかいですか。
  　青木一郎さん　　　　　　　　　　……　青木一郎さんが　一番　（せいが）　たかいです。

180

2. はると なつと あきと ふゆで、
　　どの 気候(こう)が 一番 よかったですか。
　　　あき　　　　　　　　　　　　…… あき(の 気候(こう))が 一番 よかったです。

3. あなたは フランス語と ドイツ語と
　　日本語とでは、　どれが 一番 じょうずですか。
　　　日本語　　　　　　　　　　…… 日本語が 一番 じょうずです。

4. 日本の 物(もの)で、　なにが 一番 ほしいですか。
　　　カメラ　　　　　　　　　　…… カメラが 一番 ほしいです。

5. ともだちの 中で、　だれの じどうしゃが 一番 あたらしいですか。
　　　スミスさんの　　　　　　　…… スミスさんのが 一番 あたらしいです。

6. この 中で、　どれが 一番 やすいですか。
　　　これ　　　　　　　　　　　…… これが 一番 やすいです。

10.7.10　E-J Substitution Drill

あの 店(みせ)より この 店(みせ)の ほうが きれいです。

1. more quiet　　　　　　…… あの 店(みせ)より この 店(みせ)の ほうが しずかです。
2. farther　　　　　　　 …… あの 店(みせ)より この 店(みせ)の ほうが とおいです。
3. noisier　　　　　　　 …… あの 店(みせ)より この 店(みせ)の ほうが うるさいです。
4. cooler　　　　　　　　…… あの 店(みせ)より この 店(みせ)の ほうが すずしいです。
5. hotter and more humid …… あの 店(みせ)より この 店(みせ)の ほうが むしあついです。
6. smaller　　　　　　　 …… あの 店(みせ)より この 店(みせ)の ほうが 小さいです。
7. more famous　　　　　…… あの 店(みせ)より この 店(みせ)の ほうが ゆうめいです。

10.7.11　Transformation Drill

1. 東京は 京都(と)より むしあついです。　⟶ 京都(と)は 東京ほど むしあつくありません。
2. タクシーは バスより はやいです。　⟶ バスは タクシーほど はやくありません。
3. 北海道(ほっかいどう)は ハワイより 大きいです。　⟶ ハワイは 北海道(ほっかいどう)ほど 大きくありません。
4. あなたは 青木(あおき)さんより せいが ひくいです。　⟶ 青木(あおき)さんは あなたほど せいが ひくく ありません。
5. アメリカは 日本より くだ物(もの)が ゆたかです。　⟶ 日本は アメリカほど くだ物(もの)が ゆたか じゃありません。
6. ポールさんは ぼくより 日本語が じょうずです。　⟶ ぼくは ポールさんほど 日本語が じょうずじゃありません。
7. てんぷらは すきやきより 好きです。　⟶ すきやきは てんぷらほど 好きじゃ ありません。

8. じゅうどうは からてより さかんです。——→ からては じゅうどうほど さかんじゃ
   　　　　　　　　　　　　　　　　　　　　　　ありません。

10.7.12　E-J Response Drill

1. 京都と　東京では、　どちらが　むしあついですか。
   Tōkyō　　　　　　　　　　　……（京都より）東京の　ほうが　むしあついです。
2. この　本と　その　本と、　どっちが　てきとうですか。
   this book　　　　　　　　　……（その　本より）この　本の　ほうが　てきとうです。
3. のり物は　ひこうきと　ふねと、　どっちの　ほうが　好きですか。
   airplane　　　　　　　　　　……（ふねより）ひこうきの　ほうが　好きです。
4. タイプライターと　ラジオと、　どっちが　ほしいですか。
   radio　　　　　　　　　　　……（タイプライターより）ラジオの　ほうが　ほしいです。
5. ニューヨークと　サンフランシスコとでは、
   どちらの　ほうが　ふるいですか。
   New York　　　　　　　　　……（サンフランシスコより）ニューヨークの　ほうが
   　　　　　　　　　　　　　　　　　　　　　　　　　　　ふるいです。
6. きみと　ぼくとでは、　どっちの　せいが　たかいですか。
   you　　　　　　　　　　　　……（ぼくより）きみの　ほうが　（せいが）　たかいです。
7. ゴルフと　テニスと、　どちらが　さかんですか。
   golf　　　　　　　　　　　……（テニスより）ゴルフの　ほうが　さかんです。

10.7.13　E-J Response Drill

1. 習った　外国語の　中で、どれが　一番
   やさしかったですか。
   French　　　　　　　　　　　……　フランス語が　一番　やさしかったです。
2. 日本の　四つの　島の　中で、どの　島が
   一番　ひろいですか。
   Honshū　　　　　　　　　　……　本州が　一番　ひろいです。
3. はると　なつと　あきでは、どの　きせつが
   一番　好きですか。
   autumn　　　　　　　　　　……　あきが　一番　好きです。
4. あなたが　かった　本の　中で、どれが
   一番　あたらしいですか。
   this one　　　　　　　　　　……　これが　一番　あたらしいです。
5. この　中で、どの　さんこう書の
   せつめいが　一番　くわしいですか。
   this big one　　　　　　　　……　この　大きいのが　一番　くわしいです。

6. バスと　タクシーと　でんしゃとでは、
　　どれが　一番　おそいですか。
　　bus　　　　　　　　　　　　　…… バスが　一番　おそいです。

10.8　EXERCISES

10.8.1　Make an appropriate question that fits each of the following answers:

　1. はい、　バスより　はやいでしょう。

　2. これが　一番　みじかいです。

　3. 青木さんが　一番　せいが　たかいです。

　4. いいえ、　東京は　北海道より　ずっと　むしあついです。

　5. こっちの　ほうが　ふるいでしょう。

　6. いいえ、　わたしの　こたえは　あなたの　こたえほど　よくありません。

10.8.2　Answer the following in Japanese:

　1. きょ年　見た　えいがの　中で、　なにが　一番　おもしろかったですか。

　2. せかいで、　どこへ　一番　行ってみたいですか。

　3. この　教室の　中で、　一番　せいが　たかい　人は　だれですか。

　4. アメリカで、　一番　せまい　州は　どこですか。

　5. うんどうの　中で、　なにが　好きですか。

　6. あなたが　今　一番　ほしい　物は　なんですか。

10.8.3　1. Compare two or three objects in the classroom.　Make questions and answer to these questions.

　　　2. Make comparisons concerning Japan and the United States.

　　　　　e.g.　アメリカは　日本より　ずっと　ひろいです。

10.8.4　Write the underlined *hiragana* in *kanji*:

　1. ひがしアメリカと　にしアメリカとでは　どちらの　ほうが　ふゆ　あたたかいですか。

　2. ときどき　あの　まちへ　かいものに　でかけます。

　3. きたにほんと　みなみにほんを　くらべてください。

　4. ぼくは　いろいろな　うんどうを　しますが、　スキーを　するのが　いちばん
　　　すきです。　にばんめが　スケートです。　そして、　さんばんめが　ボーリングです。

10.8.5   Write the following in *katakana*:

1. Kariforunia   3. Afurika

2. Ajia   4. Arasuka

10.9 SITUATIONAL CONVERSATION

10.9.1   Home town

A Japanese man asks an American where he is from.

The American says he is from California.

The Japanese man says he knows little about California. But he understands that California is one of the richest states in the States with lots of fruit throughout the year.

The American asks where the Japanese man's home is.

The Japanese answers he is from Kyōto, but presently living in Tōkyō. He prefers Kyōto because Kyōto is a much quieter city than Tōkyō although it is much hotter during the summer months.

10.9.2   Compare your home town with your friend's; size, climate, etc.

LESSON 11

11.1 PRESENTATION

－ 料理 －

日本料理は、 あじも いいですが、 いろや かたちも ひじょうに 美しいです。

としよりは、 だいたい、 日本料理が 好きですが、 わかい 人は、 日本料理を 食べるより*1 西洋料理や 中国料理を 食べる 方が 好きです。

11.2 DIALOG

大川 「あ、もう 六時に*2 なりました*2ね。 おそくなりますから、 そろそろ しつれいします。」

小山 「もう そんな 時間ですか*4。 いっしょに 食事しませんか。」

大川 「そうですね……。 いい 所が ありますか。」

小山 「この へんの 食堂の 食べ物は まずいから、 ごちそうは できないけど、 ぼくが 作りますよ。 外で 食べるより 自分で 料理した*5 方が ずっと いいです。」

大川 「でも、 作るのは たいへんでしょう? 外へ 行った*5 方が いいですよ。」

小山 「いえ、 すぐ できます*6。」

大川 「そうですか。 じゃあ、 わたしも 手つだいます。 小山さんは なにを 作るのが 一番 じょうずですか*7。」

小山 「カレーライスや とんかつですね。 にくと やさいが ありますから、 カレーに*8 しましょうか。」

大川 「いいですね。 ぼくは カレーが 大好きです。」

小山 「じゃあ、 カレーを 作りましょう。 でも、 たぶん 大川さんが おもう ほど おいしくありませんよ。」

186

11.3 PATTERN SENTENCES

11.3.1

NM				(Nd)	R
N	R	→	V	(no)	YORI
soto	de		taberU		

NM			Nd	R
PM	→	V	HOO	GA
jibun de		ryoori shiTA		

A	C
ii	desu

"It is better to cook by oneself than to eat out."

11.3.2

NM				Nd	R
Ni	R	→	V	NO	GA
nani	o		tsukurU		

N
ICHIBAN

Na	C		SP
joozu	desu	—	ka

"What do you make [cook] best?"

11.3.3

N	R	→	V	R	→
anata	ga		omoU	HODO	

A	E
oishiku	arimaSEN

"It is not as tasty as you may think it is."

11.4 NOTES

11.4.1 *Nihon ryoori o taberu yori seiyoo ryoori ya Chuugoku ryoori o taberu hoo ga suki desu* means "I like eating western dishes and Chinese dishes better than eating Japanese dishes." The comparative patterns introduced in Note 10.4.6 can be applied to a comparison of two actions instead of two items. The Verbs stating actions to be compared are in the Dictionary form (or TA form) of those Verbs, and, depending upon the Relational following them, the dependent Nominative *no,* that has been introduced in Lesson 6, may occur after the Dictionary form (or TA form). Thus:

Verb 1
(Dictionary form) *(no)* + *yori* + **Verb 2**
(Dictionary form) + *hoo ga* ······

Verb 2
(Dictionary form) + *no wa* + **Verb 1**
(Dictionary form) + *(no) yori* ······

sakana o taberu		niku o taberu	
jibun de tsukuru	yori	tetsudau	hoo ga ii desu
tenisu o suru		boorin'gu o suru	

niku o taberu		sakana o taberu	
tetsudau	no wa	jibun de tsukuru	(no) yori ii desu
boorin'gu o suru		tenisu o suru	

"it is better to { eat meat / help / bowl } than to { eat fish" / make by oneself" / play tennis" }

Koyama san wa doitsugo o hanasu yori furan'sugo o hanasu hoo ga joozu desu.

"Mr. Koyama can speak French better than German."

Tegami wa roomaji de kaku yori hiragana de kaku hoo ga zutto muzukashii desu nee.

"Writing a letter in *hiragana* is far more difficult (to me) than writing in *rōmaji*."

Biiru o nomu yori osake o nomu hoo ga ii desu.

"I prefer drinking *sake* to drinking beer."

A comparative question is formulated as follows:

Verb 1
(Dictionary form) + *no to* + **Verb 2**
(Dictionary form) + *no to* { *(de),* / *(de wa),* }

dochira (no hoo) / *dotchi (no hoo)* } *ga* + { **Adjective** / **adjectival Nominative** } *desu ka?*

A reply to the above question is made in one of the following ways:

Verb 1 (Dictionary form) + *hoo ga* ······ *desu*

Verb 1 (Dictionary form) + *hoo ga* + **Verb 2 (Dictionary form)** + *yori* ······ *desu*

    or **Verb 2 (Dictionary form)** + *yori* + **Verb 1 (Dictionary form)** + *hoo ga* ······ *desu*

Verb 1 (Dictionary form) + *no ga* ······ *desu*

Kabuki o miru no to Nihon no eiga o miru no to de wa, dotchi ga ii desu ka?	"Which do you like better, to see *kabuki* or a Japanese movie?"
Kabuki o miru hoo ga (Nihon no eiga o miru yori) ii desu.	"I prefer seeing *kabuki* (to seeing a Japanese movie)."
Kyooto o ken'butsu suru no to Nikkoo o ken'butsu suru no to, dochira ga omoshiroi desu ka?	"Which is more interesting, to see Kyōto or to see Nikkō?"
Kyooto o ken'butsu suru hoo ga omoshiroi desu.	"It is more interesting to see Kyōto."
Kareeraisu o tsukuru no to ton'katsu o tsukuru no to, dotchi ga hayai desu ka?	"Which is faster, to make curry and rice or pork cutlet?"
Ton'katsu o tsukuru no ga hayai desu.	"It is faster to make pork cutlet."

11.4.2 *Rokuji ni narimashita* means "it got to be six o'clock." *Narimasu* is an intransitive Verb meaning "become," "get to be," "come to be," etc. In the structure "Nominative 1 becomes Nominative 2," Nominative 2 is always followed by the goal Relational *ni*. This is also true to an adjectival Nominative.

Nominative 1 + $\begin{Bmatrix} wa \\ ga \end{Bmatrix}$ + **Nominative 2** + *ni* + *narimasu*

sen'sei		"become a teacher"
rokuji		"get to be six o'clock"
natsu		"become summer"
hatachi		"will be twenty years old"
kirei	ni narimasu	"become pretty or clean"
gen'ki		"recover; get well"
shizuka		"become quiet"
hima		"become free"
suki		"come to like"

Rainen boku wa hatachi ni narimasu may be translated as "I will be twenty years old next year." When a change is referred to, the future form of English "will be" may be expressed by using *narimasu*. Note that *narimasu* is not always equivalent to English "become."

Watakushi wa rainen nihon'go no sen'sei ni narimasu.	"I will become a Japanese teacher next year."
Ashita wa kitto hima ni narimasu.	"I will be free tomorrow, for sure."

Kono mise wa mae, kissaten deshita ga, hon'ya ni narimashita.	"This shop was a coffee shop before, but it became [changed to] a book store."
Kodomo wa byooki deshita keredo, gen'ki ni narimashita.	"The child was sick, but he got well."
Ton'katsu wa mae suki ja arimasen deshita ga, ima wa suki ni narimashita.	"I did not like pork cutlet before, but I came to like it."
Watakushi wa rainen Meriiran'do Daigaku no gakusei ni narimasu.	"I'll be a student at the University of Maryland next year."
Musuko wa isha ni narimasen deshita.	"My son didn't become a physician."

11.4.3 *Osoku narimasu* means "It is getting late," o· "It will become late." When an Adjective precedes *narimasu,* the Adjective is always in the KU form and the combination means "become such and such," "get to be such and such," "come to be such and such," etc.

Note that a Nominative is always followed by the Relational *ni* before *narimasu* while an Adjective is in the KU form before *narimasu.*

Nominative + *wa* + Adjective(*-ku*) + *narimasu*

atsuku		"become hot"
yasuku		"become inexpensive"
furuku	narimasu	"(things) get old"
ookiku		"will be larger"
hayaku		"become faster or earlier"
hoshiku		"come to want"

Natsu, kono heya wa totemo atsuku narimasu.	"This room gets very hot in summer."
Ten'ki ga yoku narimasen deshita kara, ohanami ni ikimasen deshita.	"The weather didn't get better, so I didn't go flower viewing."
Nihon'go no ben'kyoo ga omoshiroku narimashita.	"I have come to find more interest in studying Japanese."
Kono koohii wa tsumetaku narimashita kara, atsui no o kudasai.	"This coffee has become cold, so please give me a hotter one."
Sen'shuu seetaa o kaimashita ga, mata atarashii no ga hoshiku narimashita.	"I bought a sweater last week, but I got to wanting a new one again."

11.4.4 *Moo son'na jikan desu ka?* is often used as an expression equivalent to "Is it so late now?" or "Is the time up already?" This expression shows a surprise about time's passing fast. *Kon'na jikan* may also occur in the expression.

Ohirugohan desu yo.	"It's lunch."

Moo son'na jikan desu ka?	"Is it already time for lunch?"
Hachiji desu kara, isoide kudasai.	"It's eight o'clock, so please hurry."
E! Moo son'na jikan desu ka?	"My! Is it so late now?"

11.4.5 *Jibun de ryoori shita hoo ga zutto ii desu* means "It would be much better to cook by myself (than to eat out)." The Dictionary form of a Verb before *hoo ga* (*ii*) is substitutable with the TA form of the Verb (see 11.4.1). The use of the TA form makes the statement more realistic, or more emphatic.

Kotae wa roomaji de kaku hoo ga hayai desu.	"It is faster to write the answer in *rōmaji*."
Kotae wa roomaji de kaita hoo ga hayai desu.	"It is faster if you write the answer in *rōmaji*."

When the TA form of a Verb precedes *hoo ga ii,* and the statement is addressed to the hearer, the statement is normally that of advice or suggestion to the hearer and corresponds to "you'd better do such and such."

Verb(*-ta*) + *hoo ga ii* (*desu yo*)

Uchi e kaetta hoo ga ii desu yo.	"You'd better go home."
Koohii yori Kokakoora o non'da hoo ga ii desu.	"You'd better drink Coke rather than coffee."
Koyama san, isoida hoo ga ii desu yo.	"Mr. Koyama, you'd better hurry."

11.4.6 *Sugu dekimasu yo* here means "It will be ready soon." The Verb *dekimasu* has a meaning of "is ready," "is done," "is made," etc.

Gohan wa nan'ji ni dekimasu ka?	"What time will the meal be ready?"
Watakushi no rein'kooto wa dekite imasu ka? (said to a laundry man)	"Is my raincoat ready?"

11.4.7 The superlative pattern has been introduced in Lesson 10. When three or more actions instead of items are to be compared, the Dictionary form (or TA form) of a Verb followed by the dependent Nominative *no* will take the place of Nominatives representing items to be compared.

Dictionary form of Verb + *no* + {*wa* / *ga*} + *ichiban* + {Adjective / adjectival Nominative} *desu*

gitaa o hiku
tenisu o suru   } no {wa / ga} ichiban {tanoshii desu / omoshiroi desu / suki desu
kodomo to hanasu

"playing a guitar
"playing tennis   } is the most {enjoyable" / interesting" / favorable"
"talking with children

Seiyoo ryoori o tsukuru no wa ichiban muzukashii desu.

"To cook western food is the most difficult."

Watakushi wa yuumei na kooen o ken'butsu suru no ga ichiban suki desu.

"It is my favorite pastime to visit famous parks."

When several actions are given for choice, a question is formulated as follows:

Verb 1 + *no to* + **Verb 2** + *no to* + ... **Verb N** *no (to) de (wa)*, *dore ga ichiban* .... *ka?*

"of Verb 1, Verb 2, ... Verb N, which is the most ....?"

In the above pattern, Verb 1, Verb 2, ... Verb N are all in the Dictionary form (or TA form).

Nihon'go o kaku no to yomu no to kiku no to, dore ga ichiban { yasashii desu / joozu desu / suki desu } ka?

"of writing, reading, and understanding Japanese, which { is the easiest?" / are you the best at?" / do you like best?" }

Gitaa o hiku no to baiorin o hiku no to piano o hiku no to de wa, dore ga ichiban joozu desu ka?

"Which are you the most proficient in, playing a guitar, a violin, or a piano?"

Juudoo o narau no to karate o narau no to tenisu o narau no to de, dore ga ichiban muzukashii desu ka?

"Which is the most difficult, learning *jūdō*, *karate*, or tennis?"

Nikkoo e iku no to Kyooto o ken'butsu suru no to kabuki o miru no to de wa, dore ga ichiban ii desu ka?

"Of going to Nikkō, visiting Kyōto, and seeing *kabuki*, which is the best?"

11.4.8 *Karee ni shimashoo ka?* means here "Shall we make it curry and rice?" or "Shall we decide on curry and rice?" The *ni* is the Relational of goal and is followed by the transitive Verb *shimasu* "make." In the complete pattern of "make Nominative 1 into Nominative 2," Nominative 1 is followed by the Relational *o* and Nominative 2 is followed by the goal Relational *ni*. Nominative 2 may be an adjectival Nominative.

Nominative 1 + *o* + **Nominative 2** + *ni* + *shimasu*

musume		isha		"make my daughter a doctor"
musuko		sen'sei		"make my son a teacher"
kodomo	o	yuumei	ni shimasu	"make my child famous"
heya		kirei		"clean the room"
nooto		dame		"damage the notebook"
un'doo		sakan		"make sport popular"

Musuko o gun'jin ni shimashita.	"I made my son a career soldier."
Musume o isha ni shimasu.	"I will make my daughter a doctor."
Kyooshitsu o kirei ni shimashoo.	"Let's clean the classroom."

In the meaning of "making a choice," (e.g. in deciding on what dish you are going to order in a restaurant or setting the date of a meeting, etc.), *o* seldom occurs and *ni shimasu* will be usually equivalent to "I'll have (beefsteak)," or "We'll make it (Tuesday)."

Nani o tabemashoo ka?	"What shall we eat?"
Boku wa bifuteki ni shimasu.	"I will have beefsteak."
Kitanakatta kara, kokuban o kirei ni shimashita.	"I cleaned the blackboard because it was dirty."
Urusai desu nee. Shizuka ni shite kudasai.	"It is noisy. Please be quiet. [lit. Please make yourself quiet.]"

Note that the pattern N1 *o* N2 *ni shimasu* and the pattern N1 *wa* N2 *ni narimasu* form a contrast.

Compare the following:

Watakushi wa musuko o isha ni shimashita.	"I made my son a physician."
Musuko wa isha ni narimashita.	"My son became a physician."
Minoru wa heya o kirei ni shimashita.	"Minoru cleaned up the room."
Heya wa kirei ni narimashita.	"The room became clean."
Isha wa kodomo o gen'ki ni shimasu.	"A medical doctor makes a child get healthy."
Kodomo wa gen'ki ni narimasu.	"The child will get well."
Hayashi sen'sei wa kono daigaku o yuumei ni shimashita.	"Professor Hayashi made this college famous."
Kono daigaku wa yuumei ni narimashita.	"This college became famous."

When an Adjective precedes the Verb *shimasu* "make," the Adjective is in the KU form and the thing or person that is made in a certain state is followed by the Relational *o*.

Nominative + *o* + Adjective(-*ku*) + *shimasu*

oishiku atsuku nagaku osoku yasashiku } shimasu	"make (something)	{ tasty" hot" "heat" long" "lengthen" slow; late" "slow down" easy"

Compare the following:

Ryoori o oishiku shimasu.	"I will make the food tasty."

Ryoori ga oishiku narimasu.   "The food will be made tasty."

Koocha o atsuku shimashoo.   "I'll make black tea hotter."

Koocha ga atsuku narimashita.   "The black tea got hotter."

Shiken o muzukashiku shimashita.   "I made the exam difficult."

Shiken ga muzukashiku narimashita.   "The exam became difficult."

Kono tatemono o ookiku shimasu.   "They'll enlarge that building."

Kono tatemono wa ookiku
   narimashita yo.   "That building became larger."

11.4.9   *Ookawa san ga omou hodo oishiku arimasen* means "(my curry and rice) won't be as good as Mr. Ōkawa may think." The negative comparison introduced in Note 10.4.10 may be applied to comparing two actions.

$$\text{Verb 1 (Dictionary form)} + no\ wa + \text{Verb 2 (Dictionary form)} + hodo + \text{negative Predicate}$$

kaku
tsukuru   } no wa { yomu
isha ni naru   miru   } hodo { yasashiku arimasen
                            anata ga omou   omoshiroku arimasen
                            haha ga iu*   suki de wa arimasen
                                                         taihen de wa arimasen

"writing
"making   } is not as { easy
"becoming a physician   interesting   } as { reading"
                                 favorable   watching"
                                 hard   you may think"
                                                          my mother says"

* The Dictionary form of the Verb *iimasu* "say" is written *iu* but pronounced *yuu*.

Kyooto wa anata ga omou hodo
   atsuku arimasen yo.   "It is not so hot in Kyōto as you may think."

Nihon'go o hanasu no wa kiku
   hodo yasashiku arimasen.   "It is not as easy to speak Japanese as it is to hear
                                                            and understand it."

Boku no eigo wa kimi ga omou
   hodo joozu ja arimasen.   "My English is not so good as you think."

11.5   VOCABULARY

Presentation

料理 (りょうり)	ryoori	....	N	cooking; dish; food
あじ	aji	....	N	taste; flavor
いろ	iro	....	N	color

194

かたち	katachi	....	N	shape; form; appearance
ひじょうに	hijoo ni	....	Adv.	extremely
としより	toshiyori	....	N	old folks; aged person
わかい	wakai	....	A	is young
西洋	seiyoo	....	N	Western (countries); the Occident (cf. *tooyoo* "Eastern (countries); the Orient")

Dialog

大川	Ookawa	....	N	family name
に	ni	....	R	goal Relational (see 11.4.2)
なりました	narimashita	....	V	became (TA form of *narimasu ← naru*)
食事しません	shokuji shimasen	....	V	do not have a meal; do not dine (negative of *shokuji (o) shimasu ← shokuji (o) suru*)
ごちそう	gochisoo	....	N	feast; treat
ごちそうします	gochisoo shimasu	....	V	treat (one to something to eat or drink) (normal form of *gochisoo (o) suru*)
作ります	tsukurimasu	....	V	make; create; prepare; cook (normal form of *tsukuru*)
自分で	jibun de	....	PM	by oneself; for oneself
料理した	ryoori shita	....	V	cooked (TA form of *ryoori suru*)
できます	dekimasu	....	V	is ready; is done; is made (normal form of *dekiru*) (see 11.4.6)
手つだいます	tetsudaimasu	....	V	help; assist (a person to do something) (normal form of *tetsudau*)
カレーライス	kareeraisu	....	N	curry and rice
とんかつ	ton'katsu	....	N	pork cutlet
にく	niku	....	N	meat
やさい	yasai	....	N	vegetables
しましょう	shimashoo	....	V	let's make (OO form of *shimasu ← suru*) (see 11.4.8)
おもう	omou	....	V	think (Dictionary form)

Notes

さかな	sakana	....	N	fish
むすこ	musuko	....	N	son
いしゃ	isha	....	N	medical doctor; physician
いそいで	isoide	....	V	TE form of *isogimasu ← isogu* – hurry
ぐん人	gun'jin	....	N	military personnel
むすめ	musume	....	N	daughter; girl

11.6 KANJI

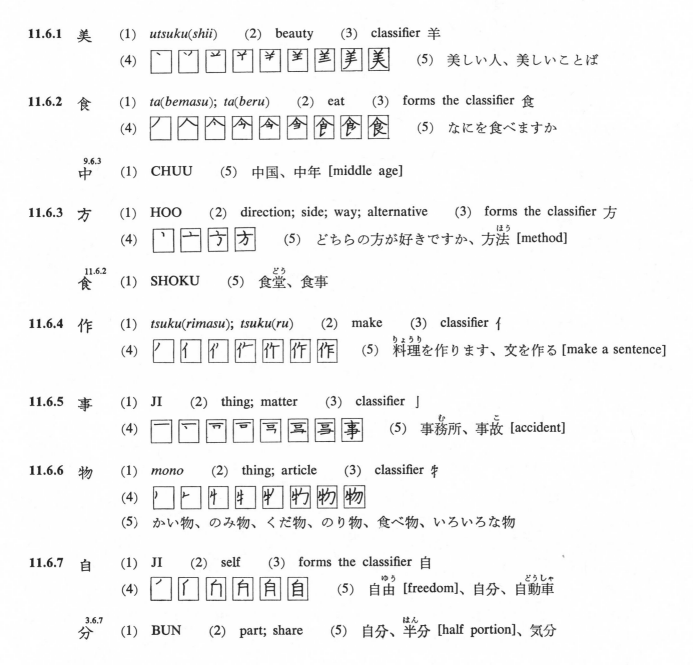

11.6.1 美　(1) *utsuku(shii)*　(2) beauty　(3) classifier 羊
(4) [stroke diagram]　(5) 美しい人、美しいことば

11.6.2 食　(1) *ta(bemasu)*; *ta(beru)*　(2) eat　(3) forms the classifier 食
(4) [stroke diagram]　(5) なにを食べますか

中 (9.6.3)　(1) CHUU　(5) 中国、中年 [middle age]

11.6.3 方　(1) HOO　(2) direction; side; way; alternative　(3) forms the classifier 方
(4) [stroke diagram]　(5) どちらの方が好きですか、方法 [method]

食 (11.6.2)　(1) SHOKU　(5) 食堂、食事

11.6.4 作　(1) *tsuku(rimasu)*; *tsuku(ru)*　(2) make　(3) classifier 亻
(4) [stroke diagram]　(5) 料理を作ります、文を作る [make a sentence]

11.6.5 事　(1) JI　(2) thing; matter　(3) classifier ⅃
(4) [stroke diagram]　(5) 事務所、事故 [accident]

11.6.6 物　(1) *mono*　(2) thing; article　(3) classifier 牜
(4) [stroke diagram]
(5) かい物、のみ物、くだ物、のり物、食べ物、いろいろな物

11.6.7 自　(1) JI　(2) self　(3) forms the classifier 自
(4) [stroke diagram]　(5) 自由 [freedom]、自分、自動車

分 (3.6.7)　(1) BUN　(2) part; share　(5) 自分、半分 [half portion]、気分

11.7 DRILLS

11.7.1 Pattern Drill

1. Wakai hito wa Nihon ryoori o taberu yori seiyoo ryoori ya Chuugoku ryoori o taberu hoo ga suki desu.

2. Soto de taberu yori jibun de ryoori shita hoo ga zutto ii desu.

3. Soto e itta hoo ga ii desu yo.

4. Koyama san wa nani o tsukuru no ga ichiban joozu desu ka?

5. Tabun Ookawa san ga omou hodo oishiku arimasen yo.

11.7.2 Transformation Drill

<u>西洋料理を　食べるより　中国料理を　食べる</u>　方が　好きです。

1. ピアノを　ひきます、ギターを
　　ひきます　　　　　　　　　　　⟶　ピアノを　ひくより、ギターを　ひく　方が
　　　　　　　　　　　　　　　　　　　　好きです。

2. ふねに　のります、ひこうきに　のります⟶　ふねに　のるより　ひこうきに　のる　方が
　　　　　　　　　　　　　　　　　　　　好きです。

3. あさごはんを　作ります、ばんごはんを　⟶　あさごはんを　作るより　ばんごはんを
　　作ります　　　　　　　　　　　　　　　　作る　方が　好きです。

4. 東京に　すみます、京都に　すみます　⟶　東京に　すむより　京都に　すむ　方が　好きです。

5. えいがを　見ます、かぶきを　見ます　⟶　えいがを　見るより　かぶきを　見る　方が
　　　　　　　　　　　　　　　　　　　　　好きです。

6. 図書館で　しらべます、うちで　　　⟶　図書館で　しらべるより　うちで　しらべる
　　しらべます　　　　　　　　　　　　　　方が　好きです。

7. ドイツ語で　はなします、フランス語で　⟶　ドイツ語で　はなすより　フランス語で　はなす
　　はなします　　　　　　　　　　　　　　方が　好きです。

8. ポピュラーを　聞きます、ジャズを　⟶　ポピュラーを　聞くより　ジャズを　聞く　方が
　　聞きます　　　　　　　　　　　　　　好きです。

11.7.3 Transformation Drill

<u>ビールを　のむのは　てんぷらを　食べるより</u>　いいです。

1. 日本語を　はなします、日本語を　⟶　日本語を　はなすのは　日本語を　書くより
　　書きます　　　　　　　　　　　　　　いいです。

2. 東京へ　行きます、京都を　けんぶつ　⟶　東京へ　行くのは　京都を　けんぶつするより
　　します　　　　　　　　　　　　　　　　いいです。

3. 料理を　作ります、外で　食べます　⟶　料理を　作るのは　外で　食べるより　いいです。

4. ぎんこうに　つとめます、デパートで　⟶　ぎんこうに　つとめるのは　デパートで
　　はたらきます　　　　　　　　　　　　　はたらくより　いいです。

5. 本を　読みます、おんがくを　聞きます　⟶　本を　読むのは　おんがくを　聞くより　いい
　　　　　　　　　　　　　　　　　　　　　です。

6. バスに　のります、あるきます　⟶　バスに　のるのは　あるくより　いいです。

11.7.4 Transformation Drill

<u>わたしは　カレーライスを　作るのが　一番</u>　じょうずです。

1. ピアノを　ひきます　⟶　わたしは　ピアノを　ひくのが　一番　じょうずです。

2. 日本語で　はなします　　→　わたしは　日本語で　はなすのが　一番　じょうずです。

3. かん字を　書きます　　→　わたしは　かん字を　書くのが　一番　じょうずです。

4. テニスを　します　　→　わたしは　テニスを　するのが　一番　じょうずです。

5. から手を　します　　→　わたしは　から手を　するのが　一番　じょうずです。

6. フランス語を　読みます　→　わたしは　フランス語を　読むのが　一番　じょうずです。

7. 中国料理を　作ります　→　わたしは　中国料理を　作るのが　一番　じょうずです。

11.7.5　Transformation Drill

1. 手つだいます、　自分で　作ります　　→　手つだうのは　自分で　作るほど　むずかしく
ありません。

2. フランス語を　習います、　日本語を
習います　　→　フランス語を　習うのは　日本語を　習うほど
むずかしくありません。

3. ひらがなで　書きます、　かん字で
書きます　　→　ひらがなで　書くのは　かん字で　書くほど
むずかしくありません。

4. ここから　うちまで　はしります、
ともだちが　おもいます　　→　ここから　うちまで　はしるのは　ともだちが
おもうほど　むずかしくありません。

5. 日本の　しんぶんを　読みます、
小山さんが　いいます　　→　日本の　しんぶんを　読むのは　小山さんが
いうほど　むずかしくありません。

6. 学校の　先生に　なります、　いしゃに
なります　　→　学校の　先生に　なるのは　いしゃに　なるほど
むずかしくありません。

11.7.6　Expansion Drill

1. 好きです。　　……　好きです。
ふねに　のる　方が　　……　ふねに　のる　方が　好きです。
ひこうきに　のるより　　……　ひこうきに　のるより　ふねに　のる　方が　好きです。
いもうとは　　……　いもうとは　ひこうきに　のるより　ふねに　のる　方が
好きです。

2. ずっと　はやいです。　　……　ずっと　はやいです。
ははが　作った　方が　　……　ははが　作った　方が　ずっと　はやいです。
わたしが　作るより　　……　わたしが　作るより　ははが　作った　方が　ずっと
はやいです。
料理は　　……　料理は　わたしが　作るより　ははが　作った　方が　ずっと
はやいです。

3. 一番　じょうずです。　　……　一番　じょうずです。
日本語を　はなすのが　　……　日本語を　はなすのが　一番　じょうずです。
外国語の　中で　　……　外国語の　中で　日本語を　はなすのが　一番　じょうず
です。

スミスさんは	……	スミスさんは 外国語の 中で 日本語を はなすのが 一番 じょうずです。

4. 一番 おそかったです。 …… 一番 おそかったです。

じゅぎょうに 来るのが …… じゅぎょうに 来るのが 一番 おそかったです。

学生の 中で …… 学生の 中で じゅぎょうに 来るのが 一番 おそかった です。

青木(あおき)さんは …… 青木(あおき)さんは 学生の 中で じゅぎょうに 来るのが 一番 おそかったです。

5. やさしくありません。 …… やさしくありません。

森(もり)さんが いうほど …… 森(もり)さんが いうほど やさしくありません。

学校の 先生に なるのは …… 学校の 先生に なるのは 森(もり)さんが いうほど やさしく ありません。

6. たいへんではありません。 …… たいへんではありません。

あなたが おもうほど …… あなたが おもうほど たいへんではありません。

ドイツ語を 習うのは …… ドイツ語を 習うのは あなたが おもうほど たいへんでは ありません。

11.7.7 Response Drill

1. おんがくを 聞くのと 本を 読むのと、
   どっちが 好きですか。

   おんがくを 聞く …… おんがくを 聞く 方が 好きです。

2. ひらがなを 書くのと 読むのと、
   どっちの 方が やさしいですか。

   ひらがなを 読む …… ひらがなを 読む 方が やさしいです。

3. 日曜日(よう)に 行くのと 土曜日(よう)に 行くのと、
   どっちの 方が つごうが いいですか。

   土曜日(よう)に 行く …… 土曜日(よう)に 行く 方が つごうが いいです。

4. 中国料理(りょうり)を 作るのと 西洋料理(せいようりょうり)を 作るのと
   日本料理(りょうり)を 作るのとで、 どれが 一番
   たいへんですか。

   日本料理(りょうり)を 作る …… 日本料理(りょうり)を 作るのが 一番 たいへんです。

5. えい語を はなすのと フランス語を はなすのと
   ドイツ語を はなすのとでは、 どれが 一番
   じょうずですか。

   えい語を はなす …… えい語を はなすのが 一番 じょうずです。

6. バスで 来るのと タクシーで 来るのと
でんしゃで 来るのとでは、 どれが 一番
はやいですか。
でんしゃで 来る　　　　　　　　　…… でんしゃで 来るのが 一番 はやいです。

11.7.8　Transformation Drill

A. 1. 西洋料理を 作ります、 中国料理を
作ります
　→ 西洋料理を 作るのは 中国料理を 作るほど
やさしくありません。

2. テニスを します、 ゴルフを
します
　→ テニスを するのは ゴルフを するほど
やさしくありません。

3. 日本語を 習います、 フランス語を
習います
　→ 日本語を 習うのは フランス語を 習うほど
やさしくありません。

4. ひらがなを 書きます、 ローマ字を
書きます
　→ ひらがなを 書くのは ローマ字を 書くほど
やさしくありません。

5. 日本語で はなします、 先生が
おもいます
　→ 日本語で はなすのは 先生が おもうほど
やさしくありません。

B. 1. にくを 食べます、 さかなを
食べます
　→ にくを 食べるのは さかなを 食べるほど
好きじゃありません。

2. 本を 読みます、 おんがくを
聞きます
　→ 本を 読むのは おんがくを 聞くほど
好きじゃありません。

3. えいがを 見ます、 テレビを
見ます
　→ えいがを 見るのは テレビを 見るほど
好きじゃありません。

4. べんきょうを します、 青木さんが
おもいます
　→ べんきょうを するのは 青木さんが
おもうほど 好きじゃありません。

5. かい物を します、 あなたが
いいます
　→ かい物を するのは あなたが いうほど
好きじゃありません。

11.7.9　Transformation Drill

1. もう 六時です。　　　　　　　　→ もう 六時に なりました。

2. とても げん気です。　　　　　　→ とても げん気に なりました。

3. うんどうが さかんです。　　　　→ うんどうが さかんに なりました。

4. 林さんは 先生です。　　　　　　→ 林さんは 先生に なりました。

5. むすめは きれいです。　　　　　→ むすめは きれいに なりました。

6. 井上先生は ゆうめいです。　　　→ 井上先生は ゆうめいに なりました。

7. おとうとが びょう気です。　　　→ おとうとが びょう気に なりました。

8. すきやきが 大好きです。　　　　→ すきやきが 大好きに なりました。

9. ともだちは いしゃです。　　　　→ ともだちは いしゃに なりました。

10. 教室は しずかです。　　　　　　→ 教室は しずかに なりました。

200

11.7.10 Transformation Drill

1. きょうは　天気が　わるいです。 ⟶ きょうは　天気が　わるくなりました。
2. 一郎くんは　せいが　たかいです。 ⟶ 一郎くんは　せいが　たかくなりました。
3. みち子さんは　美しいです。 ⟶ みち子さんは　美しくなりました。
4. とても　むしあついですね。 ⟶ とても　むしあつくなりましたね。
5. 子どもたちは　かわいいです。 ⟶ 子どもたちは　かわいくなりました。
6. この　辞書は　ふるいです。 ⟶ この　辞書は　ふるくなりました。
7. こんしゅうは　いそがしいです。 ⟶ こんしゅうは　いそがしくなりました。
8. しけんが　むずかしいです。 ⟶ しけんが　むずかしくなりました。
9. 日本語の　べんきょうが　おもしろい ⟶ 日本語の　べんきょうが　おもしろく
　　です。 　　なりました。

11.7.11 Transformation Drill

1. しけんは　やさしいです。 ⟶ しけんを　やさしくします。
2. 教室は　きれいです。 ⟶ 教室を　きれいに　します。
3. せつめいは　くわしいです。 ⟶ せつめいを　くわしくします。
4. しゅくだいは　おおいです。 ⟶ しゅくだいを　おおくします。
5. 子どもの　へやは　ひろいです。 ⟶ 子どもの　へやを　ひろくします。
6. コーヒーは　あついです。 ⟶ コーヒーを　あつくします。

11.7.12 Transformation Drill

1. 日本語が　じょうずです。 ⟶ 日本語が　じょうずに　なりました。
2. しごとが　いそがしいです。 ⟶ しごとが　いそがしくなりました。
3. 教科書が　あたらしいです。 ⟶ 教科書が　あたらしくなりました。
4. 森さんは　大学の　先生です。 ⟶ 森さんは　大学の　先生に　なりました。
5. デパートが　きれいです。 ⟶ デパートが　きれいに　なりました。
6. わたしの　ともだちは　いしゃです。 ⟶ わたしの　ともだちは　いしゃに　なりました。

11.7.13 Response Drill

1. ばんごはんは　なんに　しましたか。

　　ビフテキ　　　　　　　……　（ばんごはんは）　ビフテキに　しました。
　　さかな　　　　　　　　……　（ばんごはんは）　さかなに　しました。
　　中国料理　　　　　　　……　（ばんごはんは）　中国料理に　しました。
　　あたたかい　料理　　　……　（ばんごはんは）　あたたかい　料理に　しました。
　　あなたが　好きな　食べ物　……　（ばんごはんは）　あなたが　好きな　食べ物に　しました。

2. りょこうに 行くのは いつに しますか。
　 らいしゅうの 木曜日　　…… （りょこうに 行くのは）らいしゅうの 木曜日に します。
　 四月　　　　　　　　　…… （りょこうに 行くのは）四月に します。
　 らい年の あき　　　　　…… （りょこうに 行くのは）らい年の あきに します。
　 あしたの ごご 三時　　　…… （りょこうに 行くのは）あしたの ごご 三時に します。

3. けんぶつする 所は どこに しましょうか。
　 京都　　　　　　　　　…… （けんぶつする 所は）京都に しましょう。
　 じんじゃか おてら　　　…… （けんぶつする 所は）じんじゃか おてらに しましょう。
　 しずかな 町　　　　　　…… （けんぶつする 所は）しずかな 町に しましょう。
　 ちかい 所　　　　　　　…… （けんぶつする 所は）ちかい 所に しましょう。

11.7.14　E-J Expansion Drill

1. いいです。　　　　　　　　　　　　…… いいです。
　 it's better to eat at home　　　　　　…… うちで 食べる 方が いいです。
　 than to eat out　　　　　　　　　　…… 外で 食べるより うちで 食べる 方が いいです。

2. おもしろいです。　　　　　　　　　…… おもしろいです。
　 preparing by oneself is more interesting　…… 自分で 作る 方が おもしろいです。
　 than helping　　　　　　　　　　　…… 手つだうより 自分で 作る 方が おもしろいです。
　 as for cooking　　　　　　　　　　…… 料理は 手つだうより 自分で 作る 方が おもしろいです。

3. 好きです。　　　　　　　　　　　　…… 好きです。
　 I like to listen to jazz best　　　　　…… ジャズを 聞くのが 一番 好きです。
　 among various kinds of music　　　　…… いろいろな おんがくの 中で ジャズを 聞くのが 一番 好きです。

4. たのしいです。　　　　　　　　　　…… たのしいです。
　 talking with Paul is the most enjoyable　…… ポールさんと はなすのが 一番 たのしいです。
　 of Paul, Michiko, and Ikuo　　　　　…… ポールさんと みち子さんと いくおさんとでは、ポールさんと はなすのが 一番 たのしいです。

11.7.15　E-J Substitution Drill

いもうとは 先生に なりました。
1. a college student　　　　　…… いもうとは 大学生に なりました。

202

2. big   …… いもうとは　大きくなりました。

3. pretty   …… いもうとは　きれいに　なりました。

4. healthy   …… いもうとは　げん気に　なりました。

5. a junior student   …… いもうとは　三年生に　なりました。

6. famous   …… いもうとは　ゆうめいに　なりました。

7. a librarian   …… いもうとは　図書館員に　なりました。

8. busy   …… いもうとは　いそがしくなりました。

11.7.16　E-J Substitution Drill

へやを　あたたかくしました。

1. wide   …… へやを　ひろくしました。

2. small (narrow)   …… へやを　せまくしました。

3. cool   …… へやを　すずしくしました。

4. clean   …… へやを　きれいに　しました。

5. dirty   …… へやを　きたなくしました。

6. a dining room   …… へやを　食堂に　しました。

7. new   …… へやを　あたらしくしました。

8. beautiful   …… へやを　美しくしました。

11.8　EXERCISES

11.8.1　Answer the following in Japanese:

1. ここから　図書館へ　行くのと　食堂へ　行くのと、　どっちの　方が　とおいですか。
2. あなたは　なんに　なりたいですか。
3. きのうの　ひるごはんは　なんに　しましたか。
4. おんがくを　聞くのと　本を　読むのとでは、　どっちが　好きですか。
5. らいしゅうの　日曜日に、　えいがへ　行くのと　町へ　食事に　行くのと　うちに
　　いるのとでは、　どれが　一番　いいですか。
6. 自分の　へやを　いつ　きれいに　しましたか。

11.8.2　Express the following ideas in Japanese:

1. I prefer drinking black tea to drinking coffee.
2. I wanted to be (become) a school teacher, but I could not become a teacher.
3. My father wanted to make me a career soldier, but I did not become one.

4. My Japanese is not as good as you may think.

5. You'd better hurry.

6. Mr. Smith speaks Japanese better than any other language.

11.8.3 Insert an appropriate word in each blank using one of the given words:

こと、 ほど、 より、 の中で、 物、 に、 の

1. 日本の　大学では　から手を　する（　）テニスを　する　方が　さかんです。

2. 日本語を　習う（　）は　ポールさんが　おもう（　）やさしくありません。

3. むすこを　ぐん人（　）したかったんですが、　むすこは　いしゃ（　）なりました。

4. 一年生（　）だれが　一番　はしる（　）が　はやいですか。

5. 日本で　どんな（　）を　かいたいですか。

11.8.4 Carry on the following conversation in Japanese:

— At a restaurant —

Yamada: I'll treat you today.

Katō: Thank you.

Yamada: What shall we order?

Katō: Let's see.... I'll have pork cutlet and (boiled) rice.

Yamada: I'll have fish today. I didn't care for fish before, but I've come to like it.

Katō: Will the dishes be ready soon?

Yamada: Are you in a hurry?

Katō: Yes, I am.

Yamada: (To the waitress) Pardon me, please bring one pork cutlet and this dish (pointing at a menu).

Waitress: Yes, sir.

Yamada: Please hurry.

Waitress: Yes. Shall I bring coffee now?

Yamada: Yes, please.

Katō: Please bring mine later.

11.8.5 Write the following underlined *hiragana* in *kanji*:

1. しょくじに　うちへ　かえります。

2. じぶんで　つくる　ほうが　はやいです。

3. うつくしい　しょく堂で　たべた　ほうが　おいしいです。

4. のみもの

11.9 SITUATIONAL CONVERSATION

11.9.1 Dinner

Three friends are discussing what they will have for dinner.
A asks where they should eat: at home, at a restaurant, or at a cafeteria nearby.
B wants to eat at the cafeteria nearby.
C invites A and B to his home. He would like to know what the other two want to eat.
A says he would like to eat *sukiyaki*.
B wants to eat *tempura*.
C decides to cook *sukiyaki* which can be cooked faster than *tempura*.

11.9.2 Father and daughter

A girl wants to become a music instructor.
Her father recommends that she becomes a physician.
The daughter says that she would like to be a music instructor because to become a physician is more difficult than to become a music instructor, and, in addition, it takes more time.
The father then tells the daughter that she'd better take piano lessons.

11.9.3 Conversation at the dinner table.

LESSON 12

— Review —

12.1 PATTERN

12.1.1 Permission and Prohibition

a. Verb

この　はこを　あけて		
えい語で　こたえて		
まどを　しめて	（も）	いいです
そこに　すわって		かまいません
急行に　のって		
いしゃに　なって		
黒板の　そばに　たって		
辞書を　つかって	は	いけません
あとで　手つだって		だめです
そう　おもって		
おとうさんを　つれてきて		
自分で　料理して		
これを　テーラーさんに　わたして		
へやを　きたなくして		

ひらがなで　こたえて		
まどを　あけて		
ここに　すわって		
子どもを　つれていって	（も）	いいですか
料理を　手つだって		かまいませんか
ドアを　しめて		
とんかつを　作って		
しけんを　わたして		

いいえ、	………………………………	は	いけません
	………………………………		だめです

えんぴつを　つかって		
先生に　なって		
ははに　わたして		
ともだちに　あって	は	いけませんか
かぞくを　つれていって		だめですか
しゃしょうに　聞いて		
この　紙に　書いて		
黒板の　前に　たっていて		

いいえ、	……………………………………	いいです
	…………………………………… （も）	かまいません

b. **Adjective**

わかくて		
むしあつくて		
やさいは　ふるくて		
にくは　すくなくて		いいです
のみ物は　まずくて	（も）	かまいません
教室は　ひろくて		
子どもの　へやは　せまくて		
しけんは　ながくて		
せつめいが　みじかくて		いけません
書くのが　おそくて	は	だめです
せいが　ひくくて		
おきる　時間が　はやくて		
学生が　おおくて		

天気が　わるくて		
へやは　せまくて		
せいが　ひくくて		
しけんは　ながくて		いいですか
辞書は　ふるくて	（も）	かまいませんか
おちゃは　つめたくて		
べんきょうする　所が　うるさくて		
来る　時間が　おそくて		

| いいえ、 | ……………………………………
…………………………………… | は | いけません
だめです |

| 教室が　きたなくて
学校が　とおくて
もんだいは　みじかくて
食事が　まずくて
コーヒーが　なくて
にくは　ふるくて
せいが　たかくて | は | いけませんか
だめですか |

| いいえ、 | ……………………………………
…………………………………… | （も） | いいです
かまいません |

c. Copula

| 先生は　外国人
手つだう　人は　大川さん
図書館員は　テーラーさん
のり物は　タクシー
スージーさんの　うしろ | | （も） | いいです
かまいません |
| 教室の　外
食事は　さかな
あさごはんは　にく
かん字が　へた
しごとが　ひま | で | は | いけません
だめです |

| 二年生
女の　人
わかい　いしゃ
あの　まどぐち
あさって
ローマ字
日本語が　へた | で | （も） | いいですか
かまいませんか |

いいえ、　｜……………………　｜で｜は｜いけません
　　　　　｜……………………　｜　　　｜だめです

あの　日本人
この　こたえ
やすい　カメラ
まどの　そば
たて物の　外　　　　　　　　　　　で｜は｜いけませんか
店員^{てんいん}は　みち子さん　　　　　　　　｜だめですか
ひるごはんは　中国料理^{りょうり}
ひらがなが　へた

いいえ、　｜………………　｜で｜（も）｜いいです
　　　　　｜………………　｜　　　　｜かまいません

12.1.2　Negative Imperative

まどを　あけ
しけんを　はじめ
ローマ字で　こたえ
ドアを　しめ
それと　これを　くらべ
そこに　すわら
でんしゃに　のら
食事を　作ら
いしゃに　なら
つくえの　上に　たた
じゅぎょうを　やすま　　　　　ないで｜ください
万年筆^{ひつ}を　つかわ
あなたは　手^てつだわ
そう　おもわ
日本語で　はなさ
あまり　いそが
子どもを　つれてこ
今　料理^{りょうり}し
東京へ　行か
うちへ　かえら

ごちそうし きたなくし		ないで　ください

12.1.3　Superative Expression

a.　Nominative

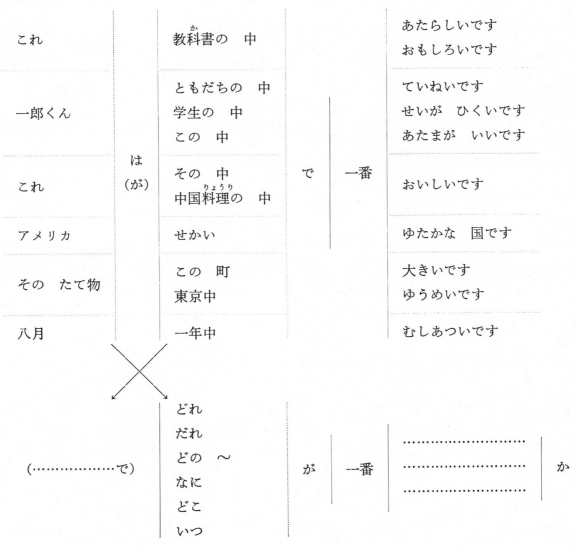

これ	教科書の　中		あたらしいです おもしろいです
一郎くん	ともだちの　中 学生の　中 この　中		ていねいです せいが　ひくいです あたまが　いいです
これ	その　中 中国料理の　中	は (が) ～ で 一番	おいしいです
アメリカ	せかい		ゆたかな　国です
その　たて物	この　町 東京中		大きいです ゆうめいです
八月	一年中		むしあついです

(…………で)	どれ だれ どの　～ なに どこ いつ	が　一番	…………………… …………………… …………………… か

210

ポピュラー		クラシック		ジャズ	
これ		それ		あれ	
にっこう	と	京都	と	なら	の中で、
みち子さん		かず子さん		けい子さん	（と）では、
日曜日		火曜日		木曜日	

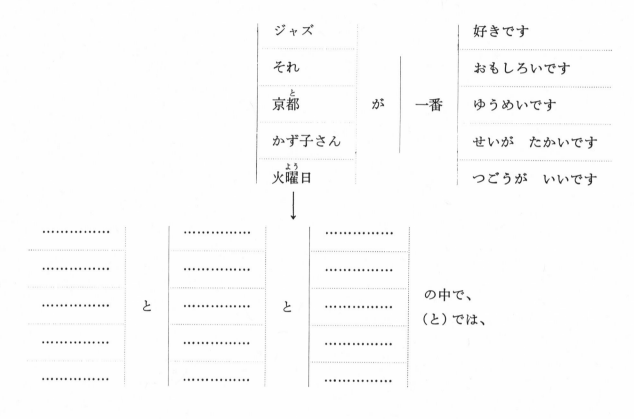

ジャズ			好きです
それ			おもしろいです
京都	が	一番	ゆうめいです
かず子さん			せいが　たかいです
火曜日			つごうが　いいです

↓

………………		………………		………………	
………………		………………		…………	
………………	と	………………	と	…………	の中で、
………………		………………		…………	（と）では、
………………		………………		…………	

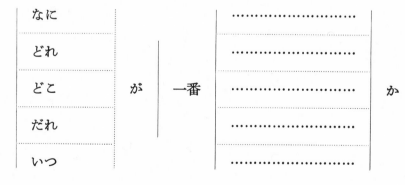

なに			………………………	
どれ			………………………	
どこ	が	一番	………………………	か
だれ			………………………	
いつ			………………………	

b. **Adjective**

c. **Verb**

…………｜ の ｜と｜ ………… ｜ の ｜と｜ ………… ｜ の ｜（と）では、

なにを する				
なにを 作る	の	が	一番	いいです	か
なんに なる				好きです	

12.1.4 Comparative Expression

a. Nominative

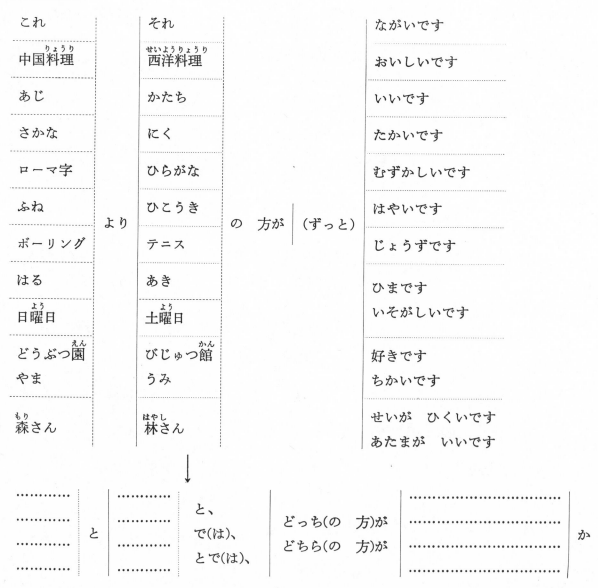

これ	それ	ながいです
中国料理（ちゅうごくりょうり）	西洋料理（せいようりょうり）	おいしいです
あじ	かたち	いいです
さかな	にく	たかいです
ローマ字	ひらがな	むずかしいです
ふね	ひこうき	はやいです
ボーリング	テニス	じょうずです
はる	あき	ひまです
日曜日（にちようび）	土曜日（どようび）	いそがしいです
どうぶつ園（えん）	びじゅつ館（かん）	好きです
やま	うみ	ちかいです
森さん（もり）	林さん（はやし）	せいが ひくいです／あたまが いいです

より　……　の 方が　（ずっと）

………… と ………… と、／で(は)、／とで(は)、　どっち(の 方)が／どちら(の 方)が　………… か

b. Verb

	より		方が（ずっと）	
ローマ字で こたえる		ひらがなで こたえる		むずかしいです
フォークを つかう		はしを つかう		たいへんです
まどを あける		ドアを あける		すずしいです
いしゃに なる		大学の 先生に なる		いいです
東京に すむ		京都に すむ		たのしいです
ぎんこうで はたらく		図書館で はたらく		
うちで まつ		大学で まつ		つごうが いいです
北海道へ 行く		九州へ 行く		好きです
バスで 行く		タクシーに のった		はやいです
たっている		いすに すわった		いいです
ほかの 人が 料理する		あなたが 料理した		じょうずです

```
……………          ……………       と、
……………  の と  ……………  の  では、    どっち（の 方）が   ………………
……………          ……………       とでは、   どちら（の 方）が   ………………   か
                                                              ………………
```

c. "had better"

いそいだ
すぐ うちへ かえった
ぐん人に なった
まどを しめた
しけんを はじめた
三時に また 来た   方が ｜ いいです（よ）
大学で しらべた
東京駅で おりた
あの 先生に あった
自分で 作った

214

12.1.5 Negative Comparison

a. Nominative

京都	この 町	むしあつくありません
カリフォルニア州	ニューヨーク州	さむくありません
この 本は	あなたの 本	おもしろくありません
ぼくの うち	井上さんの うち	大きくありません
うちの いぬ	この いぬ	小さくありません
大川さん	青木さん	美しくありません / わかくありません
この 公園	上野公園	ゆうめいじゃありません
わたしの ことば	林さんの ことば	ていねいではありません
ここの コーヒー	きっさ店の コーヒー	おいしくありません
ラジオ	カメラ	ほしくありません
すきやき	てんぷら	好きじゃありません
日本料理	中国料理	きらいではありません

（は ... ほど）

b. Verb

この 料理	あなたが 作る	おいしくありません
すきやき	てんぷらを 食べる	好きじゃありません
中国語	日本語を 習う	やさしくありません
かん字	ひらがなを 書く	むずかしくありません
ジョージさんの 日本語	みんなが いう	じょうずではありません
わたしの かいわ	ポールさんが おもう	おもしろくありません
東京を けんぶつする	京都を けんぶつする	たのしくありません
ピアノを ひく	ギターを ひく	へたではありません

（は ... の ... ほど）

テニスを　する			スケートを　する		好きではありません
えいがを　見る			テレビを　見る		きらいではありません
しんぶんを　読む	の	は	ざっしを　読む	ほど	むずかしくありません
はしを　つかう			あなたが　おもう		たいへんではありません
日本文学を　しらべる			アメリカ文学を　しらべる		

12.1.6 "become," "get," etc.

わたくし		図書館員		
むすめ		いしゃ		
むすこ		ぐん人		
一郎くん	は	大学生	に	
おとうと	(が)	ゆうめい		
あの　人		きれい		
べんきょう		好き		なります
中国語		じょうず		
せつめい		くわしく		
セーター		たかく		
ぼくの　うち	は	あたらしく		
青木さん	(が)	えらく		
かえる　時間		おそく		
しごと		いそがしく		

....	は	なんに		なりますか
....	(が)	どう		

216

12.1.7 "make"

		に	
むすこ		ぐん人	
むすめ		いしゃ	
子ども		大学の　先生	
あの　人		ともだち	
へや		しずか	
うち	を	るす	します
国	(は)	ゆたか	
うんどう		さかん	
教室（しつ）		ひろく	
サイズ		大きく	
コーヒー		あつく	
とんかつ		おいしく	

		なんに	
…………	を	なんに	しますか
…………	(は)	どう	

12.2　OTHERS

12.2.1　Relational *dake* "only"

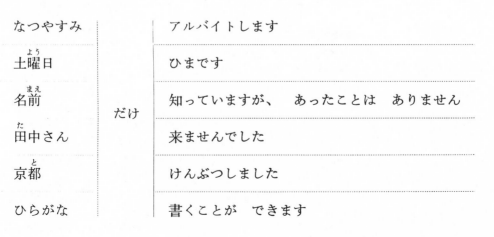

なつやすみ		アルバイトします
土曜日（よう）		ひまです
名前（まえ）	だけ	知っていますが、　あったことは　ありません
田中さん（た）		来ませんでした
京都（と）		けんぶつしました
ひらがな		書くことが　できます

12.2.2 Relational *keredomo* "although"

この　へやは　むしあつい（です）		まどを　あけないでください
しけんは　みじかい（です）		あなたが　おもうほど　やさしくありません
ぼくの　うちは　あたらしくない（です）		とても　いいです
えいがを　見たかった（です）		おかねが　ありませんでした
日本語は　へたです		はなしてもかまいませんか
あの　店は　きれいです		この　店の　方が　しずかです
けさ　天気が　へんでした	けれども、 けれど、 けど、	さんぽに　行きました
これは　おとうとの　本です		つかってもかまいません
一郎くんの　うちへ　行きました		一郎くんは　るすでした
バスは　タクシーほど　はやくありません		バスに　のった　方が　いいですよ
辞書を　見てもいいです		さんこう書を　見てはだめです
ここで　あそんではいけません		にわで　あそんでいいです
これは　この　中で　一番　たかかった（です）		あまり　よくありません
料理は　へたです		ぼくが　ごちそうしますよ

12.2.3 Location Nominative

a.

この その あの		中	が （は）	きたないです
やね		上	に	いました
いす その　はこ	の	うしろ 下	を	見ましたか
テーブル		上	で	書いてください

a.

うち へや		中 外	が (は)	しずかです
つくえ デパート 学校(こう) 教会(きょうかい) 木(き)	の	そば 前(まえ) うしろ	に	あります います たっています
井上さん(いのうえ) あの 木(き)		そば	へ	来てください
図書館(としょかん)		前(まえ) うしろ	まで	あるきましょう

b.

駅 大学 どうぶつ園(えん) デパート おてら ぼくの うち 教科書(か) ノート 紙	の	中 そば 外 前(まえ) うしろ 上 下	の	店(みせ) 食堂(どう) きっさ店(てん) 本や 万年筆(ひつ) 物

c.

上 下	が (は)	きたないです
そば 中	に	います すわりました
うしろ 外	を	きれいに しましょう

前 上	で	書いています
中	へ	はいりましょう
そば 前	まで	行ってみます

12.3 AURAL COMPREHENSION

ポール　　「中村先生。　ぼくは　先生の　学生ではありませんけれど、　先生の　日本文学の
　　　　　　じゅぎょうを　聞いてもいいでしょうか。」

中村先生　「ええ、　いいですよ。　けれど、　うしろの　せきに　すわってください。　黒板の
　　　　　　そばには　すわらないでください。　あまり　よく　できない　学生が　すわります
　　　　　　から………。」

ポール　　「はい、　わかりました。」

中村先生　「わたしの　学生は　ポールくんほど　日本語が　できません。」

ポール　　「そうですか。　ぼくも、　いろいろな　外国語を　習ったことが　ありますが、　日本語が
　　　　　　一番　むずかしかったです。」

中村先生　「そうでしょうね。　あ、　じゅぎょうを　はじめる　時間に　なりました。　いそいだ
　　　　　　方が　いいですね。」

LESSON 13

13.1 PRESENTATION

ー 東京の　みち ー

東京は　人口が　ひじょうに　多いです。　電車や　バスや　地下鉄は　いつも　こんでいます。　自動車、　タクシー、　バス、　トラックなど、　たくさんの　のり物が　せまい　みちを*1　はしっています。

13.2 DIALOG

木村　「田中さん、　すみませんが、　フランス大使館へ　行く　みちを　教えて　ください。」

田中　「フランス大使館なら*2、　よく　知っていますけど、　車に　のって　いきますか*3。」

木村　「とおければ*4、　タクシーか　バスで　行きますけど、　ちかいんでしょう？」

田中　「ちょっと　とおいですよ。　十五番の　バスで　行けば*5、　大使館の　そばに　とまります*6。　二つ目で　おりれば*5、　すぐ　わかりますよ。」

木村　「十五番の　バスですね？　停留所は　どこですか。」

田中　「この　とおりの　二番目の　かどを*1　左へ　まがります。　ほら、　今　あかい*7　自転車が　はしってきますね*3。　あの　かどです。」

木村　「ええ、　わかります。」

田中　「それから、　まっすぐ　五十メートルぐらい　あるいていきます*3。　すると、　右に　しろい　たて物が　あります。　停留所は　その　たて物の　入口の　前です。」

木村　「どうも　ありがとうございました。」

13.3 PATTERN SENTENCES

13.3.1

A	N	R
semai	michi	O

→

V	E
hashitte	imasu

"They are running along the narrow streets."

13.3.2

N	C
Furan'su Taishikan	NARA

,

Adv.
yoku

→

V	E
shitte	imasu

"If it is (about) the French Embassy, I am very familiar with it."

13.3.3

A
tooKEREBA

,

N	R
takushii	de

→

V
ikimasu

"If it is far, I'll go by taxi."

13.3.4

N	R
basu	de

→

V
ikEBA

,

N	R	N	R
taishikan	no	soba	ni

→

V
tomarimasu

"If you go by bus, it will stop near the embassy."

13.4 NOTES

13.4.1 *Semai michi o hashitte imasu* means "It is running along the narrow street." The Relational *o* is used after a place Nominative when a motion takes place through the place. It is often translated as "through (the place)," "along (the street)," "at (the corner)," etc. Note that the Verb following this Relational *o* is not a transitive Verb but a Verb of motion to cover a certain distance or space, such as *arukimasu* "walk," *ikimasu* "go," *magarimasu* "turn," etc.

Gin'za michi	}	o	{	arukimasu hashirimasu	"walk "run	}	along through	{	the Ginza" the street"
eki no mae	}		{	ikimasu kimasu	"go "come	}		{	the front of the station"
kado	}		{	magarimasu	"turn	}	(at)	{	the corner"

Hiroi michi o hashitte imasu.	"It is running on the wide street."
Ichiroo kun ga deguchi no soba o aruite imashita.	"Ichirō was walking near the exit."
Ano kado o magarimashoo.	"Let's turn at that corner."

13.4.2 *Furan'su Taishikan nara, yoku shitte imasu* means "If it is the French Embassy, I know it well." *Nara* is the provisional of the Copula *desu ← da*. The original form of *nara* is *naraba* and it is called the BA form of the Copula *da*. *Nara* occurs before a comma, as a provisional clause, and the clause is equivalent to "if it is the case that or of ...." or "provided that it is true ...." *Nara* may occur after a Verb or an Adjective as well as a Nominative, but only the case of a Nominative preceding *nara* will be dealt with in this lesson. When the subject occurs in the provisional clause, the subject should be followed by the emphatic subject Relational *ga*. (In a dependent clause, the subject is always followed by *ga*.) When the subject of the dependent clause is at the same time the subject of the final clause, the subject may be followed by the Relational *wa*.

(*moshi*) + (**Nominative** + *ga*) + **Nominative** + *nara,* ......

aoi no		"it is the blue one, .."
asatte		"it is the day after tomorrow, .."
anata ga kirai	} *nara, ...*	"if" "you don't like it, .."
setsumei ga tekitoo		"the explanation is adequate, .."

In the provisional clause, the Adverb *moshi* may occur as a signal of a supposition, and it functions to emphasize the provisional or suppositional meaning of the clause.

Doyoobi nara, tsugoo ga ii n desu ga.	"I'll be available if it is Saturday."
Moshi hima nara, issho ni ikimasen ka?	"If you are free, won't you go with us?"
Nihon'go no jugyoo nara, moo owarimashita yo.	"If you are talking about the Japanese lesson, it is already finished."
Kono kuroi kutsu ga nisen'en nara, totemo yasui desu yo.	"If these black shoes cost 2,000 yen, they are very cheap."

The negative provisional expression of a copular Predicate is formed by transforming the plain negative form of the Copula. The plain negative of the Copula is formed replacing *arimasen* in *ja arimasen* by the Extender *nai*. When these are transformed into the BA form, the Relational *wa* in *de wa nai* should always be deleted.

~ ja arimasen ⟶ ~ ja nai ⟶ ~ ja nakereba

~ de wa arimasen ⟶ ~ de (wa) nai ⟶ ~ de nakereba

aki de nakereba	"if it is not fall"
tekitoo na hon ja nakereba	"if it is not an adequate book"
Byooki de nakereba, zehi kite kudasai.	"If you are not sick, please come by all means."

13.4.3   *Kuruma ni notte ikimasu* means "I am going by car." The TE form of Verbs such as *norimasu* "ride," *arukimasu* "walk," *hashirimasu* "run" may be followed by the Extender *ikimasu, kimasu,* or *kaerimasu,* and the combinations mean how one goes, comes, goes back or comes back, etc. They may be translated into various English expressions.

notte		ikimasu	"go		riding"
aruite	·	kimasu	"come		walking"
hashitte		kaerimasu	"go (come) back"		running"

Chikatetsu ni notte ikimasen ka?   "Won't you go by subway?"

Shin'juku Eki kara aruite kimashita.   "I walked here from Shinjuku Station."

Mainichi uchi made hashitte kaerimasu.   "I run home every day."

Hikooki ni notte ikitakatta desu.   "I wanted to go by airplane."

13.4.4   *Tookereba, takushii de ikimasu* means "If it is far, I'll take a taxi." *Tookereba* is the BA form or the provisional form of the Adjective *tooi.* The BA form of an Adjective is formed regularly by replacing *-i* with *-kereba.*

Adjective(-*i*) ⟶ **Adjective(-*kereba*)**

chika*i*		chika*kereba*
hiro*i*	⟶	hiro*kereba*
sema*i*		sema*kereba*
yo*i*		yo*kereba*

Like the provisional clause of the Copula explained in Note 13.4.2, the subject in the clause is followed by the Relational *ga,* and the Adverb *moshi* may occur.

(***moshi***) + (**Nominative** + ***ga***) + **Adjective(-*kereba*)**, ⋯⋯

ten'ki ga yokereba,....	"if the weather is good,...."
eiga ga nagakereba,....	"if the movie is long,...."
uchi ga furukereba,....	"if the house is old,...."
sei ga hikukereba,....	"if he is short,...."
heya ga semakereba,....	"if the room is small,...."

Saizu ga chiisakereba, ookii no o sashiagemasu.   "If the size is small, I'll give you a big(ger) one."

Moshi ten'ki ga warukereba, aruku yori kuruma ni notta hoo ga ii desu ne.   "Provided that the weather is bad, we'd better ride in a car than walk."

Atsukereba, nomimono wa tsumetai mono no hoo ga ii deshoo.   "If it is hot, cold drinks may be preferable."

The negative provisional form of an Adjective "if something is not so" is formed by transforming the plain negative form of an Adjective, which is the combination of the KU form of an Adjective plus the Extender *nai.* The Extender *nai* is the plain equivalent of the Extender *arimasen.* The BA form of the Extender *nai* is formed in the same way as that of Adjectives.

Adjective(-*ku*) + *nai* ⟶ **Adjective(-*ku*) + *nakereba*

shiroku arimasen ⟶ shiroku nai ⟶ shiroku nakereba   "if it is not white"

hikuku arimasen ⟶ hikuku nai ⟶ hikuku nakereba   "if someone is not short"

nagaku arimasen ⟶ nagaku nai ⟶ nagaku nakereba   "if it is not long"

Amari furuku nakereba, kaitai n desu ga.	"If it is not too old, I would like to buy it."
Koohii ga hoshiku nakereba, koocha ka Kokakoora wa doo desu ka?	"If you don't want coffee, how about black tea or a Coke?"

13.4.5 *Basu de ikeba, taishikan no soba ni tomarimasu* means "If you go by bus, the bus will stop near the embassy." *Ikeba* is the BA form or the provisional form of the Verb *iku* and occurs as a non-final Predicate of the provisional clause meaning "if one does such and such, ..."

The BA form of Verbs is constructed in the following ways:

(1) Vowel Verb . . . . . . Stem form plus -*reba*

orimasu/oriru ⟶ orireba
akemasu/akeru ⟶ akereba
dekimasu/dekiru ⟶ dekireba
mimasu/miru ⟶ mireba
oshiemasu/oshieru ⟶ oshiereba

(2) Consonant Verb . . . . . . Base form plus -*eba*

ikimasu/iku ⟶ ikeba
komimasu/komu ⟶ komeba
tomarimasu/tomaru ⟶ tomareba
tachimasu/tatsu ⟶ tateba
kashimasu/kasu ⟶ kaseba

(3) Irregular Verb

shimasu/suru ⟶ sureba
kimasu/kuru ⟶ kureba

(*moshi*) + (**Nominative** + *ga*) + { **Verb(-*reba*),** ⋯⋯⋯ or **Verb(-*eba*),** ⋯⋯⋯

Nihon'go ga wakareba, Nihon o yoku shiru koto ga dekimasu.	"If you understand the Japanese language, you will be able to know Japan better."
Sono kado o magareba, sugu eki desu yo.	"If you turn that corner, the station is right there."
Moshi ame ga fureba, tenisu wa shimasen.	"If it should rain, we are not going to play tennis."

The negative provisional form of a Verb "if one does not do such and such" is made by transforming the plain negative form of the Verb into the BA form of the adjectival Derivative -*nai*.

Pre-Nai form of Verb + -*nai* ——→ Pre-Nai form of Verb + -*nakereba*

ikanai	——→ ikanakereba	"if I don't go"
komanai	——→ komanakereba	"if it doesn't get crowded"
tomaranai	——→ tomaranakereba	"if it doesn't stop"
shinai	——→ shinakereba	"if it doesn't do"
oshienai	——→ oshienakereba	"if you don't teach"

Chikatetsu de iku koto ga dekinakereba, takushii ni notte ikimashoo.　"If we can not go by subway, let's go by taxi."

Ame ga furanakereba, ashita no hoo ga ii desu.　"Tomorrow will be better if it doesn't rain."

13.4.6　*Taishikan no soba ni tomarimasu* is "It stops near the embassy." The Verb *tomarimasu* is an intransitive Verb meaning "stop," or "come to a halt." The place Nominative indicating the place where something stops may be followed by the Relational *ni* or *de*. As explained in Note 9.4.2, *ni* is used when the location is stressed, while *de* is used to emphasize the action. Therefore, when a train or a bus stops at a station or a bus stop, the Relational *ni* will be used.

Koko de tomatte kudasai.　"Please stop here."

Kyuukoo wa kono eki ni tomarimasu ka?　"Does an express stop at this station?"

Basu wa juuji gofun ni kono teiryuujo ni tomarimasu.　"The bus will stop at this bus stop at 10:05."

13.4.7　*Akai* is an Adjective meaning "is red." Here are some Adjectives of color:

akai	"is red"	aoi	"is blue"
shiroi	"is white"	kiiroi*	"is yellow"
kuroi	"is black"	chairoi*	"is brown"

* These Adjectives are derived from Nominatives *kiiro* and *chairo*. Therefore, "is yellow" and "is brown" may be expressed using their adjectival forms *kiiroi (desu)* and *chairoi (desu)* or Nominatives of color *kiiro* and *chairo* plus *desu*.

Akai jidoosha ga hoshii desu.　"I want a red car."

Kutsu wa chairokute mo ii desu ka? (chairo de mo)　"Is it all right if the shoes are brown?"

When the names of color are expressed, *aka, shiro, kuro, ao, kiiro,* and *chairo* stand as Nominatives describing colors.

Aka ga suki desu.　"I like red (color)."

Kinoo katta seetaa no iro wa kiiro desu.　"The color of the sweater I bought yesterday is yellow."

The Nominative for "color" is *iro*, and *don'na iro* or *nani iro* are used to ask "what kind of color?" or "what color?"

Anata no kuruma wa nani iro desu ka?   "What color is your car?"

Don'na iro no kaado deshita ka?   "What color was the card?"

13.5 VOCABULARY

Presentation

みち	michi	....	N	street; road; way
人口	jin'koo	....	N	population
地下鉄	chikatetsu	....	N	subway (lit. underground railway)
こんで	kon'de	....	V	TE form of *komimasu ← komu* – get crowded
トラック	torakku	....	N	truck
を	o	....	R	through; along; at; in; on (see 13.4.1)

Dialog

木村	Kimura	....	N	family name
田中	Tanaka	....	N	family name
大使館	taishikan	....	N	embassy (cf. *taishi* "ambassador")
教えて	oshiete	....	V	TE form of *oshiemasu ← oshieru* – teach; instruct; tell; show
なら	nara	....	C	if it is a ~ (BA form of *desu ← da*) (see 13.4.2)
車	kuruma	....	N	car; automobile
とおければ	tookereba	....	A	if it is far (BA form of *tooi*) (see 13.4.4)
行けば	ikeba	....	V	if one goes (BA form of *iku*) (see 13.4.5)
とまります	tomarimasu	....	V	stop (normal form of *tomaru*) (intransitive Verb) (see 13.4.6)
おりれば	orireba	....	V	if one gets off (BA form of *oriru*)
停留所	teiryuujo	....	N	bus stop; car stop
とおり	toori	....	N	avenue; street
かど	kado	....	N	corner; turn
左	hidari	....	N	left
まがります	magarimasu	....	V	turn (normal form of *magaru*)
ほら	hora	....	SI	look!; there!
あかい	akai	....	A	is red (see 13.4.7)
自転車	jiten'sha	....	N	bicycle
まっすぐ	massugu	....	Adv.	straight
すると	suruto	....	SI	thereupon; and just then
右	migi	....	N	right

しろい	shiroi	.... A	is white
入口 (いり)	iriguchi	.... N	entrance (cf. *deguchi* "exit")
	Notes		
ならば	naraba	 C	(see 13.4.2)
出口	deguchi	.... N	exit
あおい	aoi	.... A	is blue
もし	moshi	.... Adv.	if; provided (see 13.4.2)
くろい	kuroi	.... A	is black
ない	nai	.... E	plain equivalent of *arimasen* (see 13.4.2)
なければ	nakereba	.... E	BA form of *nai* (see 13.4.2)
きいろい	kiiroi	.... A	is yellow
ちゃいろい	chairoi	.... A	is brown
あか	aka	.... N	red
しろ	shiro	.... N	white
くろ	kuro	.... N	black
あお	ao	.... N	blue
きいろ	kiiro	.... N	yellow
ちゃいろ	chairo	.... N	brown

13.6 KANJI

13.6.1 多 (1) *oo(i)* (2) abundant; many (3) classifier 夕

(4) ［丿］［ク］［夕］［夕］［多］［多］ (5) 本が多いです、人口(こう)が多い

13.6.2 電 (1) DEN (2) lightening; electricity (3) classifier 雨(あめ)

(4) ［一］［冂］［冖］［雨］［雨］［雨］［雨］［雫］［雪］［雪］［電］

(5) 電車、電気 [electricity]

13.6.3 車 (1) SHA (2) wheel; vehicle (3) forms the classifier 車

(4) ［一］［冖］［冃］［冐］［百］［亘］［車］ (5) 自動車、電車

13.6.4 動 (1) DOO (2) move (3) classifier 力(ちから) [power]

(4) ［丿］［冖］［冃］［冃］［台］［台］［車］［車］［重］［動］［動］

(5) 動物園(ぶつえん)、自動的(てき) [automatic]、運動(うん)

9.6.2 教 (1) *oshi(emasu); oshi(eru)* (2) teach; instruct; inform; tell

(5) 日本語を教えます、みちを教えてください

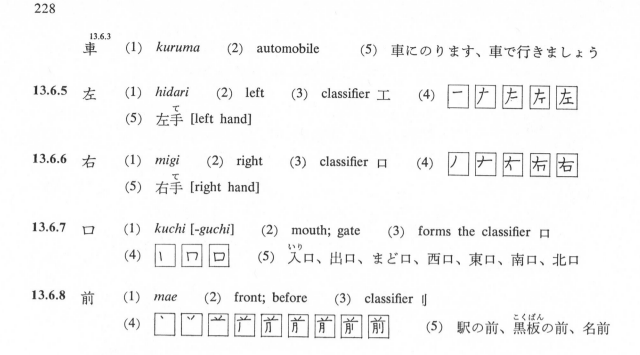

13.6.3 車 (1) *kuruma* (2) automobile (5) 車にのります、車で行きましょう

13.6.5 左 (1) *hidari* (2) left (3) classifier 工 (4) 一 ナ た 右 左
(5) 左手 [left hand]

13.6.6 右 (1) *migi* (2) right (3) classifier 口 (4) ノ ナ 大 右 右
(5) 右手 [right hand]

13.6.7 口 (1) *kuchi* [-*guchi*] (2) mouth; gate (3) forms the classifier 口
(4) 丨 冂 口 (5) 入口、出口、まど口、西口、東口、南口、北口

13.6.8 前 (1) *mae* (2) front; before (3) classifier ⺉
(4) ` ⺍ ⺌ 丷 产 产 前 前 前 (5) 駅の前、黒板の前、名前

13.7 DRILLS

13.7.1 Pattern Drill

1. Jidoosha, takushii, basu, torakku nado, takusan no norimono ga semai michi o hashitte imasu.

2. Furan'su Taishikan nara, yoku shitte imasu kedo, kuruma ni notte ikimasu ka?

3. Tookereba, takushii ka basu de ikimasu kedo, chikai n deshoo?

4. Juugoban no basu de ikeba, taishikan no soba ni tomarimasu.

5. Futatsume de orireba, sugu wakarimasu yo.

6. Kono toori no niban'me no kado o hidari e magarimasu.

13.7.2 Transformation Drill

1. 京都は きれいです。 　⟶　 京都が きれいなら、 いっしょに 行って みましょう。

2. その 店は しずかです。 　⟶　 その 店が しずかなら、 いっしょに 行って みましょう。

3. あなたは ひまです。 　⟶　 あなたが ひまなら、 いっしょに 行って みましょう。

4. ふるい おてらです。 　⟶　 ふるい おてらなら、 いっしょに 行って みましょう。

5. おもしろい えいがです。 　⟶　 おもしろい えいがなら、 いっしょに 行って みましょう。

6. あそこは　ゆうめいです。 　　　 —→　あそこが　ゆうめいなら、　いっしょに　行って
　　　　　　　　　　　　　　　　　　　　　　　みましょう。

7. きれいな　公園です。 　　　　　　 —→　きれいな　公園なら、　いっしょに　行って
　　　　　　　　　　　　　　　　　　　　　　　みましょう。

8. にっこうは　大好きです。 　　　　 —→　にっこうが　大好きなら、　いっしょに　行って
　　　　　　　　　　　　　　　　　　　　　　　みましょう。

13.7.3　Transformation Drill

1. 大使館は　とおいです。 　　　　　 —→　大使館が　とおければ、　行きたくありません。

2. その　えいがは　つまらないです。 —→　その　えいがが　つまらなければ、　行きたく
　　　　　　　　　　　　　　　　　　　　　　ありません。

3. 天気は　わるいです。 　　　　　　 —→　天気が　わるければ、　行きたくありません。

4. 東京は　むしあついです。 　　　　 —→　東京が　むしあつければ、　行きたく
　　　　　　　　　　　　　　　　　　　　　　ありません。

5. へやは　きたないです。 　　　　　 —→　へやが　きたなければ、　行きたくありません。

6. きっさ店は　うるさいです。 　　　 —→　きっさ店が　うるさければ、　行きたく
　　　　　　　　　　　　　　　　　　　　　　ありません。

7. みちが　せまいです。 　　　　　　 —→　みちが　せまければ、　行きたくありません。

8. 時間が　おそいです。 　　　　　　 —→　時間が　おそければ、　行きたくありません。

9. 自転車が　ないです。 　　　　　　 —→　自転車が　なければ、　行きたくありません。

13.7.4　Transformation Drill

1. 十五番の　バスに　のります。 　　 —→　十五番の　バスに　のれば、　すぐ
　　　　　　　　　　　　　　　　　　　　　　わかります。

2. まど口に　行きます。 　　　　　　 —→　まど口に　行けば、　すぐ　わかります。

3. しゃしょうに　聞きます。 　　　　 —→　しゃしょうに　聞けば、　すぐ　わかります。

4. この　本を　読みます。 　　　　　 —→　この　本を　読めば、　すぐ　わかります。

5. うちへ　かえります。 　　　　　　 —→　うちへ　かえれば、　すぐ　わかります。

6. 図書館で　しらべます。 　　　　　 —→　図書館で　しらべれば、　すぐ　わかります。

7. 井上さんに　あいます。 　　　　　 —→　井上さんに　あえば、　すぐ　わかります。

8. 四つ目の　停留所で　おります。 　 —→　四つ目の　停留所で　おりれば、　すぐ
　　　　　　　　　　　　　　　　　　　　　　わかります。

9. ぼくの　うちへ　来ます。 　　　　 —→　ぼくの　うちへ　来れば、　すぐ　わかります。

13.7.5　Transformation Drill

1. カレーライスは　好きじゃありません。 　　　　カレーライスが　好きじゃなければ、
　　作りません。 　　　　　　　　　　　 —→　　　　作りません。

2. びょう気ではありません。　　　　　　　⎫
　　やまへ　行きます。　　　　　　　　　⎬ → びょう気でなければ、　やまへ　行きます。

3. セーターは　きいろではありません。　⎫　　セーターは　きいろでなければ、　ほしく
　　ほしくありません。　　　　　　　　　⎬ →　　　ありません。

4. わかくありません。　　　　　　　　　⎫　　わかくなければ、　から手を　することは
　　から手を　することは　できません。⎬ →　　　できません。

5. おそくありません。　　　　　　　　　⎫
　　あるいていきましょう。　　　　　　　⎬ → おそくなければ、　あるいていきましょう。

6. 地下鉄は　はやくありません。　　　　⎫　　地下鉄が　はやくなければ、　タクシーで
　　タクシーで　行きましょう。　　　　　⎬ →　　　行きましょう。

13.7.6　Transformation Drill

1. バスは　こみません。　　　　　　　　⎫　　バスが　こまなければ、　バスに　のって
　　バスに　のっていきましょう。　　　　⎬ →　　　いきましょう。

2. いそぎません。　　　　　　　　　　　⎫
　　おそくなりますよ。　　　　　　　　　⎬ → いそがなければ、　おそくなりますよ。

3. まい日　日本語を　べんきょうしません。⎫　まい日　日本語を　べんきょうしなければ、
　　じょうずに　なりません。　　　　　　⎬ →　　　じょうずに　なりません。

4. てきとうな　本が　見つかりません。　⎫　　てきとうな　本が　見つからなければ、
　　図書館員に　聞いてください。　　　　⎬ →　　　図書館員に　聞いてください。

5. あした　うちに　いません。　　　　　⎫　　あした　うちに　いなければ、　たぶん　大学に
　　たぶん　大学に　います。　　　　　　⎬ →　　　います。

6. しゅくだいは　ありません。　　　　　⎫　　しゅくだいが　なければ、　自分で　べんきょう
　　自分で　べんきょうしてください。　　⎬ →　　　してください。

7. 林さんは　手つだいません。　　　　　⎫　　林さんが　手つだわなければ、　だれが
　　だれが　手つだいますか。　　　　　　⎬ →　　　手つだいますか。

8. 日本語が　できません。　　　　　　　⎫　　日本語が　できなければ、　えい語で
　　えい語で　はなしてもいいです。　　　⎬ →　　　はなしてもいいです。

13.7.7　Combination Drill

1. 学校の　入口です。　　　　　　　　　⎫
　　あの　かどに　あります。　　　　　　⎬ → 学校の　入口なら、　あの　かどに　あります。

2. 日本語です。　　　　　　　　　　　　⎫　　日本語なら、　テーラーさんが　一番
　　テーラーさんが　一番　じょうずです。⎬ →　　　じょうずです。

3. あの 店は しずかです。
あそこで やすみましょう。
⎫
⎬→
⎭
あの 店が しずかなら、 あそこで
やすみましょう。

4. 天気が わるいです。
うみへ 行きたくありません。
⎫
⎬→
⎭
天気が わるければ、 うみへ 行きたく
ありません。

5. 急行の 方が はやいです。
急行に のっていきましょう。
⎫
⎬→
⎭
急行の 方が はやければ、 急行に のって
いきましょう。

6. ここから あるいていきます。
十分ぐらい かかります。
⎫
⎬→
⎭
ここから あるいていけば、 十分ぐらい
かかります。

7. その かどを まがります。
すぐ わかりますよ。
⎫
⎬→
⎭
その かどを まがれば、 すぐ
わかりますよ。

8. 電車が こみます。
出かけません。
⎫
⎬→
⎭
電車が こめば、 出かけません。

9. ハワイと カリフォルニアを
くらべます。
ハワイの 方が あついでしょう。
⎫
⎬→
⎭
ハワイと カリフォルニアを くらべれば、
ハワイの 方が あついでしょう。

10. まい日 日本語を べんきょうします。
じょうずに なります。
⎫
⎬→
⎭
まい日 日本語を べんきょうすれば、
じょうずに なります。

13.7.8 E-J Substitution Drill

A. コーヒーなら、 ほしいです。

1. if it is a red car ...... あかい 車なら、 ほしいです。
2. if it is a movie ticket ...... えいがの きっぷなら、 ほしいです。
3. if it is a famous thing ...... ゆうめいな 物なら、 ほしいです。
4. if it is curry and rice ...... カレーライスなら、 ほしいです。
5. if it is pretty ...... きれいなら、 ほしいです。
6. if that book is famous ...... その 本が ゆうめいなら、 ほしいです。

B. ちかければ、 タクシーに のっていきます。

1. if it is cold ...... さむければ、 タクシーに のっていきます。
2. if it is inexpensive ...... やすければ、 タクシーに のっていきます。
3. if it is late ...... おそければ、 タクシーに のっていきます。
4. if it is all right ...... よければ、 タクシーに のっていきます。
5. if I'm busy ...... いそがしければ、 タクシーに のっていきます。
6. if the weather is bad ...... 天気が わるければ、 タクシーに のっていきます。
7. if the office is far ...... 事務所が とおければ、 タクシーに のっていきます。

C. この　とおりを　まがれば、　すぐ　わかります。

1. if you walk about three minutes ...... 三分ぐらい　あるけば、　すぐ　わかります。

2. if you speak in Japanese ...... 日本語で　はなせば、　すぐ　わかります。

3. if you ask a train conductor ...... しゃしょうに　聞けば、　すぐ　わかります。

4. if you read a newspaper ...... しんぶんを　読めば、　すぐ　わかります。

5. if you study every day ...... まい日　べんきょうすれば、　すぐ　わかります。

6. if you check it at the library ...... 図書館で　しらべれば、　すぐ　わかります。

7. if you get off at the third stop ...... 三つ目の　停留所で　おりれば、　すぐ　わかります。

13.7.9 Transformation Drill

A. 一等に　のりましょう。　　　　　　⟶　一等に　のっていきましょう。

1. 地下鉄に　のります。　　　　　　⟶　地下鉄に　のっていきます。

2. 出口まで　あるきました。　　　　⟶　出口まで　あるいていきました。

3. 大学の　前まで　はしりました。　⟶　大学の　前まで　はしっていきました。

4. 事務所まで　タクシーに　のりませんか。　⟶　事務所まで　タクシーに　のっていきませんか。

5. 停留所まで　はしりましょう。　　⟶　停留所まで　はしっていきましょう。

B. 天気が　いいから、　あるきます。　⟶　天気が　いいから、　あるいてかえります。

1. まい日　バスに　のります。　　　⟶　まい日　バスに　のってかえります。

2. 大学から　うちまで　はしりました。　⟶　大学から　うちまで　はしってかえりました。

3. うちの　前まで　車に　のりました。　⟶　うちの　前まで　車に　のってかえりました。

4. 公園の　中を　あるきましょう。　⟶　公園の　中を　あるいてかえりましょう。

5. 大使館の　そばを　はしりました。　⟶　大使館の　そばを　はしってかえりました。

C. あの　かどまで　はしりました。　⟶　あの　かどまで　はしってきました。

1. ひこうきに　のります。　　　　　⟶　ひこうきに　のってきます。

2. 三つ目の　停留所まで　あるきましたか。　⟶　三つ目の　停留所まで　あるいてきましたか。

3. その　とおりを　二十メートルぐらい　はしりました。　⟶　その　とおりを　二十メートルぐらい　はしってきました。

4. うちから　事務所まで　あるきます。　⟶　うちから　事務所まで　あるいてきます。

5. タクシーに　のってください。　　⟶　タクシーに　のってきてください。

13.7.10 Substitution Drill

あの　みちを　あるいていきます。

1. この　とおり　　　　　　　　　......　この　とおりを　あるいていきます。

2. あの　たて物の　うしろ　　　　　......　あの　たて物の　うしろを　あるいていきます。

3. その　自動車の　前　　　　　　　......　その　自動車の　前を　あるいていきます。

4. はしってきました　　　　……　その　自動車の　前を　はしってきました。
5. 公園の　中　　　　……　公園の　中を　はしってきました。
6. あの　せまい　みち　　　　……　あの　せまい　みちを　はしってきました。
7. まがってください　　　　……　あの　せまい　みちを　まがってください。
8. 三つ目の　かど　　　　……　三つ目の　かどを　まがってください。

13.7.11　Expansion Drill

1. あるいていきます。　　　　……　あるいていきます。
   五十メートルぐらい　　　　……　五十メートルぐらい　あるいていきます。
   停留所まで　　　　……　停留所まで　五十メートルぐらい　あるいていきます。
   大学の　そばから　　　　……　大学の　そばから　停留所まで　五十メートルぐらい
   　　　　　　あるいていきます。
   まい日、　　　　……　まい日、　大学の　そばから　停留所まで　五十メートル
   　　　　　　ぐらい　あるいていきます。

2. はしってかえりました。　　　　……　はしってかえりました。
   まっすぐ　　　　……　まっすぐ　はしってかえりました。
   うちまで　　　　……　うちまで　まっすぐ　はしってかえりました。
   あの　かどから　　　　……　あの　かどから　うちまで　まっすぐ　はしって
   　　　　　　かえりました。
   ポールと　いっしょに　　　　……　ポールと　いっしょに　あの　かどから　うちまで　まっすぐ
   　　　　　　はしってかえりました。

3. のってきました。　　　　……　のってきました。
   急行に　　　　……　急行に　のってきました。
   大阪から　　　　……　大阪から　急行に　のってきました。
   おととい　　　　……　おととい　大阪から　急行に　のってきました。
   ブラウンさんは　　　　……　ブラウンさんは　おととい　大阪から　急行に　のって
   　　　　　　きました。

4. とまりますか。　　　　……　とまりますか。
   前に　　　　……　前に　とまりますか。
   大使館の　　　　……　大使館の　前に　とまりますか。
   十五番の　バスは　　　　……　十五番の　バスは　大使館の　前に　とまりますか。

5. やすみましょう。　　　　……　やすみましょう。
   あそこで　　　　……　あそこで　やすみましょう。
   しずかなら、　　　　……　しずかなら、　あそこで　やすみましょう。
   あの　きっさ店が　　　　……　あの　きっさ店が　しずかなら、　あそこで　やすみましょう。

6. かいたいです。 ...... かいたいです。

  その さんこう書を ...... その さんこう書を かいたいです。

  くわしければ、 ...... くわしければ、 その さんこう書を かいたいです。

  せつめいが ...... せつめいが くわしければ、 その さんこう書を
                     かいたいです。

7. あります。 ...... あります。

  左に ...... 左に あります。

  その 店は ...... その 店は 左に あります。

  あるいていけば、 ...... あるいていけば、 その 店は 左に あります。

  まっすぐ ...... まっすぐ あるいていけば、 その 店は 左に あります。

  この とおりを ...... この とおりを まっすぐ あるいていけば、 その 店は
                     左に あります。

13.7.12 E-J Response Drill

1. どんな いろの 自動車に のってきましたか。

  in a red car ...... あかい 自動車に のってきました。

2. 東京行の バスは どこに とまりますか。

  near that white building ...... あの しろい たて物の そばに とまります。

3. あおい 車は どこへ 行きましたか。

  turned to the left at the second corner ...... 二つ目の かどを 左へ まがりました。

4. 十五番の バスの 停留所は どこですか。

  in front of the entrance of the department ...... デパートの 入口の 前です。
    store

5. あした うみへ 行きましょうか。

  yes, if the weather is good ...... ええ、 天気が よければ、 （うみへ）
                                       行きましょう。

6. 火曜日に 出かけることが できますか。

  no, if it is Tuesday ...... いいえ、 火曜日なら、 出かけることが
                              できません。

7. タクシーに のっていきますか。

  yes, if the train is crowded ...... はい、 電車が こんでいれば、タクシーに
                                       のっていきます。

13.7.13 Substitution Drill (Review)

1. 大使館へ　行く　みちを　教えてください。

   木村さんが　駅に　つく　時間　　　　…… 木村さんが　駅に　つく　時間を　教えて
   　　　　　　　　　　　　　　　　　　　　　　ください。

2. 電車が　こんでいない　時間　　　　…… 電車が　こんでいない　時間を　教えて
   　　　　　　　　　　　　　　　　　　　　　　ください。

3. この　急行が　とまる　駅　　　　…… この　急行が　とまる　駅を　教えてください。

4. 大阪行が　出る　所　　　　…… 大阪行が　出る　所を　教えてください。

5. 田中先生が　教えている　大学　　　　…… 田中先生が　教えている　大学を　教えて
   　　　　　　　　　　　　　　　　　　　　　　ください。

6. あなたが　行った　びじゅつ館の　名前　…… あなたが　行った　びじゅつ館の　名前を
   　　　　　　　　　　　　　　　　　　　　　　教えてください。

7. かず子さんの　しらべた　もんだい　…… かず子さんの　しらべた　もんだいを
   　　　　　　　　　　　　　　　　　　　　　　教えてください。

8. さんこう書を　かった　本やの　名前　…… さんこう書を　かった　本やの　名前を
   　　　　　　　　　　　　　　　　　　　　　　教えてください。

13.8 EXERCISES

13.8.1 Insert an appropriate Relational in each blank:

1. あかい　自動車(　　)　大使館(　　)　前(　　)　とまりました。

2. せまい　みち(　　)　はしらないでください。

3. 田中さん(　　)　あの　ちゃいろい　たて物(　　)　左(　　)　たっています。

4. 三つ目(　　)　かど(　　)　右(　　)　まがりましょう。

5. バス(　　)　地下鉄(　　)　のってきます。

6. この　とおり(　　)　タクシー(　　)　行けば、　二十分ぐらいです。

13.8.2 Express the following ideas in Japanese:

1. Please turn to the right at the fourth corner.

2. If you go riding on that bus, the embassy is in front of the next stop.

3. If it rains, I won't come.

4. If the coffee is cold, I'll make it hotter.

5. Mr. Tanaka does not come walking down that street. He comes riding a bicycle.

6. Please walk straight about two hundred meters down this street.

236

13.8.3 Direct the way to your home or dormitory from where you are now.

13.8.4 Using the illustration below, tell the way to:

     a. bank   b. the Tanaka residence   c. church   d. bookstore   e. bus stop

13.8.5 Write the following underlined *hiragana* in *kanji*:

1. でんしゃや　じどうしゃが　でぐちの　まえを　はしっています。
2. みぎにも　ひだりにも　くるまが　とまっています。
3. とうきょうは　じん口が　おおいです。
4. みちを　おしえてください。

13.8.6 Write the following in *katakana*:

1. torakku   2. kareeraisu

13.9 SITUATIONAL CONVERSATION

13.9.1 Direction to the U.S. Embassy

A stranger and an employee at the bakery talk about the way to the U.S. Embassy. The stranger
  does not know the direction.
The employee at the bakery gives the directions to the stranger.
The stranger would like to know how long it takes to get there by taxi.
The employee answers that if the stranger goes by taxi, it will take about seven minutes, but it will
  take twenty minutes by bus.

13.9.2 In a taxi

A taxi driver asks where his passenger wants to go.
The passenger says he wants to go to Shinjuku.
Arriving at the Shinjuku district, the passenger directs the driver: turn to the left at the next corner
  and go straight for 300 meters.
The driver says he cannot turn to the left at that corner.
Then the passenger asks the driver to stop in front of a tobacco store near the corner.

13.9.3 Carry on a conversation acting as a taxi driver and his passenger going to a particular destination.

LESSON 14

郵便はがき

日本郵便 7

千代田区　神田　神保町

青木一郎様

二丁目　五番十七号

九月三日

杉並区　荻窪三丁目七六

山本美智子

東京都　新宿区　三光町

3-18-6

木村　実　様

NIPPON 15

七月七日

横浜市　中区　新栄町三六〇

ポール・ブラウン

東京都　千代田区　神田　神保町

二丁目　五番　十七号

青木一郎様

NIPPON 15

–14.1 PRESENTATION

― 山のぼり ―

お元気ですか。

さっそくですが、来月の 一日と 二日、富士山に

のぼるつもりですが、あなたも いらっしゃいませんか。

ぼくの ほかに 山田さんと 石井さんも 行くはずです。

電車の きっぷを 買わなければなりませんから、

今月の 二十八日までに 電話で 返事を くだされば、

つごうが いいんですが。

ぼくの 電話番号は 四五一―五八九二です。

では、よい 返事を 待っています。

さようなら

七月二十四日

木下

パターソン様

14.2 DIALOG

パターソン 「もしもし、 パターソンですが……。」

木下 「あ、 パターソンさん、 待っていました。 いっしょに
いらっしゃいますか。」

パターソン 「ええ、 ぜひ つれていってください。」

木下 「それは よかった。 二十九日に なれば、 くわしい こと^{*8}が わかる
はずです。」

パターソン 「じゃあ、 会う 時間や 場所は あとで 知らせてください。」

木下 「ええ。 山の 上は かなり さむいから、 ぼくは セーターを
持っていくつもりです。 パターソンさんも セーターか ジャンパーを
持っていった 方が いいですよ。」

パターソン 「おべんとうは?」

木下 「出かける 日^{*9}の よるの べんとうは 持っていかなければ
なりませんね。 おかしや くだ物は いっしょに 買いますから、
持ってこなくてもいい^{*5}ですけど……。」

パターソン 「わかりました。」

14.3 PATTERN SENTENCES

14.3.1

NM			Nd	C
N	R	V	TSUMORI	desu
Fujisan	ni →	noborU		

"We are planning to climb Mt. Fuji."

14.3.2

NM				Nd	C
N	R		V	HAZU	desu
Ishii san	mo	→	ikU		

"Mr. Ishii is supposed to go, too."

14.3.3

N	R		V + Da		V
kippu	o	→	kawaNAKEREBA	⟶	NARIMASEN

"We have to buy tickets."

14.4 NOTES

14.4.1 *Sassoku desu ga, ...* "I'll come to the point at once" is often used in telephone conversation or in correspondence. This expression is used frequently in Japanese because many Japanese think it is a lack of courtesy to start talking about the subject without giving sufficient (to the Japanese people's mind) preliminary remarks, such as comments on weather, health, etc.

14.4.2 *Tsuitachi* is "the first day of the month." Here are the days of the month:

1	tsuitachi	11	juu ichinichi	21	nijuu ichinichi
2	futsuka	12	juu ninichi	22	nijuu ninichi
3	mikka	13	juu san'nichi	23	nijuu san'nichi
4	yokka	14	juu yokka	24	nijuu yokka
5	itsuka	15	juu gonichi	25	nijuu gonichi
6	muika	16	juu rokunichi	26	nijuu rokunichi
7	nanoka	17	juu shichinichi	27	nijuu shichinichi
8	yooka	18	juu hachinichi	28	nijuu hachinichi
9	kokonoka	19	juu kunichi	29	nijuu kunichi
10	tooka	20	hatsuka	30	san'juunichi
				31	san'juu ichinichi

The counter for "day" is *-nichi*. Except *tsuitachi,* the above words may be used also for the number of days; *futsuka* can be "the second day of the month," or "two days," *mikka* "the third day," or "three days." *Ichinichi* is used for "a day." *Nan'nichi* can be "what day of the month?" or "how many days?" The *kanji* for *tsuitachi, futsuka, mikka,* etc. are all written 一、二、三、etc., plus 日、regardless of their pronunciation. To tell the date, the year comes first, and then comes the month, and day comes last. If the day of the week occurs, it comes after the day.

一九六七年十二月二十四日
八月五日木曜日

242

Anata no tan'joobi wa itsu desu ka?	"What day is your birthday?"
Juuichigatsu juu san'nichi desu.	"It's November 13."
Kon'getsu no itsuka ni shiken ga arimasu.	"We'll have an exam on the 5th of this month."
Pataason san ga Nihon e kuru hi wa nan'nichi desu ka?	"What day is the day when Mr. Patterson is coming to Japan?"
Nan'nichi gurai Kyooto ni iru tsumori desu ka?	"About how many days are you planning to stay in Kyōto?"

14.4.3 *Fujisan ni noboru tsumori desu* means "I intend to climb Mt. Fuji." The *tsumori* is a dependent Nominative meaning "intention," "will," "plan," etc., and it is always preceded by a Nominative Modifier. The Nominative Modifier preceding *tsumori* can be the Dictionary form of a Verb, or the plain negative form of a Verb. The *tsumori* may be followed by the Copula *desu* or *deshita*. When the *deshita* is used after *tsumori* the context usually implies that a person had the intention of doing such and such in the past but failed to do it. When the sentence of intention is a statement, it is normally the speaker's intention, but it can be that of a second or a third person. *Tsumori* in other structural environment will be introduced in later volumes.

(Predicate Modifier) + Dictionary form of Verb
(Predicate Modifier) + plain negative form of Verb } + *tsumori* + { *desu* / *deshita* }

Fujisan ni noboru
kuni e kaeru
seetaa o kau
den'wa o suru
Nakamura san ni au
umi de oyogu
Fujisan ni noboranai
kuni e kaeranai
seetaa o kawanai
den'wa o shinai
Nakamura san ni awanai
umi de oyoganai
} tsumori { desu / deshita }

"I am planning to" / "I was planning to" / "I am not planning to" / "I wasn't planning to" { "climb Mt. Fuji" / "go home" / "buy a sweater" / "telephone" / "meet Mr. Nakamura" / "swim in the sea" }

Raishuu no nichiyoobi ni doko e iku tsumori desu ka?	"Where do you intend to go next Sunday?"
Kyoo wa gojikan gurai uchi de ben'kyoo suru tsumori deshita ga, dekimasen deshita.	"I was planning to study for about five hours at home today, but I couldn't."
Boku wa kotoshi no natsuyasumi ni kuni e kaeranai tsumori desu.	"I do not intend to go home during this summer vacation."
Kinoo wa dekakenai tsumori deshita ga, chotto rusu ni shimashita.	"I (originally) didn't intend to go out yesterday, but I was out for a while."

14.4.4 *Yamada san mo iku hazu desu* means "Mr. Yamada is supposed to go, too," or "Mr. Yamada is expected to go, too." The *hazu* is a dependent Nominative meaning "expectation," and is always followed by a Nominative Modifier. In general, it indicates the objective "expectation" of the speaker concerning some action, happening, state, etc., outside the speaker's immediate control. In other words, the use of *hazu* does not reflect subjective "guesswork," but rather, reflects some objective understanding on the part of the speaker. The *hazu* is usually used to state the speaker's expectation of someone else's doing such and such or being such and such, but it can also refer to, on some limited occasions, the speaker's own doing or being such and such.

Compare: Watakushi wa Doitsu e iku tsumori desu.
Watakushi wa Doitsu e iku hazu desu.

This pattern of expectation will be often equivalent to "is expected to," "is supposed to," "should (not in the meaning of obligation)," etc. The *hazu* may occur in various structural environments, but only the following will be introduced in this lesson. Not only a Verb but also an Adjective may occur as a Nominative Modifier before *hazu*, while an Adjective usually does not occur before *tsumori*, but only *hazu* with a Verb will be introduced in this lesson.

(Predicate Modifier) + **Dictionary form**
(Predicate Modifier) + **plain negative imperfect form**} of Verb + *hazu* + {*desu* / *deshita*}

(Predicate Modifier) + **TA form**
(Predicate Modifier) + **plain negative perfect form**} of Verb + *hazu* + *desu*

The difference between *iku hazu deshita* and *itta hazu desu* lies in whether the speaker has the expectation at present or had it in the past. *Iku hazu deshita* refers to the expectation that the speaker had in the past, while *itta hazu desu* is the present expectation concerning someone else's having done something. *Iku hazu deshita* means "he was expected to go [but he didn't]," and *itta hazu desu* means "he is supposed to have gone."

Musuko wa rainen isha ni naru hazu desu.	"My son is supposed to be a medical doctor next year."
Kyoo tomodachi ga san'nin uchi e kuru hazu deshita.	"Three friends were expected to come to my house today."
Yamamoto san wa kinoo jugyoo o yasun'da hazu desu.	"Mr. Yamamoto is supposed to have been absent from school yesterday."
Kinoshita san wa Fujisan ni noboranakatta hazu desu yo.	"Mr. Kinoshita supposedly did not climb Mt. Fuji."

14.4.5 *Kawanakereba narimasen* means "I have to buy it." *Kawanakereba* is the BA form of the plain negative of *kau*, namely *kawanai*, and is followed by *narimasen* "it won't do" to form the pattern meaning "obligation," or "necessity." The BA form of the plain negative Adjective, and the BA form of the plain negative Copula may also occur before *narimasen*. The plain negative form of Adjectives and plain negative form of the Copula are formed by replacing the Extender *arimasen* by *nai*.

ookiku arimasen = ookiku na*i* ⟶ ookiku na*kereba*

∼ ja arimasen = ∼ ja na*i* ⟶ ∼ ja na*kereba*

∼ de wa arimasen = ∼ de wa na*i* ⟶ ∼ de* na*kereba*

kaimasen = kawana*i* ⟶ kawana*kereba*

BA form of {**plain negative of Verb** / **plain negative of Adjective** / **plain negative of Copula**} + *narimasen* (*ikemasen*)

Ikemasen "it won't do" is substitutable for *narimasen* in the above pattern and in the pattern of

-te wa ikemasen, although the combinations of -nakereba narimasen and -te wa ikemasen are more commonly used than other combinations.

ikanakereba kakanakereba minakereba			go" write" see"
atsuku nakereba omoshiroku nakereba yoku nakereba	narimasen	"(one) has to "(it)	be hot" be interesting" be good"
∼ ja nakereba ∼ de* nakereba			be such and such"

* As explained in Note 13.4.2, *wa* never occurs here.

The answer to a question *-nakereba narimasen ka?* "Do [I] have to (do) ....?" is expressed by an expression of permission: "it is all right if you don't (do it)" or "you don't have to (do it)" *(shi)nakute mo ii desu.*

Asa goji ni okinakereba narimasen ka?	"Do I have to get up at five in the morning?"
Iie, goji ni okinakute mo ii desu.	"No, you don't have to."
Kinoshita san ni hi o shirasenakute mo ii desu ka?	"Is it unnecessary to inform Mr. Kinoshita of the date?"
Iie, shirasenakereba narimasen yo.	"No, you have to inform him."

14.4.6 *Nijuu hachinichi made ni* means "by the 28th." *Made ni* is a double Relational consisting of the time Relational *made* and another time Relational *ni*, and follows a time Nominative. It means "not later than the time given," or "by the time given."
While *made* means that an action or a state continues till the designated time, *made ni* indicates that an action should be completed by the time.

Juu gonichi made ni repooto o kakimasu.	"I'll write a report by the fifteenth."
Suiyoobi made ni shite kudasai.	"Please do it by Wednesday."
Natsu made ni Nihon e iku tsumori desu.	"I intend to go to Japan by the summer."

14.4.7 In giving a telephone number, one syllable numerals such as *ni, shi, go* are preferrably replaced by *nii, yon, goo,* and *shichi* replaced by *nana* to avoid possible confusions.

ichi, nii, san, yon, goo, roku, nana, hachi, kyuu, juu

Tookyoo nii-yon-ichi no nana-goo-nii-kyuu   Tōkyō 241-7529

14.4.8 *Kuwashii koto* means "detailed matters." In addition to the meaning "act" as a nominalizer, the dependent Nominative *koto* may mean "matter," or "intangible thing," always preceded by a Nominative Modifier. Note the difference between *koto* and *mono* "tangible thing" or "article." Compare:

Omoshiroi koto o kikimashita.   "I heard about an interesting matter."

Omoshiroi mono o mimashita.   "I saw an interesting thing."

anata no		"matters concerning you"
sono	koto	"that matter"
ii		"something good"
wakaranai		"matters that one doesn't understand"

14.4.9 *Hi* is a Nominative meaning "day." Like *jikan* "time" or "hour," *hi* may also be preceded by a Nominative Modifier and mean "the day when something happens," or "such and such day." *Hi* may be followed by various Relationals including the time Relationals such as *ni, made, made ni,* etc.

yuki no		"a snowy day"
sono		"that day"
atsui		"a hot day"
shizuka na	hi	"a quiet day"
gakkoo no owaru		"the day when school will be over"
ame ga futte ita		"the day when it was raining"

Dekakeru hi wa nan'nichi desu ka?   "What day is the day when you leave?"

Yuki no hi ni gakkoo e ikimashita ga, jugyoo wa arimasen deshita.   "I went to school on a snowy day, but there were no classes."

Totemo atsui hi ni Kyooto e ikimashita.   "I went to Kyōto on a very hot day."

Michiko san ga kuru hi wa raishuu no suiyoobi desu.   "The day when Michiko is coming is next Wednesday."

14.5 VOCABULARY

Presentation

山のぼり	yama nobori	....	N	mountain climbing (this may be followed by (*o*) *suru* to form a verbal expression)
一日	tsuitachi	....	N	the first day of the month
二日	futsuka	....	N	the second day of the month; two days
富士山	Fujisan	....	N	Mt. Fuji
のぼる	noboru	....	V	climb; go up (Dictionary form)
つもり	tsumori	....	Nd	intention; planning (see 14.4.3)
いらっしゃいません	irasshaimasen	....	V	do not come; do not go (*irasshaimasu* is polite equivalent of *kimasu* or *ikimasu* and normal form of *irassharu*)
はず	hazu	....	Nd	expected to (do); supposed to (do) (see 14.4.4)
なりません	narimasen	....	V	it won't do (see 14.4.5)
二十八日	nijuu hachinichi	....	N	the twenty-eighth day; twenty-eight days

246

までに	made ni	....	R	by (see 14.4.6)
くだされば	kudasareba	....	V	if one gives (to me) (BA form of *kudasaru*)
番号	ban'goo	....	N	(sequential) number
二十四日	nijuu yokka	....	N	the twenty-fourth day; twenty-four days
木下	Kinoshita	....	N	family name
パターソン	Pataason	....	N	Patterson

Dialog

二十九日	nijuu kunichi	....	N	the twenty-ninth day; twenty-nine days
なれば	nareba	....	V	if it becomes (BA form of *naru*)
こと	koto	....	Nd	matter; thing (intangible) (see 14.4.8)
場所	basho	....	N	place
知らせて	shirasete	....	V	TE form of *shirasemasu* ← *shiraseru* – inform; let one know
かなり	kanari	....	Adv.	quite
ジャンパー	jan'paa	....	N	casual jacket; jumper
べんとう	ben'too	....	N	lunch; meal to take out
日	hi	....	N	day (see 14.4.9)
いかなければ	ikanakereba	....	V	BA form of *ikanai* (see 14.4.5)

Notes

三日	mikka	....	N	the third day of the month; three days
四日	yokka	....	N	the fourth day of the month; four days
五日	itsuka	....	N	the fifth day of the month; five days
六日	muika	....	N	the sixth day of the month; six days
七日	nanoka	....	N	the seventh day of the month; seven days
八日	yooka	....	N	the eighth day of the month; eight days
九日	kokonoka	....	N	the ninth day of the month; nine days
十日	tooka	....	N	the tenth day of the month; ten days
十四日	juu yokka	....	N	the fourteenth day of the month; fourteen days
二十日	hatsuka	....	N	the twentieth day of the month; twenty days
日	-nichi	....	Nd	counter for day (see 14.4.2)
一日	ichinichi	....	N	a day
たんじょう日	tan'joobi	....	N	birthday
およぐ	oyogu	....	V	swim (Dictionary form)

14.6 KANJI

来 ^{3.6.3}   (1) RAI   (2) coming   (5) 来年、来月、来しゅう [cf. 先月、先しゅう]

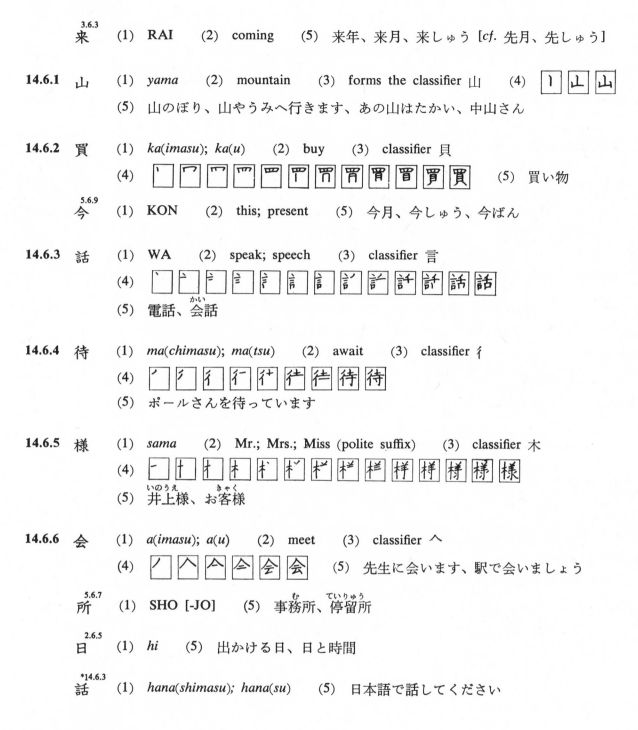

14.6.1   山   (1) *yama*   (2) mountain   (3) forms the classifier 山   (4) 丨 凵 山

     (5) 山のぼり、山やうみへ行きます、あの山はたかい、中山さん

14.6.2   買   (1) *ka(imasu); ka(u)*   (2) buy   (3) classifier 貝

     (4) 買   (5) 買い物

今 ^{5.6.9}   (1) KON   (2) this; present   (5) 今月、今しゅう、今ばん

14.6.3   話   (1) WA   (2) speak; speech   (3) classifier 言

     (4) 話

     (5) 電話、会話

14.6.4   待   (1) *ma(chimasu); ma(tsu)*   (2) await   (3) classifier 彳

     (4) 待

     (5) ポールさんを待っています

14.6.5   様   (1) *sama*   (2) Mr.; Mrs.; Miss (polite suffix)   (3) classifier 木

     (4) 様

     (5) 井上様、お客様

14.6.6   会   (1) *a(imasu); a(u)*   (2) meet   (3) classifier 𠆢

     (4) 会   (5) 先生に会います、駅で会いましょう

所 ^{5.6.7}   (1) SHO [-JO]   (5) 事務所、停留所

日 ^{2.6.5}   (1) *hi*   (5) 出かける日、日と時間

話 ^{*14.6.3}   (1) *hana(shimasu); hana(su)*   (5) 日本語で話してください

14.7 DRILLS

14.7.1 Pattern Drill

1. Raigetsu no tsuitachi to futsuka, Fujisan ni noboru tsumori desu ga, anata mo irasshaimasen ka?

2. Boku no hoka ni Yamada san to Ishii san mo iku hazu desu.

3. Den'sha no kippu o kawanakereba narimasen.

4. Nijuu kunichi ni nareba, kuwashii koto ga wakaru hazu desu.

5. Yama no ue wa kanari samui kara, boku wa seetaa o motte iku tsumori desu.

6. Dekakeru hi no yoru no oben'too wa motte ikanakereba narimasen ne.

14.7.2 Transformation Drill

1. べんとうを 持っていきます。 　　　 ⟶ 　べんとうを 持っていくつもりです。

2. 大学で 日本語を 習います。 　　　 ⟶ 　大学で 日本語を 習うつもりです。

3. ニューヨークで 教えます。 　　　 ⟶ 　ニューヨークで 教えるつもりです。

4. わたしは 今しゅう 行きます。 　　　 ⟶ 　わたしは 今しゅう 行くつもりです。

5. ぼくは いしゃに なります。 　　　 ⟶ 　ぼくは いしゃに なるつもりです。

6. これから、 えい語で 話します。 　　　 ⟶ 　これから、 えい語で 話すつもりです。

7. 日曜日に うみで およぎます。 　　　 ⟶ 　日曜日に うみで およぐつもりです。

8. あさっての あさ 出かけます。 　　　 ⟶ 　あさっての あさ 出かけるつもりです。

9. 石井さんに 会います。 　　　 ⟶ 　石井さんに 会うつもりです。

10. 富士山に のぼります。 　　　 ⟶ 　富士山に のぼるつもりです。

14.7.3 Transformation Drill

1. 国へ かえりません。 　　　 ⟶ 　国へ かえらないつもりです。

2. さけを のみません。 　　　 ⟶ 　さけを のまないつもりです。

3. 京都は けんぶつしません。 　　　 ⟶ 　京都は けんぶつしないつもりです。

4. 自分では 料理しません。 　　　 ⟶ 　自分では 料理しないつもりです。

5. 日本語では 話しません。 　　　 ⟶ 　日本語では 話さないつもりです。

6. 電車に のりません。 　　　 ⟶ 　電車に のらないつもりです。

7. 花見に 行きません。 　　　 ⟶ 　花見に 行かないつもりです。

8. ぼくは から手を しません。 　　　 ⟶ 　ぼくは から手を しないつもりです。

9. べんとうは 持っていきません。 　　　 ⟶ 　べんとうは 持っていかないつもりです。

10. 山に のぼりません。 　　　 ⟶ 　山に のぼらないつもりです。

14.7.4 Transformation Drill

1. じゅぎょうを やすむつもりでした。 　　　 ⟶ 　じゅぎょうを やすまないつもりでした。

2. 日本語を 習うつもりでした。 　　　 ⟶ 　日本語を 習わないつもりでした。

3. ぐん人に なるつもりでした。 　　　 ⟶ 　ぐん人に ならないつもりでした。

4. デパートで　アルバイトするつもり　　　→　　デパートで　アルバイトしないつもりでした。
　　でした。

5. きょうは　買い物に　行くつもりでした。　→　　きょうは　買い物に　行かないつもりでした。

6. ひこうきに　のるつもりでした。　　　　　→　　ひこうきに　のらないつもりでした。

7. ははに　知らせるつもりでした。　　　　　→　　ははに　知らせないつもりでした。

8. べんとうは　持ってくるつもりでした。　　→　　べんとうは　持ってこないつもりでした。

14.7.5　Mixed Drill

1. 中国料理を　作ることが　　　　　　　→　　中国料理を　作るつもりでしたが、　作ることが
　　できませんでした。　　　　　　　　　　　　できませんでした。

2. 返事を　書くことが　できませんでした。→　　返事を　書くつもりでしたが、　書くことが
　　　　　　　　　　　　　　　　　　　　　　　　できませんでした。

3. 青木さんに　知らせることが　　　　　　→　　青木さんに　知らせるつもりでしたが、
　　できませんでした。　　　　　　　　　　　　知らせることが　できませんでした。

4. タクシーに　のってくることが　　　　　→　　タクシーに　のってくるつもりでしたが、
　　できませんでした。　　　　　　　　　　　　のってくることが　できませんでした。

5. さんこう書を　読むことが　できません　→　　さんこう書を　読むつもりでしたが、読むことが
　　でした。　　　　　　　　　　　　　　　　　できませんでした。

6. あかい　車を　買うことが　できません　→　　あかい　車を　買うつもりでしたが、買うことが
　　でした。　　　　　　　　　　　　　　　　　できませんでした。

7. ごご　十時に　ねることが　できません　→　　ごご　十時に　ねるつもりでしたが、ねることが
　　でした。　　　　　　　　　　　　　　　　　できませんでした。

8. とんかつを　食べることが　できません　→　　とんかつを　食べるつもりでしたが、　食べる
　　でした。　　　　　　　　　　　　　　　　　ことが　できませんでした。

14.7.6　Transformation Drill

1. いもうとが　電話を　します。　　　　　→　　いもうとが　電話を　するはずです。

2. わたしたちは　大学で　会います。　　　→　　わたしたちは　大学で　会うはずです。

3. あねは　今ばん　うちに　います。　　　→　　あねは　今ばん　うちに　いるはずです。

4. 急行は　五時に　つきます。　　　　　　→　　急行は　五時に　つくはずです。

5. 石井さんも　いらっしゃいます。　　　　→　　石井さんも　いらっしゃるはずです。

6. ポールさんは　日本語が　わかります。　→　　ポールさんは　日本語が　わかるはずです。

7. ジャックさんは　きょう　しゅくだいを　→　　ジャックさんは　きょう　しゅくだいを
　　持ってきます。　　　　　　　　　　　　　　持ってくるはずです。

8. 田中さんが　駅で　待っています。　　　→　　田中さんが　駅で　待っているはずです。

9. あさと　よるは　電車が　こみます。　　→　　あさと　よるは　電車が　こむはずです。

10. 京都まで　一時間　かかります。　　　　→　　京都まで　一時間　かかるはずです。

14.7.7 Transformation Drill

1. おとうとは 今ばん 出かけません。 　—→ 　おとうとは 今ばん 出かけないはずです。

2. バスは よる こみませんよ。 　—→ 　バスは よる こまないはずですよ。

3. 一郎くんは えいがを 見ません。 　—→ 　一郎くんは えいがを 見ないはずです。

4. ブラウンさんは おさけを のみません。 —→ 　ブラウンさんは おさけを のまないはずです。

5. 山田先生は 日本語を 教えません。 　—→ 　山田先生は 日本語を 教えないはずです。

6. 先生は あさって 大学へ 　　　　　—→ 　先生は あさって 大学へ いらっしゃらない
　　いらっしゃいません。 　　　　　　　　　　はずです。

7. むすこは ぐん人に なりません。 　—→ 　むすこは ぐん人に ならないはずです。

8. みち子さんは 今、うちに いませんよ。 —→ 　みち子さんは 今、うちに いないはずですよ。

9. あの 人は ドイツへ りょこう 　　　—→ 　あの 人は ドイツへ りょこうしない
　　しません。 　　　　　　　　　　　　　　　　はずです。

10. きょうは じゅぎょうが ありません。 —→ 　きょうは じゅぎょうが ないはずです。

14.7.8 Transformation Drill

1. 富士山に のぼりました。 　　　　　—→ 　富士山に のぼったはずです。

2. おたくの そばを あるいていきました。 —→ 　おたくの そばを あるいていったはずです。

3. 日本の 物を 買いました。 　　　　　—→ 　日本の 物を 買ったはずです。

4. 林先生に 会いました。 　　　　　　—→ 　林先生に 会ったはずです。

5. 名前と 所を 書きました。 　　　　　—→ 　名前と 所を 書いたはずです。

6. 図書館で しらべました。 　　　　　—→ 　図書館で しらべたはずです。

7. その 本は 大学に ありました。 　　—→ 　その 本は 大学に あったはずです。

8. けい子さんは およぎに 行きました。 —→ 　けい子さんは およぎに 行ったはずです。

9. 一郎くんは 二つ目の かどを 　　　—→ 　一郎くんは 二つ目の かどを まがった
　　まがりました。 　　　　　　　　　　　　　　はずです。

10. パターソンさんに 出かける 日を 　—→ 　パターソンさんに 出かける 日を 知らせた
　　知らせました。 　　　　　　　　　　　　　　はずです。

14.7.9 Transformation Drill

1. あには ネクタイを 買いませんでした。—→ 　あには ネクタイを 買わなかったはずです。

2. ははは 買い物に 出かけませんでした。—→ 　ははは 買い物に 出かけなかったはずです。

3. おかねを かしませんでした。 　　　—→ 　おかねを かさなかったはずです。

4. その ことは 知りませんでした。 　—→ 　その ことは 知らなかったはずです。

5. 返事を もらいませんでした。 　　　—→ 　返事を もらわなかったはずです。

6. ひらがなは 教えませんでした。 　　—→ 　ひらがなは 教えなかったはずです。

7. あそこに　自転車は　ありませんでした。 —→ あそこに　自転車は　なかったはずです。
8. いもうとは　しんかん線に　のって —→ いもうとは　しんかん線に　のっていかなかった
　　いきませんでした。 はずです。

14.7.10　Transformation Drill

A. 1. 来月の　十五日に　来ます。 —→ 来月の　十五日に　来なければなりません。
2. ひらがなと　かん字を　つかいます。 —→ ひらがなと　かん字を　つかわなければ
　　　　　　　　　　　　　　　　　　　なりません。
3. ジョージさんに　あした　会います。 —→ ジョージさんに　あした　会わなければ
　　　　　　　　　　　　　　　　　　　なりません。
4. あの　かどを　まがります。 —→ あの　かどを　まがらなければなりません。
5. 月曜日までに　返事を　書きます。 —→ 月曜日までに　返事を　書かなければ
　　　　　　　　　　　　　　　　　　　なりません。
6. 会う　場所を　知らせます。 —→ 会う　場所を　知らせなければなりません。
7. 学校へ　おべんとうを　持って —→ 学校へ　おべんとうを　持っていかなければ
　　いきます。 なりません。
8. へやを　きれいに　します。 —→ へやを　きれいに　しなければなりません。
9. バスに　のってかえります。 —→ バスに　のってかえらなければなりません。
10. いしゃを　よびます。 —→ いしゃを　よばなければなりません。

B. 1. 辞書は　あたらしいです。 —→ 辞書は　あたらしくなければなりません。
2. コーヒーは　あついです。 —→ コーヒーは　あつくなければなりません。
3. 子どもが　行く　学校は　ちかいです。—→ 子どもが　行く　学校は　ちかくなければ
　　　　　　　　　　　　　　　　　　　なりません。
4. レポートは　ながいです。 —→ レポートは　ながくなければなりません。
5. しけんの　紙は　しろいです。 —→ しけんの　紙は　しろくなければなりません。

C. 1. 先生に　会うのは　火曜日です。 —→ 先生に　会うのは　火曜日でなければ
　　　　　　　　　　　　　　　　　　　なりません。
2. 店員の　ことばは　ていねいです。 —→ 店員の　ことばは　ていねいでなければ
　　　　　　　　　　　　　　　　　　　なりません。
3. アルバイトを　するのは —→ アルバイトを　するのは
　　なつやすみです。 なつやすみでなければなりません。
4. 教室は　しずかです。 —→ 教室は　しずかでなければなりません。
5. 東京へ　しごとに　行くのは —→ 東京へ　しごとに　行くのは
　　来しゅうです。 来しゅうでなければなりません。

14.7.11 Expansion Drill

1. のぼるつもりです。   ……   のぼるつもりです。

   富士山に   ……   富士山に　のぼるつもりです。

   来年、   ……   来年、　富士山に　のぼるつもりです。

   ぼくは   ……   ぼくは　来年、　富士山に　のぼるつもりです。

2. 行くつもりです。   ……   行くつもりです。

   買いに   ……   買いに　行くつもりです。

   かぶきの　きっぷを   ……   かぶきの　きっぷを　買いに　行くつもりです。

   あした   ……   あした　かぶきの　きっぷを　買いに
               行くつもりです。

   わたくしは   ……   わたくしは　あした　かぶきの　きっぷを　買いに
               行くつもりです。

3. アルバイトは　しないつもりです。 …… アルバイトは　しないつもりです。

   いそがしければ、   ……   いそがしければ、　アルバイトは　しないつもりです。

   べんきょうが   ……   べんきょうが　いそがしければ、　アルバイトは
               しないつもりです。

   わたしは   ……   わたしは　べんきょうが　いそがしければ、
               アルバイトは　しないつもりです。

4. つかわないつもりでした。   ……   つかわないつもりでした。

   えい語を   ……   えい語を　つかわないつもりでした。

   教室の　中では   ……   教室の　中では　えい語を　つかわないつもりでした。

   ぼくは   ……   ぼくは　教室の　中では　えい語を
               つかわないつもりでした。

5. 話しました。   ……   話しました。

   日本人が　大ぜい　来ましたから、 …… 日本人が　大ぜい　来ましたから、　話しました。

   話さないつもりでしたが、   ……   話さないつもりでしたが、　日本人が　大ぜい
               来ましたから、　話しました。

   日本語では   ……   日本語では　話さないつもりでしたが、　日本人が
               大ぜい　来ましたから、　話しました。

14.7.12 Substitution Drill

月曜日までに　レポートを　持ってきてください。

  1. ごご　三時   ……   ごご　三時までに　レポートを　持ってきてください。

  2. 三月六日   ……   三月六日までに　レポートを　持ってきてください。

3. 今月の　二十日　　　　　　…… 今月の　二十日までに　レポートを　持ってきて
　　　　　　　　　　　　　　　　　　　ください。

4. 来しゅうの　土曜日　　　　…… 来しゅうの　土曜日までに　レポートを　持ってきて
　　　　　　　　よう　　　　　　　　　　　よう
　　　　　　　　　　　　　　　　　　　ください。

5. あさって　　　　　　　　　…… あさってまでに　レポートを　持ってきてください。

6. ゆうがた　　　　　　　　　…… ゆうがたまでに　レポートを　持ってきてください。

14.7.13　Substitution Drill

くわしい　ことなら、　あの　人に　聞いてみてください。

1. わからない　　　　　　　　…… わからない　ことなら、　あの　人に　聞いてみて
　　　　　　　　　　　　　　　　　　　ください。

2. 車の　　　　　　　　　　　…… 車の　ことなら、　あの　人に　聞いてみてください。

3. むずかしい　　　　　　　　…… むずかしい　ことなら、　あの　人に　聞いてみて
　　　　　　　　　　　　　　　　　　　ください。

4. しゅくだいの　　　　　　　…… しゅくだいの　ことなら、　あの　人に　聞いてみて
　　　　　　　　　　　　　　　　　　　ください。

5. みち子さんの　　　　　　　…… みち子さんの　ことなら、　あの　人に　聞いてみて
　　　　　　　　　　　　　　　　　　　ください。

6. 日本語の　　　　　　　　　…… 日本語の　ことなら、　あの　人に　聞いてみて
　　　　　　　　　　　　　　　　　　　ください。

7. ゆうめいな　　　　　　　　…… ゆうめいな　ことなら、　あの　人に　聞いてみて
　　　　　　　　　　　　　　　　　　　ください。

8. その　　　　　　　　　　　…… その　ことなら、　あの　人に　聞いてみてください。

14.7.14　E-J Response Drill

1. なん日まで　大学で　べんきょうしなければなりませんか。

　　June 15th　　　　　　　　…… 六月十五日まで　大学で　べんきょうしなければ
　　　　　　　　　　　　　　　　　　　なりません。

2. あなたの　おかあさんの　たんじょう日は　いつですか。

　　April 20th　　　　　　　　…… ははの　たんじょう日は　四月二十日です。

3. りょこうは　いつ　するつもりですか。

　　from September 1st through 8th　…… りょこうは　九月一日から　八日まで　するつもり
　　　　　　　　　　　　　　　　　　　です。

4. しんかん線の　きっぷは　いつまでに　買わなければなりませんか。
　　　　　せん

　　by June 3rd　　　　　　　…… しんかん線の　きっぷは　六月三日までに
　　　　　　　　　　　　　　　　　　せん
　　　　　　　　　　　　　　　　　　買わなければなりません。

5. なん時までに おたくへ 行きましょうか。

by four o'clock tomorrow afternoon ...... あしたの ごご 四時までに 来てください。

6. あなたが アルバイトする 日は いつですか。

Monday, Thursday and Friday ...... わたしが アルバイトする 日は 月曜日と 木曜日と 金曜日です。

7. しけんが あった 日は いつでしたか。

December 19th ...... しけんが あった 日は 十二月十九日でした。

8. スミスさんが 日本に ついた 日は なん日ですか。

May 22nd, 1967 ...... 千九百六十七年五月二十二日です。

14.7.15 E-J Transformation Drill

1. 石井さんは ふゆやすみに 国へ かえりません。

Mr. Ishii is not supposed to ...... 石井さんは ふゆやすみに 国へ かえらないはずです。

2. 天気が よければ、 うみへ あそびに 行きます。

I intend to ...... 天気が よければ、 うみへ あそびに 行くつもり です。

3. 火曜日までに しゅくだいを 持ってきますか。

do I have to ...... 火曜日までに しゅくだいを 持ってこなければ なりませんか。

4. スージーさんは あしたの あさ、 電話を くれます。

Susie is supposed to ...... スージーさんは あしたの あさ、電話を くれるはず です。

5. 来年 東京大学で 日本語を べんきょうします。

I am planning to ...... 来年 東京大学で 日本語を べんきょうする つもりです。

6. こたえは ひらがなと かたかなで 書きます。

I had to ...... こたえは ひらがなと かたかなで 書かなければ なりませんでした。

14.7.16 Review Drill

1. あの かどを 左へ まがります。 すぐ わかるはずですよ。 ⟶ あの かどを 左へ まがれば、 すぐ わかるはずですよ。

2. 二十三日に うちへ 来ます。 田中さんに 会うことが できるはず です。 ⟶ 二十三日に うちへ 来れば、 田中さんに 会うことが できるはずです。

3. あの 図書館で さがします。 いい 本が 見つかるはずです。 → あの 図書館で さがせば、 いい 本が 見つかるはずです。

4. 天気が いいです。 いもうとと いっしょに うみへ 行くはずです。 → 天気が よければ、 いもうとと いっしょに うみへ 行くはずです。

5. いそぎます。 三時までに 東京駅に つくはずです。 → いそげば、 三時までに 東京駅に つくはずです。

6. あかい くつが ほしいです。 あの 店で うっているはずです。 → あかい くつが ほしければ、 あの 店で うっているはずです。

7. 京都です。 おとうとは きょ年 行ったはずです。 → 京都なら、 おとうとは きょ年 行ったはずです。

8. 木下さんです。 りょこうに 出かけたはずです。 → 木下さんなら、 りょこうに 出かけたはずです。

14.8 EXERCISES

14.8.1 Make appropriate questions that will lead to the following answers:

1. はい、 そう するつもりです。
2. 山田さんが 来るはずです。
3. 三月三日に のぼったはずです。
4. 青木さんを つれていくつもりでした。
5. いいえ、 場所は 知らせなくてもいいです。
6. ええ、 そう しなければなりません。
7. 十日までに かえらなければなりません。

14.8.2 Answer the following in Japanese:

1. あなたの たんじょう日は なん月なん日ですか。
2. あなたが この 学校へ 来た 日は いつでしたか。
3. 日本語の じゅぎょうは いつから いつまでですか。
4. 来しゅうの 日曜日に なにを するつもりですか。
5. きょうの しゅくだいは なん日までに しなければなりませんか。
6. あなたが 国へ かえる 日は いつですか。

14.8.3 Write the following letter in Japanese:

July 6th, 1968

Dear Mr. Ishii:

How are you?
If the weather is nice, Mr. Yamada and I are planning to go to the seaside on July 18th. Won't you go with us? I cannot swim well, but Mr. Yamada can swim very well. You have to bring your lunch and snacks. If it rains on the 18th, Mr. Yamada is supposed to come to my house. Please let me know by telephone whether this is convenient.

So long,

Ikuo Watanabe

14.8.4 Write the following underlined *hiragana* in *kanji*:

1. <u>らいげつ</u>　<u>やま</u>へ　<u>いく</u>つもりですから、　<u>こんげつ</u>、　いろいろな　<u>もの</u>を
   <u>かわ</u>なければなりません。

2. お<u>客</u>さまに　<u>でんわ</u>を　しなければなりません。　ちょっと　<u>まって</u>ください。

3. <u>じ務</u>しょで　<u>あう</u>　<u>ひ</u>は　<u>なんにち</u>ですか。

4. <u>木下</u>さんには　あとで　<u>はなし</u>ます。

14.8.5 Write the following in *katakana*:

1. Pataason　　　　　　　2. jan'paa

14.9 SITUATIONAL CONVERSATION

14.9.1 Planning for mountain climbing

A young boy asks his friend if he has ever climbed mountains.
The friend says he has never climbed any mountains.
Then the young boy tells the friend that if the weather is nice next Sunday, he intends to go to
  Mt. Fuji.
The friend agrees with those plans but wants to know who else will be going with them.
The young man mentions two friends by name and says they are supposed to go with them.
The friend asks what he should take with him, such as clothes, food, snacks, etc.
The young boy replies he is planning to take a jacket or a sweater since it is cold on the mountain,
  and advises bringing a meal for the departure night.

14.9.2 Carry on a conversation about your plan for next Sunday.

14.9.3 Write a letter inviting your friend to a dinner, a movie, or *kabuki*.

LESSON 15

— Review Drill and Exercise —

15.1 REVIEW DRILL (Lessons 13 & 14)

15.1.1 Intention

きょう　東京へ　行く
木下さんに　知らせる
大学で　日本語を　教える
富士山に　のぼる
なつやすみに　およぐ
山田先生に　会う
みやげを　持ってかえる
子どもを　つれてくる

わたくし
しゅ人
いもうと
は
（が）

一日中　うちに　いない
国へ　かえらない
自転車に　のらない
辞書や　さんこう書を　つかわない
べんとうを　持っていかない
一郎くんに　いわない

つもり　です　でした

15.1.2 Expectation

さくらは　三月か　四月に　さく
急行は　ここに　とまる
きょうは　ドイツ語の　しけんが　ある

パターソンさんは　うちに　いない
木村さんは　およぐことが　できない
ごごは　電車が　こまない

はず　です　でした

あの　かどを　まがった
青木さんは　その　山に　のぼった
駅員に　知らせた

はず　です

この　もんだいは　教えなかった
万年筆は　買わなかった
木下さんは　ハワイへ　行かなかった

| | はず | です |

15.1.3　Obligation

a.　Verb

あしたは　かぜで　しごとを　やすま
四時に　ともだちに　会わ
ことばを　ていねいに　話さ
いろいろな　物を　買わ
この　本を　いもうとに　わたさ
いしゃを　よば
かりた　教科書を　かえさ
かないを　つれていか
しゅくだいを　持ってこ
はしを　つかわ
まいばん　べんきょうし
料理を　作るのを　手つだわ

| | なければ | なりません (いけません) |

b.　Adjective

学生が　多いから、教室は　ひろく
さんぽなら、天気が　よく
いろいろな　うん動を　するつもりなら、　わかく
ぼくの　買う　自転車は　あかく
子どもに　やる　本は　やさしく

| | なければ | なりません (いけません) |

c.　Nominative + Copula

ことばは　ていねい
べんきょうする　へやは　しずか
花見に　行くのは　ゆうがた
山のぼりは　七月
会う　場所は　駅

| | で / じゃ | なければ | なりません (いけません) |

15.1.4 Provisional Clause

a. Verb

あの　かどを　左へ　まがれば、	停留所は　右に　あります
地下鉄に　のっていけば、	十分ぐらい　かかります
（もし）この　もんだいが　わかれば、	つぎの　もんだいは　やさしくなります
北海道と　九州を　くらべれば、	北海道の　方が　ひろいです
一時に　はじめれば、	五時までに　おわります

電車が　こまなければ、	電車で　来た　方が　いいですよ
（もし）およぐことが　できなければ、	山に　のぼりませんか
先生が　行かなければ、	あなたも　行ってはいけません
よし子さんは、図書館に　いなければ、	うちに　いるはずです
（もし）知らなければ、	こたえなくてもかまいません

b. Adjective

（もし）天気が　よければ、	さんぽに　行きましょう
辞書が　ふるければ、	あたらしいのを　買った　方が　いいです
（もし）気分が　わるければ、	ここで　やすんでください
たかければ、	そんな　物は　買わないでください
へやが　きたなければ、	きれいに　してください
（もし）しゅくだいが　なければ、	えいがを　見に　行きたいです

こうちゃが　ほしくなければ、	なにが　ほしいですか
ちかくなければ、	タクシーに　のらなければなりません
（もし）せつめいが　くわしくなければ、	ほかの　さんこう書を　かりなければ　なりません
うるさくなければ、	あの　へやを　つかいましょう

c. Nominative + Copula

しごとが　たいへんなら、	手つだいましょうか
とんかつが　好きなら、	ごちそうしますよ
テニスなら、	よし子さんが　一番　じょうずです
青木くんの　電話番号なら、	ぼくが　知っています
来月の　七日なら、	とても　つごうが　いいです

260

ゆうめいじゃなければ、	あまり　見たくありません
そこが　しずかじゃなければ、	しずかな　所を　さがしましょう
日曜日じゃなければ、	ぼくは　行くことが　できません
びょう気でなければ、	じゅぎょうを　やすまないでください
木下さんでなければ、	あの　人は　たぶん　小山さんでしょう

15.1.5 Relational

a. *made ni* "by"

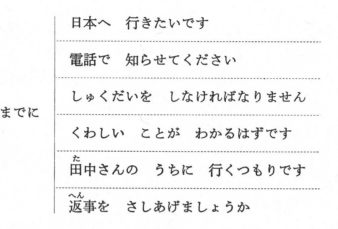

千九百六十八年八月		日本へ　行きたいです
来月の　二十五日		電話で　知らせてください
今しゅうの　金曜日	までに	しゅくだいを　しなければなりません
あしたの　ゆうがた		くわしい　ことが　わかるはずです
ごご　一時半		田中さんの　うちに　行くつもりです
なん日		返事を　さしあげましょうか

b. *o* "through"

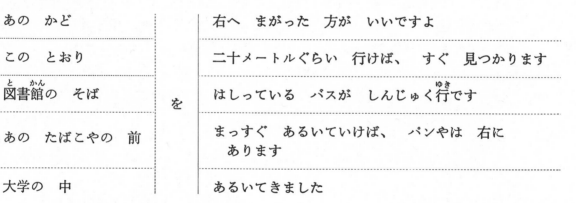

あの　かど		右へ　まがった　方が　いいですよ
この　とおり		二十メートルぐらい　行けば、　すぐ　見つかります
図書館の　そば	を	はしっている　バスが　しんじゅく行です
あの　たばこやの　前		まっすぐ　あるいていけば、　パンやは　右に　あります
大学の　中		あるいてきました

15.2 EXERCISES

15.2.1　Connect each of the A Group expressions with appropriate B Group expressions and give the English equivalent. There will be one or more choices.

A Group

1. まどを　あけないで
2. あそこに　たっている
3. 日本の　カメラを　買った
4. この　へやを　つかっても
5. さくらは　三月か　四月に　さく
6. ブラウンさんは　日本語を　話す
7. ここで　あそんでは
8. ぼくは　来年　ヨーロッパへ　行く
9. 学校の　先生に　なる
10. あしたは　六時に　おきなければ
11. あなたの　本を　見せて

B Group

a. ことが　ありますか。
b. ください。
c. 人は　スミスさんです。
d. ことが　できますか。
e. いけません。
f. 方が　好きです。
g. つもりです。
h. かまいませんか。
i. 一番　いいです。
j. はずです。
k. いいです。
l. なりません。

15.2.2　Insert an appropriate Relational:

1. 山田さんの　くつは　わたし(　)(　)　大きいでしょう。
2. きのう(　)　あさ、　上野公園(　)　花見(　)　行きました。
3. あの　きれいな　きっさ店(　)　はいってみましょう。
4. へたで(　)　かまいません(　)、　ひらがな(　)　かん字(　)　つかってください。
5. 料理の　中(　)、　なに(　)　作るの(　)　一番　じょうずですか。
6. 図書館(　)　前(　)　左(　)　まがってください。
7. 十番線(　)　出る　電車(　)　のっていけば、　すぐ　わかりますよ。
8. おととい　あなた(　)　会いたかったんですが、　どうして　しごと(　)　やすみましたか。
9. 大阪行(　)　急行(　)　なん時(　)　この　駅(　)　つきますか。
10. 千九百六十六年(　)は　東京(　)　すんでいましたが、　今は、　京都(　)　すんでいます。
11. えんぴつ(　)　書いて(　)いけません。
12. 山(　)　のぼる(　)　うみ(　)　行った　方(　)　おもしろいです。
13. てきとうな　本(　)　見つかりません。
14. かぜ(　)　気分(　)　わるい(　)、　じゅぎょう(　)　やすみません。

15. 木村さん（　）　持っている　本は　ことば（　）　とても　むずかしいです。

16. おたく（　）　大学（　）　なん分ぐらい　かかりますか。

17. いしゃ（　）　なる（　）　ぐん人（　）　なりたかったんです。

18. 七月七日まで（　）　国（　）　かえるつもりです。

19. あの　しろい　たて物（　）　前（　）　たっていて（　）いいですか。

20. きのう　買った　物（　）　ぜんぶ（　）　三千八百円でした。

21. 東京は　あなた（　）　おもう（　）　さむくありません。

15.2.3 Compose sentences in Japanese by using the words or phrases given below, and state your original ideas in English:

e.g. ずっと　……　京都の　方が　ずっと　むしあついです。

1. つもり	8. ～なければなりません	15. ～に　なりました
2. はず	9. ～ければ	16. ～に　しましょう
3. ～ことは　ありませんか	10. ～より　～の　方が	17. かなり
4. いけません	11. だけ	18. ちょうど
5. ～ことが　できますか	12. 一番	19. だいたい
6. ほど	13. ～から　～まで	20. 会えば
7. ～なら	14. ～たい(ん)です	

15.2.4 Correct the errors in the following sentences:

1. 前、　東京駅の　そばで　すんでいました。
2. 教室の　中を　きれいに　なりました。
3. 日本語で　話したことが　できますか。
4. ちかいければ、　あるいていきましょう。
5. あの　食堂の　カレーライスは　おいしいつもり　です。
6. 井上さんが　はたらいています　事務所は　大阪に　あります。
7. おそくてはかまいませんから、　もんだいも　こたえも　書いてください。
8. 自分で　作るより　レストランで　食べるの　方が　いいです。
9. 会う　時間や　場所は　すぐ　知らせればなりません。
10. びょう気から、　学校を　やすみました。

15.2.5 Combine each pair of the following, transforming the first sentence of each pair into the provisional clause "if . . . ," and then give the English equivalent for each of the combined sentences:

1. 来しゅうの　日曜日の　ごごです。

えいがを　見に　行きたいです。

2. 日本語を　話すことが　できます。

日本の　ことを　よく　知ることが　できます。

3. 七月十五日です。

ひまですから、　いっしょに　出かけましょう。

4. タクシーの　方が　はやいです。

タクシーに　のります。

5. 電車に　のってきません。

一時間ぐらい　かかりますよ。

6. あまり　たかくありません。

買いたいですねえ。

15.2.6　Make appropriate questions that will lead to the following answers:

1. はい、　一ど　行ったことが　あります。
2. これが　一番　おもしろいです。
3. いいえ、　子どもを　つれてこないでください。
4. ハワイの　方が　ずっと　あたたかいです。
5. はい、　できません。
6. 二十分ぐらい　かかるはずです。

15.2.7　Complete each sentence by inserting, in each blank, one of the Adverbs listed below:

まだ、　もし、　たいへん、　もう、　大ぜい、　ゆっくり、　ぜひ、　まっすぐ、
よく (well; often)

1. この　みちを　（　　）二十メートルぐらい　行けば、　たばこやは　右に　あります。
2. 子どもが　（　　）いますから、　（　　）うるさいです。
3. のみ物は　（　　）ほしくありません。
4. わたくしは　かぶきを　（　　）見に　行きます。
5. （　　）あした　ひまなら、　（　　）うちへ　あそびに　来てください。
6. 日本語は　（　　）へたですから、　（　　）わかりません。（　　）話してください。

15.2.8　Transform the code sentence according to the given English sentences:

A.　日本語を　教えます。

1. I want to teach Japanese.

2. I don't want to teach Japanese.

264

3. I wanted to teach Japanese.

4. I didn't want to teach Japanese.

5. I had to teach Japanese.

6. I'll go to teach Japanese.

7. I can't teach Japanese.

8. I have taught Japanese once.

9. I'm planning to teach Japanese next week.

10. The man who is teaching me Japanese is Mr. Itō.

B. スミスさんは　きょういく学を　べんきょうします。

1. Mr. Smith is studying education now.

2. Mr. Smith is supposed to study education.

3. Mr. Smith tried to study education.

4. Mr. Smith, please study education.

5. Mr. Smith, please don't study education.

6. Mr. Smith has never studied education.

C. 富士山に　のぼります。

1. You'd better climb Mt. Fuji rather than go to the seaside.

2. If it is Mt. Fuji, you must not climb.

3. May I climb Mt. Fuji next month?

4. To climb Mt. Fuji is not as easy as Mr. Tanaka says.

5. If you climb Mt. Fuji, you have to be absent from work for three days.

6. If you like mountain climbing, please try to climb Mt. Fuji.

7. The mountain I climbed last week is Mt. Fuji.

D. 天気が　いいです。

1. The weather will become better tomorrow.

2. If the weather is not good, I prefer to stay at home.

3. Do you mind if the weather is not good?

E. そこは　しずかです。

1. If that place is quiet, let's read books there.

2. If that place is not quiet, let's try to find (some) other place.

3. I'm living in a quiet place.

15.2.9 Connect each of the A group words with its antonym listed in the B group.

A Group	B Group
南	すくない
小さい	習う
先生	大きい
来る	左
買う	外
上	うる
多い	前
中	女
教える	北
山	下
東	行く
男	来年
右	学生
	うみ
	西

15.2.10 Write the following in *hiragana*. Use *kanji* when italicized:

1. Sore o *mi*sete kudasai.

2. Anata no o kite mimasu.

3. Watakushi no *yon*'da san'koo*sho* wa kore desu.

4. Wakaranakatta mon'dai o shirabetai n desu.

5. Kore o *yon*'da koto ga arimasu ka?

6. *Mae* no *tokoro* ni sun'de imasu.

7. Nan'*ji* ni *i*kimashoo ka?

8. *Soto* de *ta*beru yori *jibun* de ryoori shita *hoo* ga ii desu.

9. Nani o *tsuku*ru no ga *ichiban* joozu desu ka?

10. Anata ga omou hodo oishiku arimasen.

11. Sakura wa yuumei na *hana* desu.

12. Kooen e *hana* o *mi* ni *i*kimasu.

13. Totemo ii *ten'ki* desu.

14. Zehi *mi*tai desu.

15. *Kin'yoobi* ni anata ni *a*itakatta n desu.

16. Kabuki o *mi*taku arimasen.

17. Jugyoo o yasumitaku arimasen deshita.

18. Osokute mo kamaimasen.

19. Kotae dake de mo ii n desu.

20. Ji*sho* o tsukatte wa ikemasen.

21. Ji*sho* o tsukawanaide kudasai.

22. Kyuukoo ga *Oo*saka ni tsuku *jikan* wa *shichiji* desu.

23. Tama ni kyuukoo ni noranai *hito* ga imasu.

24. Sono *naka* de *ichiban oo*kii no wa *Hon*'shuu desu.

25. *Kyoo*to no *hoo* ga zutto kirei desu.

26. Kariforunia wa hoka no shuu yori yutaka desu.

27. *Kyoo*to wa *Tookyoo* hodo urusaku arimasen.

28. Semai michi o hashitte imasu.

29. Furan'su Taishikan nara, yoku *shi*tte imasu.

30. Tookereba, takushii de *i*kimasu.

31. Basu de *i*keba, taishikan no soba ni tomarimasu.

32. Fujisan ni noboru tsumori desu.

33. Ishii san mo *i*ku hazu desu.

34. Kippu o *ka*wanakereba narimasen.

15.2.11 Replace the *hiragana,* which are underlined, by *kanji*:

1. ひがし、　にし、　みなみ、　きた

2. うえ、　した、　みぎ、　ひだり

3. げつ曜、　か曜、　すい曜、　もく曜、　きん曜、　ど曜、　にち曜

4. 田中せんせいは　だいがくで　にほんごを　おしえています。　ぼくは
　　がいこくぶんがくを　ならっています。

5. この　きょう室に　おとこが　じゅうはち人、　おんなが　きゅう人　います。
　　おとこの　ほうが　おおいです。

6. らいげつの　ようかに　じどうしゃで　やまへ　いくつもりです。

7. えきの　そばの　しょく堂で　しょくじを　しました。

8. いま、　よじ　にじっぷんです。

9. あなたの　すきな　おんがくを　ききましょう。

10. かみに　なまえと　ところを　かいてください。

11. せんきゅうひゃくろくじゅうよねんに　この　まちへ　きました。

12. でんわで　しらせてください。

13. とうきょう行の　でんしゃは　なんばん線から　でますか。

14. あの　ちいさい　きっさ店で　まっています。

15. うつくしい　ものを　もっていますね。　みせてください。

16. ちゅうごくごを　はなすことが　できますか。

15.3　AURAL COMPREHENSION

　　しばらくですが、　お元気ですか。　ぼくも　かぞくも　みんな　元気です。　北海道は
今、　たいへん　さむいですが、　あなたの　所は　どうですか。　きのうも、
五十センチぐらい　ゆきが　ふりましたから、　ことしの　ふゆは　スキーが　よく
できます。

　　今月の　二十六日ごろから　三十日ごろまで、　スキーに　来ませんか。　おとうとや
いもうとも　来しゅうから　学校が　ふゆやすみに　なるはずですから、　みんなで　一日中
スキーを　しましょう。　もし、　スキーを　したことが　なければ、　ぼくが　あなたの
先生に　なりますよ。　ポールさんは　うん動が　好きですから、　スキーも　きっと
すぐ　じょうずに　なりますよ。

　　来る　日と　駅に　つく　時間を　知らせてください。　みんなで　駅まで　行きます。
　　では、　いい　返事を　待っています。

　　　　　　　　　　　　　　　　　　　　　　　　　　　さようなら

十二月十五日

　　　　　　　　　　　　　　　　　　　　　　　　　　　鈴　木

ポール　様

APPENDIX I

ABBREVIATIONS

A	....	Adjective	*furui, kuwashii, hirokute*
Adv.	....	Adverb	*zutto, taihen*
B	....	Base	*mitsukar(imasu), tabe(ru), atarashi(i)*
C	....	Copula	*desu, de, na*
D	....	Derivative	
⎰ Da	....	adjectival Derivative	*-nai, -tai*
⎱ Dv	....	verbal Derivative	*-masu, -mashoo*
E	....	Predicate Extender	*(-te) imasu, (-te) kudasai, (de wa) nai*
I	....	Inflection	*(mitsukar)i(masu), (atarashi)i*
N	....	Nominative	
⎧ Na	....	adjectival Nominative	*taihen, teinei*
⎪ Nd	....	dependent Nominative	*koto, no, tsumori, hazu, -doru, -ban*
⎨ Ni	....	interrogative Nominative	*dochira, dotchi, dore*
⎩ N	....	ordinary Nominative	*kudamono, ototoi, tsuitachi*
NM	....	Nominative Modifier	*kirei na (hana), tsugi no eki de oriru (hito)*
P	....	Predicate	
PC	....	Pre-Copula	*n (desu)*
PM	....	Predicate Modifier	(Adverb, time Nominative, N+R, number)
PN	....	Pre-Nominative	*don'na, son'na*
R	....	Relational	
⎰ Rc	....	clause Relational	*kara, keredomo*
⎱ Rp	....	phrase Relational	*yori, made ni, ni*
S	....	Sentence	
SI	....	Sentence Interjective	*anoo, eeto*
SP	....	Sentence Particle	*ka, yo, ne, nee*
V	....	Verb	*iku, arukeba, yasun'da*

APPENDIX II

SENTENCE STRUCTURE

$$S = SI + PM \left\{ \begin{array}{l} (NM)^{*1} \left\{ \begin{array}{l} PN \\ N + (R)^{*2} \\ Adv.^* \\ P^{*4} \end{array} \right\}^{*3} + N + (R) \\ (Adv.) + Adv. + (R) \\ P^{*6} + (R) \end{array} \right\} \Big/\!\!\Big/ P \left\{ \begin{array}{l} V\{B + I + D\} \\ A\{B + I + D\} \\ (NM) + N + (R) + C \end{array} \right\} + (R) + (E)^{*7} + (PC)^{*8} + (C)^{*9} \right\} + SP$$

*1 (NM) = NM optional

*2 (R) = R optional

*3 Adv. is only followed by Na such as *kirei,* adverbially used N such as *san'nin, kyoo,* or place N such as *ushiro, ue.*

*4 limited to final-clause Predicate such as *iku, itta.*

*5 { } = specification or limitation

*6 limited to TE, KU, TARI, Stem forms. R is obligatory for TARI, Stem forms, but optional for TE, KU forms.

*7 (E) = E optional

*8 (PC) = PC optional

*9 (C) = C optional

APPENDIX III

RELATIONALS

Relational		Lesson	Functions	Example Sentences
dake	Rp	9	limitation [only; just; no more than]	*Kotae dake kaite kudasai.* *Kono kudamono wa Kariforunia ni dake arimasu.*
de	Rp	1	totalizing	*Mittsu de hyakuen desu.* *Zen'bu de ikura desu ka?*
	Rp	3	cause [because of]	*Kaze de gakkoo o yasumimashita.*
	Rp	10	designation of scope [among; of]	*Sono naka de ichiban ookii desu.* *Amerika de ichiban yuumei na hito wa dare desu ka?*

270

Relational		Lesson	Functions	Example Sentences
hodo	Rp	10	[as much as]	*Watakushi wa anata hodo joozu ja arimasen.*
kara	Rc	5	reason [because; since]	*Sugu kimasu kara, matte ite kudasai.*
kedo *keredo* *keredomo*	Rc	10	reversal [but; although; however]	*Takai keredo, sore ni shimasu.*
made	Rp	6	time or place of goal [until; as far as]	*Eki made arukimashoo.* *Asa goji made ben'kyoo shimashita.*
made ni	Rp	14	[by (the time given); not later than]	*Tooka made ni hen'ji o kudasai.*
mo	Rp	9	[even]	*Itte mo ii desu ka?*
ni	Rp	2	target time [at; in; on]	*Yoji ni dekakemashoo.*
	Rp	3	direction [to]	*Uchi ni kaeritai desu.*
	Rp	5	purpose (of going) [for; to]	*San'po ni ikimasen ka?* *Gohan o tabe ni kaerimashita.*
	Rp	11	goal (to become) (to make) (to choose)	*Sen'sei ni naritai n desu.* *Kirei ni shimashoo.* *Ban'gohan wa bifuteki ni shimasu.*
no	Rp	6	follows the subject in a Nominative Modifier	*Kyuukoo no tsuku jikan o shitte imasu ka?*
o	Rp	13	place through which action has taken place [through; along; in, etc.]	*Kono toori o tsugi no kado made arukimasu.*
yori	Rp	10	comparison [than]	*Kyooto yori Tookyoo no hoo ga ookii desu.*

APPENDIX IV

CONJUGATION TABLE

— Form —

1. Verb

a. Vowel Verb

ageru I, 12	ireru II, 1	kureru I, 12	oshieru II, 13	tsureru II, 3
akeru II, 9	iru I, 4	miru I, 4	sashiageru II, 1	tsutomeru II, 2
dekakeru I, 9	kariru I, 7	miseru II, 1	shimeru II, 9	wakareru II, 10
dekiru II 5, 11	kiru II, 1	neru II, 3	shiraberu II, 7	wasureru I, 5
deru II, 6	kotaeru II, 9	okiru II, 3	shiraseru II, 14	
hajimeru II, 9	kuraberu II, 10	oriru II, 6	taberu I, 3	

a. 1 Conjugation

Neutral					Plain	
Stem Form	Base Form	TE Form	BA Form	Pre-Nai Form	Dictionary Form	TA Form
tabe(masu)	tabe	tabe*te*	tabe*reba*	tabe(nai)	tabe*ru*	tabe*ta*
mi(masu)	mi	mi*te*	mi*reba*	mi(nai)	mi*ru*	mi*ta*

a. 2 Tense & Negation

Normal				Plain				Neutral	
Imperfect		Perfect		Imperfect		Perfect		Provisional	
Affirmative	Negative	Affirmative	Negative	Affirmative	Negative	Affirmative	Negative	Affirmative	Negative
tabemasu	tabemasen	tabe-mashita	tabemasen deshita	taberu	tabenai	tabeta	tabe-nakatta	tabereba	tabe-nakereba
mimasu	mimasen	mimashita	mimasen deshita	miru	minai	mita	minakatta	mireba	mi-nakereba

b. Consonant Verb

Group 1   /r/ group

aru	I, 4	irassharu	II, 3; 14	mitsukaru	II, 7	shiru	II, 2	wakaru	II, 2
furu	I, 11	kaeru	I, 3	naru	II, 11	suwaru	II, 9	yaru	I, 12
hairu	I, 8	kakaru	II, 6	noboru	II, 14	tomaru	II, 13		
hajimaru	II, 3	kudasaru	II, 1	noru	II, 6	tsukuru	II, 11		
hashiru	II, 6	magaru	II, 13	owaru	II, 3	uru	II, 1		

Group 2   /w/ group

au	II, 3	kau	I, 3	narau	I, 5	tsukau	II, 7
chigau	I, 5	kamau	II, 7	omou	II, 11	ukagau	II, 2; 6
iu	I, 11	morau	I, 12	tetsudau	II, 11		

Group 3   /t/ group

matsu	I, 4	motsu	II, 2	tatsu	II, 9

Group 4   /k/ group

aruku	II, 6	hiku	I, 8	itadaku	II, 1	kiku	I, 8; II, 6	tsuku	II, 6
hataraku	II, 2	iku	I, 3	kaku	I, 4	saku	II, 5		

Group 5   /s/ group

hanasu	I, 5	kaesu	II, 7	kasu	II, 7	sagasu	I, 4	watasu	II, 9

Group 6   /m/ group

komu	II, 13	nomu	I, 3	sumu	II, 2	yasumu	II, 3	yomu	I, 7

Group 7   /b/ group

asobu	II, 5	yobu	II, 5

Group 8   /g/ group

isogu	II, 11	oyogu	II, 14

Group 9   /n/ group

shinu	—

272

b. 1   Conjugation

Group	Stem Form	Base Form	TE Form	BA Form	Pre-Nai Form	Dictionary Form	TA Form
			Neutral			Plain	
1	furi(masu)	fur	futte	fureba	fura(nai)	furu	futta
2	ai(masu)	a(w)	atte	aeba	awa(nai)	au	atta
3	machi(masu)	mat	matte	mateba	mata(nai)	matsu	matta
4	aruki(masu)	aruk	aruite	arukeba	aruka(nai)	aruku	aruita
5	hanashi(masu)	hanas	hanashite	hanaseba	hanasa(nai)	hanasu	hanashita
6	komi(masu)	kom	kon'de	komeba	koma(nai)	komu	kon'da
7	asobi(masu)	asob	ason'de	asobeba	asoba(nai)	asobu	ason'da
8	isogi(masu)	isog	isoide	isogeba	isoga(nai)	isogu	isoida
9	shini(masu)	shin	shin'de	shineba	shina(nai)	shinu	shin'da

b. 2   Tense & Negation

Group	Normal Imperfect Affirmative	Normal Imperfect Negative	Normal Perfect Affirmative	Normal Perfect Negative	Plain Imperfect Affirmative	Plain Imperfect Negative	Plain Perfect Affirmative	Plain Perfect Negative	Neutral Provisional Affirmative	Neutral Provisional Negative
1	furimasu	furimasen	furimashita	furimasen deshita	furu	furanai	futta	furanakatta	fureba	fura-nakereba
2	aimasu	aimasen	aimashita	aimasen deshita	au	awanai	atta	awanakatta	aeba	awa-nakereba
3	machimasu	machimasen	machimashita	machimasen deshita	matsu	matanai	matta	mata-nakatta	mateba	mata-nakereba
4	arukimasu	arukimasen	arukimashita	arukimasen deshita	aruku	arukanai	aruita	aruka-nakatta	arukeba	aruka-nakereba
5	hanashimasu	hanashimasen	hanashimashita	hanashimasen deshita	hanasu	hanasanai	hanashita	hanasa-nakatta	hanaseba	hanasa-nakereba
6	komimasu	komimasen	komimashita	komimasen deshita	komu	komanai	kon'da	koma-nakatta	komeba	koma-nakereba
7	asobimasu	asobimasen	asobimashita	asobimasen deshita	asobu	asobanai	ason'da	asoba-nakatta	asobeba	asoba-nakereba
8	isogimasu	isogimasen	isogimashita	isogimasen deshita	isogu	isoganai	isoida	isoga-nakatta	isogeba	isoga-nakereba
9	shinimasu	shinimasen	shinimashita	shinimasen deshita	shinu	shinanai	shin'da	shina-nakatta	shineba	shina-nakereba

c.   Irregular Verb

kuru   I, 3   ben'kyoo suru   I, 9   kaimono suru   I, 4   ryokoo suru   I, 9   setsumei suru   II, 7
suru   I, 3; II, 11   den'wa suru   I, 9   kekkon suru   I, 9   ryoori suru   II, 11   shokuji suru   II, 11
arubaito suru   II, 2   gochisoo suru   II, 11   ken'butsu suru   I, 9   san'po suru   II, 5

c. 1 Conjugation

	Neutral				Plain	
Stem Form	Base Form	TE Form	BA Form	Pre-Nai Form	Dictionary Form	TA Form
ki(masu)	k	kite	kureba	ko(nai)	kuru	kita
shi(masu)	s	shite	sureba	shi(nai)	suru	shita

c. 2 Tense & Negation

Normal				Plain				Neutral	
Imperfect		Perfect		Imperfect		Perfect		Provisional	
Affirmative	Negative	Affirmative	Negative	Affirmative	Negative	Affirmative	Negative	Affirmative	Negative
kimasu	kimasen	kimashita	kimasen deshita	kuru	konai	kita	konakatta	kureba	konakereba
shimasu	shimasen	shimashita	shimasen deshita	suru	shinai	shita	shinakatta	sureba	shi-nakereba

2. Adjective

akai	II, 13	hayai	II, 6	kuwashii	II, 7	ookii	I, 7	tooi	I, 7
aoi	II, 13	hikui	II, 10	mazui	I, 8	osoi	II, 9	tsumaranai	I, 7
atarashii	II, 5	hiroi	II, 10	mijikai	II, 9	samui	I, 11	tsumetai	I, 11
atatakai	I, 11	hoshii	II, 1	mushiatsui	II, 10	semai	II, 10	urusai	I, 8
atsui	I, 11	ii	I, 7; II, 7	muzukashii	I, 7	shiroi	II, 13	utsukushii	II, 5
chairoi	II, 13	isogashii	I, 8	nagai	II, 9	subarashii	I, 9	wakai	II, 11
chiisai	I, 7	kawaii	II, 5	nai	II, 6	sukunai	II, 5	warui	I, 7
chikai	I, 7	kiiroi	II, 13	oishii	I, 8	suzushii	I, 11	yasashii	I, 7
erai	I, 7	kitanai	I, 8	omoshiroi	I, 7	takai	I, 7	yasui	I, 7
furui	II, 5	kuroi	II, 13	ooi	II, 5	tanoshii	I, 9	yoi	I, 7

1. Conjugation

Dictionary Form	Base Form	TA Form	TE Form	KU Form	BA Form
akai	aka	akakatta	akakute	akaku	akakereba

2. Tense & Negation

Normal				Plain				Neutral	
Imperfect		Perfect		Imperfect		Perfect		Provisional	
Affirmative	Negative	Affirmative	Negative	Affirmative	Negative	Affirmative	Negative	Affirmative	Negative
akai desu	akaku arimasen	akakatta desu	akaku arimasen deshita	akai	akaku nai	akakatta	akaku nakatta	akakereba	akaku nakereba

3. Adjectival Derivative

Dictionary Form	Base Form	TA Form	TE Form	KU Form	BA Form
-nai	-na	-nakatta	-nakute	-naku	-nakereba
-tai	-ta	-takatta	-takute	-taku	-takereba

4. Copula

Normal			Neutral		
Dictionary Form	TA Form	OO Form	TE Form	NA* Form	BA Form
desu	deshita	deshoo	de	na	nara(ba)

*NA Form is used only with adjectival Nominatives such as follows:

daihyooteki	II, 3	gen'ki	I, 8	joozu	I, 5	shizuka	I, 8	yutaka	II, 10
daijoobu	II, 3	hen	II, 5	kirai	I, 5	suki	I, 5	yuumei	II, 5
daikirai	I, 8	heta	I, 5	kirei	I, 8	taihen	II, 6	zan'nen	I, 9
daisuki	I, 8	hima	I, 4	sakan	II, 10	teinei	II, 1		
dame	I, 8	iroiro	II, 5	shitsurei	II, 5	tekitoo	II, 7		

APPENDIX V

PRESENTATION AND DIALOG

— Romanization and English Equivalent —

1.1 — Kaimono —

Nihon no depaato nado no ten'in no kotoba wa, taihen teinei desu. Tsugi wa ten'in to kyaku no kaiwa desu.

— Shopping —

The clerks at department stores and the like in Japan are very polite in their speech. The following is a conversation between a clerk and a customer.

1.2

Ten'in: Irasshaimase. Nani o sashiagemashoo ka /

On'na no kyaku: Rein'kooto ga hoshii n desu ga . . . .

Ten'in: Okyakusama no desu ne /

On'na no kyaku: Ee, watakushi no desu. Sore o misete kudasai.

Ten'in: Hai, doozo.

On'na no kyaku: Kono rein'kooto wa ikura desu ka /

Ten'in: San'zen roppyakuen desu.

On'na no kyaku: Chotto kite mimashoo. Sukoshi chiisai desu ne.

Ten'in: Dewa, kore wa ikaga desu ka / Yon'sen san'byakuen desu. Saizu wa choodo iı ⸃

On'na no kyaku: Ee. Jaa, kore o itadakimasu. Sore kara, hyakuen gurai no han'kachi o nimai kudasai.

Ten'in: Arigatoo gozaimasu. Rein'kooto wa hako ni iremashoo ka.

On'na no kyaku: Ee, soo shite kudasai. Sore kara, nekutai o misete kudasai.

Ten'in: Nekutai wa nikai de utte imasu.

On'na no kyaku: Jaa, ato de itte mimashoo. Zen'bu de ikura desu ka /

Ten'in: Yon'sen gohyakuen desu. Doomo arigatoo gozaimashita.

Clerk: Welcome. What shall I give to you? [What are you looking for?]

Lady customer: I want a raincoat.

Clerk: Is it for you?

Lady customer: Yes, mine [it's for me]. Please show me that one.

Clerk: Yes, here you are.

Lady customer: How much is this raincoat?

Clerk: It's 3,600 yen.

Lady customer: Let me try it on. It's a little small.

Clerk: Then, how about this? It's 4,300 yen. The size is just right.

Lady customer: All right. I'll take this, then. And, please give me two handkerchiefs for about 100 yen apiece.

Clerk: Thank you very much. Shall I put the raincoat in a box?

Lady customer: Yes, please do so. Then, show me a tie, please.

Clerk: We sell ties on the second floor.

Lady customer: Fine, I'll go and see later. How much is the total?

Clerk: It's 4,500 yen. Thank you very much.

2.1 — Daigakusei —

Ichiroo wa daigaku no yonen'sei desu. Kyooiku-gaku o ben'kyoo shite imasu.

Nihon no daigakusei wa, natsuyasumi ni yoku arubaito o shimasu. Daigaku no natsuyasumi wa shichigatsu to hachigatsu desu. Ichiroo wa shichigatsu ni arubaito o shimashita.

— College Students —

Ichirō is a senior student of a college. He is studying education.

Japanese college students often work for money during the summer vacation. The summer vacation of colleges is during July and August. Ichirō worked during July.

2.2

Hayashi: Ichiroo kun, shibaraku. *long time no see*

Ichiroo: A, Hayashi san, shibaraku desu nee.

Hayashi: Kimi wa mada gakusei deshoo /

Ichiroo: Ee, yonen desu. Hayashi san wa, ima, nan no shigoto o shite imasu ka /

Hayashi: Depaato ni tsutomete imasu.

Ichiroo: Soo desu ka. Boku mo natsuyasumi ni depaato de hatarakimashita yo /

Hayashi: Ichiroo kun, ashita no ban, uchi e kimasen ka / Yukkuri hanashimashoo.

Ichiroo: Ee, zehi ukagaimasu. *surely*

Hayashi: Watashi no tokoro wa shitte imashita ne / Ima mo mae no tokoro ni sun'de imasu.

Ichiroo: Eeto . . . . . . Shibuya deshita ne /

Hayashi: Soo, sugu wakarimasu yo. Jidoosha de kimasu ka /

Ichiroo: Iie, jidoosha wa motte imasen. Nan'ji ni ukagaimashoo ka /

Hayashi: Goji han wa doo desu ka /

Ichiroo: Ee, ii desu.

Hayashi: Dewa, goji han goro matte imasu yo /

Ichiroo: Ee. Jaa, mata ashita

Hayashi: Sayoonara

Mr. Hayashi: Ichirō, I haven't seen you for a long time.

Ichirō: Oh, Mr. Hayashi, it's been a long time since I last saw you.

Mr. Hayashi: You are still a student, aren't you?

Ichirō: Yes, I'm a senior. Mr. Hayashi, what work are you doing now?

Mr. Hayashi: I am working for a department store.

Ichirō: Oh, you are. I also worked at a department store during the summer vacation.

Mr. Hayashi: Ichirō, won't you come to my house tomorrow night? Let's talk leisurely at home.

Ichirō: Yes, I'll visit you, by all means.

Mr. Hayashi: You know my place, don't you? I am now still living at the former place [the place where

I used to live].

Ichirō:	Let me see .... It was in Shibuya, wasn't it?
Mr. Hayashi:	That's right. You'll have no trouble finding it. Are you coming by car?
Ichirō:	No, I don't have a car. What time shall I come [go]?
Mr. Hayashi:	How about five-thirty?
Ichirō:	All right, that's fine with me.
Mr. Hayashi:	Then I'll be waiting for you at about five-thirty.
Ichirō:	Yes. Then I'll see you again tomorrow.
Mr. Hayashi:	Good-bye.

3.1   — Kabuki —

"Kabuki" wa sen roppyakunen goro ni hajimarimashita. Sono koro, "kabuki" wa shomin no goraku deshita.

Ima wa, Nihon no daihyooteki na geijutsu no hitotsu desu.

   — Kabuki —

Kabuki was started around 1600. In those days it was the amusement of the common people. Now it is one of the representative arts of Japan.

3.2

Inoue:	Moshi moshi, Mori san no otaku desu ka /
Yoshiko:	Hai, soo desu.
Inoue:	Yoshiko san wa irasshaimasu ka /
Yoshiko:	Watakushi desu ga ......
Inoue:	A, Yoshiko san. Boku, Inoue desu.
Yoshiko:	Ara, kon'nichi wa
Inoue:	Kin'yoobi ni anata ni aitakatta n desu ga, gakkoo ni kimasen deshita ne / Byooki deshita ka /
Yoshiko:	Ee. Jugyoo o yasumitaku arimasen deshita ga, kaze de kibun ga warukatta n desu.
Inoue:	Mada warui n desu ka /
Yoshiko:	Iie Kinoo wa ichinichijuu nete imashita ga, kyoo wa moo daijoobu desu.
Inoue:	Sore wa yokatta desu ne. Jitsu wa, raishuu no doyoobi no kabuki no kippu o motte imasu.

278

Yoshiko san wa kabuki o mitaku arimasen ka /

Yoshiko: Ee, zehi mitai desu.

Inoue: Jaa, gogo yoji juugofun goro, Kabukiza de aimashoo. Boku wa, tomodachi o hitori tsurete ikimasu.

Yoshiko: Raishuu no doyoobi, yoji juugofun desu ne / Wakarimashita. Doomo arigatoo.

Inoue: Iie Jaa, mata

Yoshiko: Sayoonara.

Mr. Inoue: Hello, is this the Mori home?
Yoshiko: Yes, it is.
Mr. Inoue: Is Yoshiko there?
Yoshiko: This is she speaking.
Mr. Inoue: Oh, Yoshiko. This is Inoue.
Yoshiko: Oh, good afternoon.
Mr. Inoue: I wanted to see you on Friday, but you didn't come to school, did you? Were you sick?
Yoshiko: Yes. I didn't want to miss [to be absent from] the class, but I did not feel well with a cold.
Mr. Inoue: Are you still sick?
Yoshiko: No. I stayed in bed all day yesterday, but I'm all right today.
Mr. Inoue: That is good. The fact is [the reason why I've called you is], I have tickets to *kabuki* for next Saturday. Don't you want to see *kabuki*?
Yoshiko: Yes, I would like to see it very much.
Mr. Inoue: Then let's meet at the Kabuki Theater at about 4:15 in the afternoon. I'll take a friend with me.
Yoshiko: Next Saturday, at 4:15, is it? All right. Thank you.
Mr. Inoue: You are welcome. So long.
Yoshiko: Good-bye.

5.1 — Hanami —

Sakura wa yuumei na Nihon no hana desu. Daitai san'gatsu ka shigatsu ni sakimasu. Nihon no hitotachi wa, yoku iroiro na hana o mi ni ikimasu ga, toku ni sakura ga suki desu.

— Flower Viewing —

Cherry blossoms are famous Japanese flowers. Roughly speaking, they bloom in March or in April. Japanese people often go to view various flowers, but they particularly like cherry blossoms.

5.2

Jooji: Michiko san, kyoo wa subarashii ten'ki desu ne. Gogo, san'po ni ikimasen ka /

Michiko: Ee.

Jooji: Ii tokoro o shitte imasu ka /

Michiko: Ueno Kooen wa doo desu ka / Choodo ima, sakura ga saite imasu kara, ohanami ni ikimashoo ka.

Jooji: Aa, hanami desu ne. Sakura wa suki na hana desu kara, zehi mitai desu ne. Sono kooen wa don'na tokoro desu ka /

Michiko: Soo desu nee . . . . Totemo ookii kooen desu. Bijutsukan ya doobutsuen nado ga arimasu. Dakara, otona mo kodomo mo oozei asobi ni ikimasu.

Jooji: Jaa, ima wa hanami no kisetsu desu kara, hito ga toku ni ooi deshoo ne /

Michiko: Ee. . . . Jaa, Jooji san, koo shimashoo. Hajime ni, doobutsuen e ikimashoo. Soshite, yuugata ohanami o shimashoo.

Jooji: Sore ga ii desu ne / Yuugata wa tabun hito ga sukunai deshoo kara, yukkuri ohanami ga dekimasu ne /

George: Michiko, it's a wonderful day [weather] today, isn't it? Won't you go for a walk in the afternoon?
Michiko: Yes.
George: Do you know any good place [to go]?
Michiko: How about Ueno Park? Cherry blossoms are in bloom right now, so shall we go cherry blossom viewing?
George: Ah, cherry blossom viewing! Cherry blossoms are my favorite flowers, so I certainly would like to see them. What sort of place is that park?
Michiko: Let me see . . . . It is a very big park. There are an art museum, a zoo, and the like. Therefore many adults as well as many children go there to play [have a good time].
George: Well, then, as it is the cherry blossom viewing season now, there will be especially many people, won't there?
Michiko: Yes. Now, George, let's do it this way. At first, let's go to the zoo. Then let's view cherry

blossoms early in the evening.

George: That's a good idea. People will probably be scarce toward evening, so we can see cherry blossoms without hurrying.

6.1   — Norimono —

Tookyoo kara Oosaka made gohyaku gojuu rokkiro (san'byaku yon'juu rokumairu) arimasu ga, mukashi wa, taitei arukimashita kara, ryokoo suru no wa taihen deshita. Ima wa, hikooki ya Shin'kan'sen nado no hayai norimono de iku koto ga dekimasu.

       — Transportation —

It is five hundred fifty-six kilometers (three hundred forty-six miles) from Tōkyō to Ōsaka, and in the past, it was very hard to travel, because travelers generally walked that distance. Now we can go by rapid transportation facilities, such as airplanes, the New Tōkaidō Line, etc.

6.2

Gaikokujin: Chotto ukagaimasu ga, are wa Oosaka-yuki no kyuukoo desu ka /

Nihon'jin: Saa, yoku wakarimasen. Asoko ni iru ekiin ni kiite mite kudasai.

Gaikokujin: Hai, doomo arigatoo.

        *   *   *   *   *   *   *   *   *   *

Gaikokujin: Anoo, Oosaka-yuki no kyuukoo ni noritai n desu ga, nan'ban'sen kara demasu ka /

Ekiin: Nijuu ichiji ni deru kyuukoo desu ne / Juuyon'ban'sen kara desu.

Gaikokujin: Oosaka made dono gurai kakarimasu ka /

Ekiin: Yoru wa futsuukyuukoo de juujikan'han kakarimasu. Desukara, kyuukoo ga Oosaka ni tsuku jikan wa, ashita no asa shichiji nijuu happun desu.

Gaikokujin: Soo desu ka. Ittoo no seki wa mada arimasu ka /

Ekiin: Madoguchi ni wa moo nai deshoo. Notte kara, shashoo ni kiite mite kudasai. Tama ni noranai hito ya sugu oriru hito ga imasu kara ......

Gaikokujin: Jaa, soo shimasu. Doomo arigatoo.

Foreigner: Excuse me, but is that an express bound for Ōsaka?

Japanese: Well .... I don't know exactly. Please ask the station employee over there and find out.

Foreigner: All right. Thank you.

* * * * * * * * * *

Foreigner: Say, I want to take an express bound for Ōsaka. From what track does it leave?

Employee: It's an express that leaves at 2100 hours, isn't it? It leaves from Track Number 14.

Foreigner: How long does it take to Ōsaka?

Employee: The ordinary express takes ten hours and half (to Ōsaka) at night. So the time when the express arrives at Ōsaka is 7:28 tomorrow morning.

Foreigner: I see. Do you still have tickets [seats] for the first class?

Employee: I don't think they have any more at the ticket-window. After getting on the train, please ask a conductor. (He may have some) because, once in a while, there are some persons who do not take a train (after buying tickets) or some who get off a train soon (making a vacant seat).

Foreigner: Then, I'll do so. Thank you.

7.1   — Toshokan de —

Hitori no otoko no gakusei ga toshokan no kaado no tokoro de hon o sagashite imasu. Soko e, hon o nisan'satsu motta on'na no gakusei ga kimashita.

— At the Library —

A male student is looking for a book where the cards of the library are. There a female student arrives carrying two or three books with her.

7.2

Keiko: Pooru san.

Pooru: A, Keiko san, ben'kyoo desu ka /

Keiko: Ee. Ototoi karita hon o kaeshi ni kimashita. Sore ni, chotto yomitai hon mo arimasu kara ....
Pooru san wa /

Pooru: Kesa no Nihon bun'gaku no jikan ni wakaranakatta mon'dai o shirabetai n desu ga, tekitoo na hon ga mitsukarimasen.

Keiko: Kono kaado o shirabete mimashita ka /

Pooru: Ee, shirabete mimashita ga, nai n desu.

282

Keiko: Toshokan'in ni kiite mimashita ka /

Pooru: Iie, mada desu.

Keiko: Watakushi no yon'da san'koosho wa setsumei ga totemo kuwashikatta desu yo / Dai wa "Nihon Bun'gaku" desu ga, yon'da koto ga arimasu ka /

Pooru: Iie, arimasen. Koko de karita hon desu ka /

Keiko: Iie, watakushi no desu. Ima, tsukatte imasen kara, doozo.

Pooru: Jaa, kashite kudasai. Yuugata kari ni ikimasu ga, ii desu ka /

Keiko: Ee, kamaimasen.

Keiko: Paul!

Paul: Oh, Keiko, are you studying here?

Keiko: Yes. I came here to return the book I borrowed the day before yesterday. Besides, there are some books I wanted to read ... How about you?

Paul: I want to check on a matter that I could not understand in the Japanese literature class this morning, but I can't find the proper books.

Keiko: Did you check these cards?

Paul: Yes, I checked but I can't find anything.

Keiko: Did you ask the librarian?

Paul: No, not yet.

Keiko: The reference book I read had a detailed explanation. The title is "Japanese Literature." Have you ever read it?

Paul: No, I haven't. Is it the book you borrowed here?

Keiko: No, it's mine. I am not using it now, so please [I'll lend it to you].

Paul: Then please lend it to me. Is it all right if I come to get it [go to borrow it] in the evening?

Keiko: Yes, it's all right.

9.1　　　— Nihon'go no Kyooshitsu —

Kyooshitsu no naka ni, sen'sei ga hitori, gakusei ga hachinin imasu. Sen'sei wa kokuban no mae ni tatte imasu. Gakuseitachi wa, isu ni suwatte imasu. Tsukue no ue ni wa, hon ya nooto ya en'pitsu nado ga arimasu.

— Japanese Classroom —

In the classroom, there are a teacher and eight students. The teacher is standing in front of the blackboard. The students are seated on the chairs. On their desks there are books, notebooks, pencils, etc.

9.2

Sen'sei: Dewa, kore kara, kinoo naratta tokoro no shiken o shimashoo. Mazu, kami ni namae o kaite kudasai.

Gakusei (1): Sen'sei!

Sen'sei: Hai, nan desu ka /

Gakusei (1): Man'nen'hitsu o wasuremashita. En'pitsu de kaite mo ii desu ka /

Sen'sei: Ee, ii desu. Demo, kore kara wasurenai de kudasai yo /

Gakusei (2): Jisho o tsukatte mo kamaimasen ka /

Sen'sei: Iie, tsukatte wa ikemasen. Jisho mo kyookasho mo tsukawanai de kudasai. Dewa, hajimemashoo. Kokuban ni mon'dai o kakimasu kara, ima watashita kami ni kotae o kaite kudasai.

Gakusei (3): Sen'sei, kotae dake de ii n desu ka /

Sen'sei: Hai, kamaimasen.

Gakusei (3): Sore kara, roomaji de kotaete mo ii desu ka /

Sen'sei: Iie, kan'ji to kana o tsukatte kudasai. Osokute mo kamaimasen. Wakarimashita ne /

Gakusei (3): Wakarimashita.

Teacher: Well, now, let's have an examination on the part we learned yesterday. First of all, please write your name on the paper.

Student (1): Sir!

Teacher: Yes, what is it?

Student (1): I forgot [to bring] a fountain pen. May I write with a pencil?

Teacher: Yes, you may. But please don't forget from now on [to bring a fountain pen].

Student (2): Is it all right [for us] to use a dictionary?

Teacher: No, it isn't all right [for you] to use it. Don't use either the dictionary or the textbook, please. Then, let's start. I'll write the questions on the blackboard, so please write the answers on the paper I just handed to you.

Student (3): Sir, only answers will be all right?

Teacher: Yes, all right.

Student (3): And may I answer them in *rōmaji*?

Teacher: No, please use *kanji* and *kana*. I don't mind it even if it takes time. Is that clear?

Student (3): Yes.

10.1 — Nihon no Kuni —

Nihon wa yottsu no shima ni wakarete imasu. Sono naka de, ichiban ookii no wa Hon'shuu, niban'me wa Hokkaidoo, san'ban'me wa Kyuushuu, ichiban chiisai no wa Shikoku desu.

— The Country of Japan —

Japan is divided into four islands. Among them, the largest one is Honshū, the second is Hokkaidō, the third is Kyūshū, and the smallest one is Shikoku.

10.2

Aoki: Teeraa san, anata no okuni wa doko desu ka /

Teeraa: Minami Kariforunia desu.

Aoki: Kariforunia wa Kita Amerika de ichiban yutaka na shuu deshoo /

Teeraa: Ee, maa soo desu ne. Sore ni, kikoo ga ii kara, iroiro na kudamono ga ichinen'juu arimasu. Hoka no shuu yori un'doo mo sakan desu ne. Aoki san wa Kan'sai deshita ne /

Aoki: Ee, Kyooto desu.

Teeraa: Kyooto to Tookyoo to, dotchi ga suki desu ka /

Aoki: Kyooto to Tookyoo o kuraberu no wa muzukashii desu keredo, kikoo wa, Tookyoo no hoo ga ii desu ne. Kyooto wa, natsu totemo mushiatsui n desu.

Teeraa: Demo, machi wa Kyooto no hoo ga kirei deshoo /

Aoki: Mochiron, zutto kirei desu yo. Sore ni, Tookyoo hodo urusaku arimasen kara nee.

Aoki: Mr. Taylor, where is your home town?

Taylor: It's in Southern California.

Aoki: Isn't California the richest state in North America?

Taylor: Yes, something like that. Moreover, because of the nice climate, there are various kinds of fruit throughout the year. Sports (also) are more popular than in other states. You are from the Kansai area, aren't you?

Aoki: Yes, I'm from Kyōto.

Taylor: Which do you like better, Kyōto or Tōkyō?

Aoki: It is difficult to compare Kyōto with Tōkyō, but I prefer Tōkyō in climate. It's very hot and humid during the summer in Kyōto.

Taylor: But the city of Kyōto is much prettier [than the city of Tōkyō], isn't it?

Aoki: Of course, Kyōto is much prettier than Tōkyō. Besides, it is not as noisy as Tōkyō.

11.1   — Ryoori —

Nihon ryoori wa, aji mo ii desu ga, iro ya katachi mo hijoo ni utsukushii desu.

Toshiyori wa, daitai, Nihon ryoori ga suki desu ga, wakai hito wa Nihon ryoori o taberu yori

seiyoo ryoori ya Chuugoku ryoori o taberu hoo ga suki desu.

— Cooking —

Japanese food is tasty, and its colors and shapes are extremely beautiful also.

Old folks are generally fond of Japanese food; however, young people prefer eating Western or Chinese food to eating Japanese food.

11.2

Ookawa: A, moo rokuji ni narimashita ne / Osoku narimasu kara, sorosoro shitsurei shimasu.

Koyama: Moo son'na jikan desu ka / Issho ni shokuji shimasen ka /

Ookawa: Soo desu ne .... Ii tokoro ga arimasu ka /

Koyama: Kono hen no shokudoo no tabemono wa mazui kara, gochisoo wa dekinai kedo, boku ga

tsukurimasu yo. Soto de taberu yori jibun de ryoori shita hoo ga zutto ii desu.

Ookawa: Demo, tsukuru no wa taihen deshoo / Soto e itta hoo ga ii desu yo.

Koyama: Ie, sugu dekimasu.

Ookawa: Soo desu ka / Jaa, watashi mo tetsudaimasu. Koyama san wa nani o tsukuru no ga ichiban

joozu desu ka /

Koyama: Kareeraisu ya ton'katsu desu ne. ... Niku to yasai ga arimasu kara, karee ni shimashoo ka.

Ookawa: Ii desu ne. Boku wa karee ga daisuki desu.

Koyama: Jaa, karee o tsukurimashoo. Demo, tabun Ookawa san ga omou hodo oishiku arimasen yo.

Mr. Ōkawa: Oh, it's already six o'clock. It's getting late, so I'd better be leaving.

Mr. Koyama: Is it so late already? Won't you have supper with me?

Mr. Ōkawa: All right. Is there any good place (to go)?

Mr. Koyama: Food at eating places in this area is not good, so I'll cook something, though I can't give you good food. It would be much better if I cooked it myself than if we were to eat out.

Mr. Ōkawa: But it is much trouble to cook, isn't it? We'd better go out (to eat).

Mr. Koyama: No, the meal will be ready soon.

Mr. Ōkawa: Really? Then I'll help you. What do you cook best?

Mr. Koyama: Curry and rice, pork cutlet and the like. ... Since I have meat and vegetables, shall we have curry and rice?

Mr. Ōkawa: That's fine. I like curry and rice very much.

Mr. Koyama: Well, then, let's cook curry and rice. But it probably won't be as good as you may think.

13.1 — Tookyoo no Michi —

Tookyoo wa jin'koo ga hijoo ni ooi desu. Den'sha ya basu ya chikatetsu wa itsumo kon'de imasu. Jidoosha, takushii, basu, torakku nado, takusan no norimono ga semai michi o hashitte imasu.

— Streets in Tōkyō —

Tōkyō has a great population. The trains, buses, and subways are always crowded. A lot of vehicles, such as automobiles, taxis, buses, trucks, etc., are running on narrow streets.

13.2

Kimura: Tanaka san, sumimasen ga, Furan'su Taishikan e iku michi o oshiete kudasai.

Tanaka: Furan'su Taishikan nara, yoku shitte imasu kedo, kuruma ni notte ikimasu ka /

Kimura: Tookereba, takushii ka basu de ikimasu kedo, chikai n deshoo /

Tanaka: Chotto tooi desu yo. Juugoban no basu de ikeba, taishikan no soba ni tomarimasu. Futatsume de orireba, sugu wakarimasu yo.

Kimura: Juugoban no basu desu ne / Teiryuujo wa doko desu ka /

Tanaka: Kono toori no niban'me no kado o hidari e magarimasu. Hora, ima akai jiten'sha ga hashitte kimasu ne / Ano kado desu.

Kimura: Ee, wakarimasu.

Tanaka: Sore kara, massugu gojuumeetoru gurai aruite ikimasu. Suruto, migi ni shiroi tatemono ga arimasu.

Teiryuujo wa sono tatemono no iriguchi no mae desu.

Kimura: Doomo arigatoo gozaimashita.

Mr. Kimura: Excuse me, Mr. Tanaka, would you please tell me the way to the French Embassy?

Mr. Tanaka: If it is the French Embassy, I know it very well. But are you going in a car?

Mr. Kimura: If it is far (from here), I will go by taxi or bus, but it is near (from here), isn't it?

Mr. Tanaka: It is a little far. If you go by No. 15 bus, it will stop by the embassy. If you get off at the second stop, you'll find the embassy right away.

Mr. Kimura: No. 15 bus? Where is the bus stop?

Mr. Tanaka: You turn to the left at the second corner on this street. Look, there's a red bicycle coming through now, isn't there? It's that corner.

Mr. Kimura: Yes, I see.

Mr. Tanaka: And you walk down straight about fifty meters. Then there is a white building on the right. The bus stop is in front of the entrance to that building.

Mr. Kimura: Thank you very much.

14.1 — Yama Nobori —

Ogen'ki desu ka /

Sassoku desu ga, raigetsu no tsuitachi to futsuka, Fujisan ni noboru tsumori desu ga, anata mo irasshai-masen ka / Boku no hoka ni Yamada san to Ishii san mo iku hazu desu.

Den'sha no kippu o kawanakereba narimasen kara, kon'getsu no nijuu hachinichi made ni den'wa de hen'ji o kudasareba, tsugoo ga ii n desu ga.

Boku no den'wa ban'goo wa yon-goo-ichi no goo-hachi-kyuu-nii desu.

Dewa, yoi hen'ji o matte imasu.

Sayoonara

Shichigatsu nijuu yokka

Kinoshita

Pataason sama

— Mountain Climbing —

July 24

Dear Mr. Patterson:

How are you?

I'll come to the point right away. We are planning to climb Mt. Fuji on the 1st and 2nd of next month. Won't you go with us? Mr. Yamada and Mr. Ishii are supposed to go besides myself.

I must buy train tickets (in advance), so if you give me a reply on the telephone by the 28th of this month, it will be convenient.

My telephone number is 451-5892.

Then, I'll be waiting for your favorable answer.

Good-bye

Kinoshita

14.2

Pataason: Moshi moshi, Pataason desu ga . . . .

Kinoshita: A, Pataason san, matte imashita. Issho ni irasshaimasu ka /

Pataason: Ee, zehi tsurete itte kudasai.

Kinoshita: Sore wa yokatta. Nijuu kunichi ni nareba, kuwashii koto ga wakaru hazu desu.

Pataason: Jaa, au jikan ya basho wa ato de shirasete kudasai.

Kinoshita: Ee. Yama no ue wa kanari samui kara, boku wa seetaa o motte iku tsumori desu. Pataason san mo seetaa ka jan'paa o motte itta hoo ga ii desu yo.

Pataason: Oben'too wa /

Kinoshita: Dekakeru hi no yoru no ben'too wa motte ikanakereba narimasen ne. Okashi ya kudamono wa issho ni kaimasu kara, motte konakute mo ii desu kedo . . . .

Pataason: Wakarimashita.

Mr. Patterson: Hello, this is Patterson.

Mr. Kinoshita: Oh, Mr. Patterson, I have been waiting (for your call). Are you coming (going) with us?

Mr. Patterson: Yes, please take me with you by all means.

Mr. Kinoshita: That's good! We are supposed to know the details on the 29th.

Mr. Patterson: Then please let me know later of the time and place to meet.

Mr. Kinoshita: Yes. I am planning to take a sweater with me, since it is quite cold on the top of the mountain. You had better take a sweater or a jacket with you too.

Mr. Patterson: How about the meal?

Mr. Kinoshita: You have to take a meal for the night we leave. We will buy snacks and fruit [for all of us together] so you don't have to bring them, though. . . . .

Mr. Patterson: I see.

APPENDIX VI

GLOSSARY

(A)

aa	SI	5	oh; ah
Afurika	N	10	Africa
aimasu	V	3	meet (normal form of *au*) (see 3.4.7)
aji	N	11	taste; flavor
Ajia	N	10	Asia
aka	N	13	red
akai	A	13	is red (see 13.4.7)
akemasu	V	9	open (normal form of *akeru*) (transitive Verb)
an'na	PN	5	that sort of
anoo	SI	6	say; well; er-r-r-r (see 6.4.9)
ao	N	13	blue
aoi	A	13	is blue
Aoki	N	10	family name
ara	SI	3	oh; ah (used only by women)
Arasuka	N	10	Alaska
arubaito	N	2	(student's) work (for money)
arubaito shimasu	V	2	do a side-job (see 2.4.4)
arukimasu	V	6	walk (normal form of *aruku*)
asatte	N	7	the day after tomorrow
ashi	N	7	leg; foot
asobimasu	V	5	play (normal form of *asobu*) (see 5.4.9)
atama	N	10	head
atarashii	A	5	is new; is fresh
ato de	PM	1	later

(B)

-ban	Nd	6	counter for naming numbers in succession
ban'goo	N	14	(sequential) number
basho	N	14	place
basu	N	3	bus

ben'too	N	14	lunch; meal to take out
bijutsukan	N	5	art museum
boorin'gu	N	5	bowling
bun'gaku	N	7	literature
byooki	N	3	illness

(C)

chairo	N	13	brown
chairoi	A	13	is brown
chika	N	1	basement (lit. underground)
chikatetsu	N	13	subway (lit. underground railway)
choodo	Adv.	1	just; exactly

(D)

-daasu	Nd	1	dozen
dai	N	7	title
daigakusei	N	2	college student
daihyooteki	Na	3	representative
daijoobu	Na	3	all right; safe (this word is used to allay fear or doubt)
daitai	Adv.	5	roughly speaking; mostly; approximately
dake	R	9	only; just (see 9.4.7)
dame	Na	9	no good
de	R	1	totalizing (see 1.4.17)
de	R	3	because of (see 3.4.11)
de	C	9	TE form of *desu* (see 9.4.8)
de	R	10	of; among (see 10.4.1)
deguchi	N	13	exit
dekimasu	V	5	is able to; can (do); is possible (normal form of *dekiru*) (see 5.4.11 & 6.4.4)
dekimasu	V	11	is ready; is done; is made (normal form of *dekiru*) (see 11.4.6)
demasu	V	6	go out; leave (normal form of *deru*)
desukara	SI	6	therefore; so (formal form of *dakara*)
dewa	SI	1	then; well (formal equivalent of *jaa*)
-do	Nd	1	time(s)
doa	N	9	door
dochira	Ni	10	which (of the two)? (see 10.4.6)
don'na	PN	5	what sort of? (see 5.4.5)
dono gurai (dono kurai)	Ni	6	how long?; how far?; how much? (see 6.4.13)
doobutsuen	N	5	zoo
-doru	Nd	1	dollar(s) (see 1.4.11)
dotchı	Ni	10	which (of the two)? (see 10.4.6)
doyoobi	N	3	Saturday

(E)

eeto	SI	2	let me see; well

ekiin	N	6	station employee
-en	Nd	1	unit for Japanese currency (see 1.4.11)

(F)

Fujisan	N	14	Mt. Fuji
-fun	Nd	3	minute (see 3.4.16)
furui	A	5	is old (thing)
futsuka	N	14	the second day of the month; two days
futsuu	N	6	ordinary; usual; average

(G)

gaikokujin	N	6	foreigner
geijutsu	N	3	art
getsuyoobi	N	3	Monday
gochisoo	N	11	treat; feast
gochisoo shimasu	V	11	treat (one to something to eat or drink) (normal form of *gochisoo (o) suru*)
gogatsu	N	2	May
gogo	N	3	p.m.; in the afternoon (see 3.4.15)
goraku	N	3	amusement
-goro	Nd	2	about (time); approximately (see 2.4.18)
gorufu	N	5	golf
gozen	N	3	a.m.
gun'jin	N	11	military personnel; career soldier
-gurai	Nd	1	about; approximately (see 1.4.14)

(H)

hachigatsu	N	2	August
hajimarimasu	V	3	begin (intransitive Verb) (normal form of *hajimaru*)
hajime	N	5	beginning
hajimemasu	V	9	begin (transitive Verb) (normal form of *hajimeru*)
hako	N	1	box; case
-han	Nd	2	half (see 2.4.17)
hana	N	5	flower; blossom
hanami	N	5	flower viewing (usually cherry blossom viewing)
han'kachi	N	1	handkerchief
hashirimasu	V	6	run (normal form of *hashiru*)
hatarakimasu	V	2	work; labor (normal form of *hataraku*) (see 2.4.9)
hatsuka	N	14	the twentieth day of the month; twenty days
hayai	A	6	is fast; is rapid; is early
Hayashi	N	2	family name
hazu	Nd	14	expected to (do); supposed to (do) (see 14.4.4)
hen	Na	5	strange; unusual; funny
hi	N	14	day (see 14.4.9)
hidari	N	13	left
higashi	N	10	east

hijoo ni	Adv.	11	extremely
hikui	A	10	is low; is short (stature)
hiroi	A	10	is large; is wide; is spacious
hodo	R	10	as much as (see 10.4.10)
hoka	N	10	other; another; different; else (see 10.4.5)
Hon'shuu	N	10	the main island of Japan
hoo	Nd	10	alternative (see 10.4.6)
hora	SI	13	look!; there!
hoshii	A	1	want; is desirous (see 1.4.4)

(I)

ichiban	N	10	the most (see 10.4.1)
ichigatsu	N	2	January
ichinichi	N	14	a day
ichinichijuu	N	3	all day long (see 3.4.12)
Ichiroo	N	2	boy's first name
ii	A	7	is all right (see 7.4.11 & 9.4.4)
ikemasen	V	9	it won't do (see 9.4.6)
ikimasu	E	3	(see 3.4.17)
ikura	Ni	1	how much? (see 1.4.10)
imasu	E	2	normal form of *iru* (see 2.4.2)
Inoue	N	3	family name
irasshaimasu	V	3	exist; is (normal form of *irassharu*; polite equivalent of *imasu*)
irasshaimasu	V	14	come; go (polite equivalent of *kimasu* or *ikimasu*)
iremasu	V	1	put it in (normal form of *ireru*)
iriguchi	N	13	entrance
iro	N	11	color
iroiro	Na	5	various
isha	N	11	medical doctor; physician
isogimasu	V	11	hurry (normal form of *isogu*)
isu	N	9	chair
itadakimasu	V	1	get; receive (normal form of *itadaku*) (see 1.4.13)
itsuka	N	14	the fifth day of the month; five days
ittoo	N	6	first class (see 6.4.15)

(J)

jan'paa	N	14	casual jacket; jumper
ji	N	9	letter; character
jibun de	PM	11	by oneself; for oneself
jikan	N	6	time; hour
-jikan	Nd	6	hour(s) (see 6.4.14)
jin'koo	N	13	population
jiten'sha	N	13	bicycle
jitsu wa	SI	3	the fact is; the reason why .... is
Jooji	N	5	George

jugyoo	N	3	class; instruction
-juu	Nd	3	throughout
juudoo	N	5	*jūdō;* a Japanese art of self-defense
juugatsu	N	2	October
juuichigatsu	N	2	November
juunigatsu	N	2	December
juu yokka	N	14	the fourteenth day of the month; fourteen days

(K)

kaado	N	7	card
kabuki	N	3	*kabuki* performance (performed only by men)
Kabukiza	N	3	*Kabuki* Theater
kado	N	13	corner; turn
kaerimasu	E	3	(see 3.4.17)
kaeshimasu	V	7	return; give back (normal form of *kaesu*)
-kai	Nd	1	counter for floor; stories (see 1.4.15)
kaiwa	N	1	dialog; conversation
kakarimasu	V	6	require; take (normal form of *kakaru*)
kamaimasen	V	7	do not mind (see 7.4.11 & 9.4.4)
kana	N	9	Japanese syllabary
kanari	Adv.	14	quite
kan'ji	N	6	Chinese character
Kan'sai	N	10	a district including Ōsaka, Kyōto, Kōbe, etc. (cf. *Kan'too* "a district including Tōkyō, Yokohama, etc.")
kara	Rc	5	because; since (see 5.4.4)
karate	N	5	*karate;* an art of self-defense originated in the Ryūkyū Islands
kareeraisu	N	11	curry and rice
kashimasu	V	7	lend; rent (normal form of *kasu*)
katachi	N	11	shape; form; appearance
katakana	N	1	the square Japanese syllabary
kawaii	A	5	is cute
kayoobi	N	3	Tuesday
kaze	N	3	a cold
keredo(mo)	Rc	10	although (informally *kedo*) (see 10.4.8)
ki	N	9	tree
kibun	N	3	feeling (cf. feel sick, feel fine)
kiiro	N	13	yellow
kiiroi	A	13	is yellow
kikimasu	V	6	inquire (normal form of *kiku*) (see 6.4.8)
kikoo	N	10	climate
kimasu	V	1	wear (normal form of *kiru*)
kimasu	E	3	(see 3.4.17)
Kimura	N	13	family name
Kinoshita	N	14	family name

kin'yoobi	N	3	Friday
-kiro	Nd	6	short form of *kiromeetoru* – kilometer
kisetsu	N	5	season
kita	N	10	north
ko	N	1	child (usually preceded by a modifier, e.g. *otoko no ko* "boy")
kokonoka	N	14	the ninth day of the month; nine days
kokuban	N	9	blackboard
komimasu	V	13	get crowded (normal form of *komu*)
kon'na	PN	5	this sort of
kon'shuu	N	3	this week
koo	Adv.	5	in this way
kooen	N	5	park; public garden
kore kara	PM	9	from now on (see 9.4.3)
(sono)-koro	Nd	3	(those) days; (that) time
kotae	N	9	answer
kotaemasu	V	9	answer; respond (normal form of *kotaeru*)
koto	Nd	6	act; fact (see 6.4.4)
koto	Nd	14	matter; thing (intangible) (see 14.4.8)
kotoba	N	1	speech; word; language
kudamono	N	10	fruit
kudasai	E	1	please (do) (see 1.4.9)
kudasai	V	1	please give (me) (see 1.4.9)
kudasaimasu	V	1	give me (or us) (polite equivalent of *kuremasu*) (normal form of *kudasaru*) (see 1.4.9)
kugatsu	N	2	September
kurabemasu	V	10	compare (normal form of *kuraberu*) (see 10.4.7)
-kurai	Nd	1	about; approximately (see 1.4.14)
kuro	N	13	black
kuroi	A	13	is black
kuruma	N	13	car; automobile
kutsu	N	1	shoes
kuwashii	A	7	is in detail
kyaku	N	1	customer; guest; visitor
kyooiku-gaku	N	2	study of education; pedagogy
kyookasho	N	9	textbook
kyuukoo	N	6	express
Kyuushuu	N	10	Kyūshū Island

(M)

maa	SI	10	you might say; roughly; well, I think (showing some hesitation)
machi	N	10	town; city
mada	Adv.	7	(not) yet (see 7.4.8)
made	R	6	as far as; until (see 6.4.2)
made ni	R	14	by (see 14.4.6)

mado	N	9	window
madoguchi	N	6	ticket window
mae	N	9	front; before (see 9.4.1)
magarimasu	V	13	turn (normal form of *magaru*)
-mairu	Nd	6	mile
man'nen'hitsu	N	9	fountain pen
massugu	Adv.	13	straight
mazu	Adv.	9	first of all; to begin with
me	N	7	eye
-me	Nd	10	(see 10.4.3)
-meetoru	Nd	6	meter
michi	N	13	street; road; way
Michiko	N	5	girl's first name
migi	N	13	right
mijikai	A	9	is short
mikka	N	14	the third day of the month; three days
mimasu	E	1	I'll try (after TE form) (normal form of *miru*)
minami	N	10	south (see 10.4.4)
misemasu	V	1	show (normal form of *miseru*)
mitsukarimasu	V	7	is found; can find (intransitive Verb) (normal form of *mitsukaru*) (see 7.4.7)
miyage	N	3	souvenir; gift
mo	R	9	even (see 9.4.4)
mochimasu	V	2	have; hold; possess (normal form of *motsu*) (see 2.4.16)
mochiron	SI	10	of course; certainly
mokuyoobi	N	3	Thursday
mon'dai	N	7	problem; question
mono	N	10	thing (tangible)
moo	Adv.	6	(not) any more; (not) any longer (see 6.4.16)
Mori	N	3	family name
moshi	Adv.	13	if; provided (see 13.4.2)
moshi moshi	SI	3	hello (regularly used in telephone conversation)
muika	N	14	the sixth day of the month; six days
mukashi	N	6	old times
mushiatsui	A	10	is hot and humid
musuko	N	11	son
musume	N	11	daughter; girl

(N)

na	C	5	NA form of the Copula (see 5.4.1)
-nado	Nd	1	etc.; and the like
nagai	A	9	is long
nai	A	6	is nonexistent (see 6.4.17)
-nai	Da	6	negative Derivative (see 6.4.19)

nai	E	13	plain equivalent of *arimasen* (see 13.4.2)
-naide	Da	9	(see 9.4.5)
naka	N	9	inside (see 9.4.1)
(sono) naka	N	10	among (them) (see 10.4.1)
nan'ban'sen	Ni	6	what track number? (see 6.4.11)
nanoka	N	14	the seventh day of the month; seven days
nara(ba)	C	13	if it is a ~ (BA form of *desu* ← *da*) (see 13.4.2)
narimasen	V	14	it won't do (see 14.4.5)
narimasu	V	11	become (normal form of *naru*) (see 11.4.2 & 11.4.3)
nekutai	N	1	necktie
nemasu	V	3	go to bed; sleep (normal form of *neru*) (see 3.4.13)
ni	R	2	at; in; on (time Relational) (see 2.4.3)
ni	R	3	to (a place) (see 3.4.9)
ni	R	5	Relational of purpose (see 5.4.2)
ni	R	11	goal Relational (see 11.4.2)
-nichi	Nd	14	counter for day (see 14.4.2)
nichiyoobi	N	3	Sunday
nigatsu	N	2	February
nihon'jin	N	6	Japanese person
nijuu hachinichi	N	14	the twenty-eighth day; twenty-eight days
nijuu kunichi	N	14	the twenty-ninth day; twenty-nine days
nijuu yokka	N	14	the twenty-fourth day; twenty-four days
niku	N	11	meat
nishi	N	10	west
no	R	6	*no* substituting *ga* (see 6.4.7)
no	Nd	6	nominalizer (see 6.4.3)
no	Nd	10	one(s) (see 10.4.2)
noborimasu	V	14	climb; go up (normal form of *noboru*)
nomimono	N	6	a drink; a beverage
nooto	N	7	notebook
norimasu	V	6	get on; ride (normal form of *noru*) (see 6.4.10)
norimono	N	6	transportation facilities; vehicle (see 6.4.1)
notte kara	V+R	6	after getting on (see 6.4.18)
Nyuu Yooku	N	6	New York

(O)

o	R	13	through; along; at; in; on (see 13.4.1)
okimasu	V	3	get up (intransitive Verb) (normal form of *okiru*)
omoimasu	V	11	think (normal form of *omou*)
on'na	N	1	female (see 1.4.3)
ooi	A	5	are many; is much (see 5.4.10)
Ookawa	N	11	family name
Oosaka	N	2	the biggest city in western Japan
oozei	Adv.	5	many (people) (see 5.4.8)

orimasu	V	6	get off (normal form of *oriru*) (see 6.4.20)
oshiemasu	V	13	teach; instruct; tell; show (normal form of *oshieru*)
osoi	A	9	is slow; is late
otoko	N	1	male (see 1.4.3)
otona	N	5	adult; grown-ups
ototoi	N	7	the day before yesterday
owarimasu	V	3	end; finish (intransitive Verb) (normal form of *owaru*)
oyogimasu	V	14	swim (normal form of *oyogu*)

(P)

Pataason	N	14	Patterson
Pooru	N	7	Paul

(R)

raishuu	N	3	next week (see 3.4.14)
rein'kooto	N	1	raincoat
rokugatsu	N	2	June
roomaji	N	9	Roman letters
ryoori	N	11	cooking; dish; food
ryoori shimasu	V	11	cook (normal form of *ryoori suru*)

(S)

saa	SI	6	well (hesitance)
saizu	N	1	size
sakan	Na	10	flourishing; prosperous; popular
sakana	N	11	fish
sakimasu	V	5	bloom (normal form of *saku*)
sakura	N	5	cherry (tree or blossoms)
-sama	Nd	1	polite equivalent of *-san*
San Furan'shisuko	N	6	San Francisco
san'gatsu	N	2	March
san'koosho	N	7	reference book
san'po	N	5	stroll
san'po shimasu	V	5	stroll; take a walk
sashiagemasu	V	1	I give (normal form of *sashiageru*) (see 1.4.1 and 1.4.2)
seetaa	N	1	sweater
sei	N	6	height; stature
seiyoo	N	11	Western (countries); the Occident (cf. *tooyoo* "Eastern (countries); the Orient")
sekai	N	10	world
seki	N	6	seat
semai	A	10	is small; is narrow; is limited (in space)
sen	N	6	track; line
-sen'chi	Nd	6	centimeter
sen'shuu	N	3	last week
-sen'to	Nd	1	cent(s) (see 1.4.11)

setsumei	N	7	explanation
setsumei shimasu	V	7	explain (normal form of *setsumei (o) suru*)
shashoo	N	6	conductor
Shibuya	N	2	a district of Tōkyō
shichigatsu	N	2	July
shigatsu	N	2	April
shigoto	N	2	work; job
shiken	N	9	examination; test
Shikoku	N	10	Shikoku Island
shima	N	10	island
shimasu	V	11	make (normal form of *suru*) (see 11.4.8)
shimemasu	V	9	shut; close (normal form of *shimeru*)
shin'kan'sen	N	6	New Tōkaidō Line
shirabemasu	V	7	make researches (on); check up; investigate (normal form of *shiraberu*)
shirasemasu	V	14	inform; let one know (normal form of *shiraseru*)
shirimasu	V	2	get to know; come to know (normal form of *shiru*) (see 2.4.12)
shiro	N	13	white
shiroi	A	13	is white
shita	N	9	under; below (see 9.4.1)
shitsurei	Na	5	rude
shokuji	N	5	meal; dining
shokuji shimasu	V	11	have a meal; dine (normal form of *shokuji (o) suru*)
shomin	N	3	common people; populace
shukudai	N	9	homework
shuu	N	10	state
soba	N	9	vicinity; near (see 9.4.1)
son'na	PN	5	that sort of
soto	N	9	outside
suiyoobi	N	3	Wednesday
sukeeto	N	5	skate
sukii	N	5	ski
sukiyaki	N	3	*sukiyaki;* beef cooked with vegetables
sukunai	A	5	is few; is little (opposite of *ooi* – are many; is much)
sumimasu	V	2	live (normal form of *sumu*) (see 2.4.14)
supootsu shatsu	N	1	sport shirt
suruto	SI	13	thereupon; and just then
sushi	N	1	vinegar-treated rice flavored primarily with sea food, usually raw
suwarimasu	V	9	sit (normal form of *suwaru*)

(T)

tabemono	N	6	food
tachimasu	V	9	stand (normal form of *tatsu*) (see 9.4.2)
-tai	Da	3	want to (do) (see 3.4.8)
taihen	Adv.	1	very (formal equivalent of *totemo*)

taihen	Na	6	awful; hard; terrible; trouble
taishikan	N	13	embassy (cf. *taishi* "ambassador")
(o)taku	N	3	house; home (polite equivalent of *uchi*) (regularly used in telephone conversation to ask if it is Mr. So-and-so's residence)
takushii	N	6	taxi
tama ni	PM	6	occasionally; once in a while
Tanaka	N	13	family name
tan'joobi	N	14	birthday
tatemono	N	1	building
te	N	7	hand
teeburu	N	9	table
Teeraa	N	10	Taylor
teinei	Na	1	polite
teiryuujo	N	13	bus stop; car stop
tekitoo	Na	7	proper; adequate
ten'in	N	1	(shop) clerk
tenisu	N	5	tennis
tetsudaimasu	V	11	help; assist (a person to do something) (normal form of *tetsudau*)
tokoro	N	2	place; address
tomarimasu	V	13	stop (normal form of *tomaru*) (intransitive Verb) (see 13.4.6)
ton'katsu	N	11	pork cutlet
-too	Nd	6	~ class (see 6.4.15)
tooka	N	14	the tenth day of the month; ten days
toori	N	13	avenue; street
torakku	N	13	truck
toshiyori	N	11	old folks; aged person
toshokan'in	N	7	librarian; library clerk
tsugi	N	1	next; following
tsuitachi	N	14	the first day of the month
tsukaimasu	V	7	use (normal form of *tsukau*)
tsukimasu	V	6	arrive (normal form of *tsuku*)
tsukue	N	9	desk
tsukurimasu	V	11	make; create; prepare; cook (normal form of *tsukuru*)
tsumori	Nd	14	intention; planning (see 14.4.3)
tsuremasu	V	3	take (with); bring (with); accompany (normal form of *tsureru*) (see 3.4.17)
tsutomemasu	V	2	is employed; work for (an organization) (normal form of *tsutomeru*) (see 2.4.8)

(U)

ue	N	9	top; topside (see 9.4.1)
Ueno	N	5	a district of Tōkyō
ukagaimasu	V	2	visit; go (to someone's house) (normal form of *ukagau*) (see 2.4.11)
ukagaimasu	V	6	hear; inquire (normal form of *ukagau*)

un'doo	N	10	sport; physical exercise
urimasu	V	1	sell (normal form of *uru*)
ushiro	N	9	behind; back (see 9.4.1)
utsukushii	A	5	is beautiful

(W)

wakai	A	11	is young
wakaremasu	V	10	is separated; is divided (intransitive Verb) (normal form of *wakareru*)
wakarimasu	V	2	find; understand; is clear (see 2.4.15)
watashimasu	V	9	hand (normal form of *watasu*)

(Y)

yama nobori	N	14	mountain climbing (this may be followed by (*o*) *suru* to form a verbal expression)
yane	N	9	roof
yasai	N	11	vegetables
yasumi	N	2	vacation; leave; holiday; (day) off
yasumimasu	V	3	be absent (from class); take leave (normal form of *yasumu*) (see 3.4.10)
yobimasu	V	5	call (for) (normal form of *yobu*)
yokka	N	14	the fourth day of the month; four days
yoku	Adv.	2	often
yoku	Adv.	6	well; much
yonen(sei)	N	2	a senior student; fourth year student (see 2.4.1)
-yoo(bi)	Nd	3	day of the week
yooka	N	14	the eighth day of the month; eight days
yori	R	10	(more) than (see 10.4.6)
Yoshiko	N	3	girl's first name
-yuki (-iki)	Nd	6	bound for; for (see 6.4.6)
yukkuri	Adv.	2	leisurely; slowly; take one's time (see 2.4.10)
yutaka	Na	10	rich; abundant
yuugata	N	5	late afternoon; early evening
yuumei	Na	5	famous; noted

(Z)

zehi	Adv.	2	by all means; without fail
zen'bu	N	1	all; everything
zutto	Adv.	10	by far; much (more) (see 10.4.9)

APPENDIX VII

INDEX TO NOTES